Autumn

𝒜UTUMN

A SPIRITUAL BIOGRAPHY
OF THE SEASON

EDITED BY GARY SCHMIDT
AND SUSAN M. FELCH

ILLUSTRATIONS BY MARY AZARIAN

Walking Together, Finding the Way®
SKYLIGHT PATHS®
PUBLISHING
Nashville, Tennessee

Autumn:
A Spiritual Biography of the Season

2005 First Paperback Printing
2004 First Hardcover Printing

For information regarding permission to reprint material from this book, please write or
fax your request to SkyLight Paths Publishing, Permissions Department, at the address
/ fax number listed below, or e-mail your request to permissions@skylightpaths.com.

Library of Congress Cataloging-in-Publication Data
Autumn : a spiritual biography of the season / edited by Gary Schmidt and Susan M.
Felch ; illustrations by Mary Azarian.
p. cm.
Includes bibliographical references.
ISBN 1-59473-005-9 (hardcover)
1. Autumn—Literary collections. I. Schmidt, Gary D. II. Felch, Susan M., 1951–
PN6071.A97
[A88 2004]
808.8'033—dc22

2004005843

ISBN 1-59473-118-7
ISBN-13: 978-1-68336-557-0 (pbk)

Manufactured in the United States of America
SkyLight Paths, "Walking Together, Finding the Way" and colophon are trademarks
of LongHill Partners, Inc., registered in the U.S. Patent and Trademark Office.

SkyLight Paths is creating a place where people of different spiritual traditions
come together for challenge and inspiration, a place where we can help each other
understand the mystery that lies at the heart of our existence.

SkyLight Paths sees both believers and seekers as a community that increasingly
transcends traditional boundaries of religion and denomination—people wanting
to learn from each other, *walking together, finding the way.*

Walking Together, Finding the Way
Published by SkyLight Paths Publishing
An Imprint of Turner Publishing Company
4507 Charlotte Avenue, Suite 100
Nashville, TN 37209
Tel: (615) 255-2665
www.skylightpaths.com

In memory of Natalia Foos Weimer and Dottie West Weimer,
who, like Ruth, journeyed to a far country and through
their faithfulness reaped an abundant harvest
—S. M. F.

To Jenette Sikkema, who daily teaches us that late
autumn days come before the resurrections of spring
—G. S.

CONTENTS

Contents

PART THREE: Work

PART FOUR: Harvest

PREFACE

In his early days as a poet, Henry Wadsworth Longfellow crafted two poems titled, simply, "Autumn." In the first, autumn is "like a faint old man" who sits by the roadside, weary with travels. He looks around and senses a "mellow richness" in a world filled with golden robins, purple finches settling on wild cherry branches, the sounds of reaping strokes and the flail on the threshing floor. With a "sober gladness," autumn takes up the inheritance of its fruit as "the silver habit of the clouds / Comes down upon the autumn sun." Autumn, the faint old man, is satisfied, recognizing that in this fruitfulness, the gathered abundance of good work, "he shall go / To his long resting-place without a tear."

The second poem, a sonnet, proclaims a very different version of the season: It appears like a goddess, boldly blessing the land. "Thou comest, Autumn, heralded by the rain, / With banner, by great gales incessant fanned, / Brighter than brightest silks of Samarcand." Autumn stands on a bridge made of gold, stretching her royal hand out over the landscape to bless the farms in her domain, clutching a shield that is the red harvest moon. Farmers attend her steps with prayers, the flames around her altar are the sheaves of harvested grain, and the wind, "thine almoner," scatters golden leaves beneath her feet. Here there is majesty, fullness, the golden glow, and power.

A weary old man sitting by the side of the road, and a goddess glorious and beneficent, spreading her blessings over the land—the images seem paradoxical, even contradictory. But the paradox that Longfellow captures in his two poems is indeed at the heart of the season. It is a time of fullness and fertility, a time of celebrations, of harvests, of thanksgiving itself. And at the same time, it is a season in which we take up old tasks, begin routines anew after the easy living of summer, a season when, with some sadness—perhaps even despair at times—we anticipate the frozen, barren days of deep winter. There may be golden blessings being strewn about, and we recognize those; but we also recognize the weary traveler, pausing to catch breath so as to be ready for what is coming.

Henry David Thoreau captures this sense of paradox early on in *Walden*. With something like a sigh, he thinks about the many days of autumn "spent outside the town, trying to hear what was in the wind," and here we perceive the weary traveler, looking about, trying to make sense of the meaning of this season. How does autumn fit into our larger lives? But then Thoreau finishes his sentence: He is trying to hear what the wind says—and then "carry it express!" Here is the goddess strewing gold upon the land, finding meaning and generously dispersing it.

In autumn there are indeed the blazing reds and yellows of maples, the apple orchards ripe for picking, the carnival pleasures of the state fair, the fullness of barns, Thanksgiving dinner, blankets around the knees at high school football games, the lovely long shadows of the orange sun at dusk, the dry smell of leaves in the air, and the smoke of their burning. There are pumpkins and the delightful frights of Halloween, the tartness of Concord grapes, the Vs of Canada geese honking raucously overhead.

But there are too the old routines to take up again—the school bus schedule, homework, soccer practice, the mess of the woodstove (a lovely mess, but still a mess), canning applesauce. There are the cold rains taking down the last of the leaves, the snow shovels to find just in case, shorter days with darker mornings, the hunkering down against colder weather, and the knowledge that warm days are going and that snow and ice are not far behind.

Autumn is that season in between: not summer, though still somewhat like summer, and not winter, though still somewhat like winter. It is the season that does not seem to progress—like spring—as much as it juggles blazing opposites in a great circle. It is the season of work to be taken up after summer rest, and the season to harvest the work of the summer and to turn over the garden and tuck it in for its own long sleep. It is the season that grabs the attention of the moment as we take up our schedules again. And it is the season that reminds us to look ahead, to prepare for the orneriness of winter. It is the season of brilliant October leaves and drab November branches, of yellow warm days and cold crystal nights, of the unfamiliar clunkings of radiator and furnace, the smell of blankets taken out of the cedar chest, and the first touch of silver frost on the windowpane that quickly melts away—until, one morning, it doesn't.

It is the season that teaches us that our lives are made not to run in smooth and easy paths, predictable and even, always known. Our lives are messy, sometimes scheduled, sometimes random, sometimes prepared for, sometimes taken on the fly as we juggle our own blazing experiences, all of which come at us with their contradictions and with their own joys and sorrows. It is the season that teaches us that beginnings and endings are part of our experiences; though autumn represents the fulfillment of cycles, fulfillment must also bring ending. And it is the season that reminds us that maybe we are not our own; we neither mark out nor control all the paths we may take.

And like all the seasons, autumn teaches that these aspects of our lives are not negotiable—they are part of our experience in this world. School buses, soccer practice, apples, grapes—this is the stuff of our daily life. But our response to changes, renewals, endings, and the confusing mix of day-to-day moments—this is the stuff of our spiritual life.

Perhaps the first lesson of fall is just this: that paradox and rush and routine and change will come, inevitably and inexorably, as suggested in Debra Rienstra's poem, titled, like Longfellow's, "Autumn."

> *now is the wind-time, the leaf-rhyme*
> *the scattering clattering*
> *song-on-the-lawn time*
> *early eves and gray days*
> *clouds shrouding the traveled ways*
> *trees spare and cracked bare*
> *slim fingers in the air*
> *dry grass in the wind-lash*
> *waving waving as the birds pass*
> *the sky turns, the wind gusts*
> *winter sweeps in*
> *it must it must*

Since it must it must, autumn asks us to grapple with this truth that we in North America are often so eager to avoid: that life is uncertain, and that our quest to find the means to live with that knowledge is, at its deepest, a spiritual quest.

PART ONE

Change

INTRODUCTION

Early autumn is the time of state and county fairs, those great temples of communal showing off. The sights, the smells, the very air, the sounds—they never change. There is always the hawker barking out his hot dogs, always the rickety Tilt-a-Whirl run by a bored teenager, always the smell of cotton candy yielding to the smell of cow yielding to the smell of too many bodies too close yielding to the smell, the awful smell of pig. The crafts and quilts are always the same from year to year, as are the gigantic squash—and every year we say the same thing: "How could it ever grow this big? And how would you ever lift the dang thing?"

The years don't matter. The same boys are always sucking on root beer barrel candies. The same mothers are buying pastel helium balloons for the same little kids, who will be disappointed again tomorrow because all the helium will have leaked out. The same horses are winning the same ribbons; the same tractors are polished to a high sheen. Even the same music is playing, as if the fiddler had never stopped the whole livelong year, and it was only you who had gone away and so lost the notes. We go to eat the same food, touch the same plaster giants, smell the same sawdust in the same Big Top. Even the cornstalks gathered into tightly bound bundles seem to be the same ones that we saw last year, not even wilted much.

We look for and depend upon this as children—this eternality of the fair, this pleasure in the familiar and expected, this constant. But we don't grow too old before we realize that, after all, it just isn't so.

The pies really are new each year, as is the sawdust sprinkled on the ground beneath them. The plaster giants are starting to look in need of repainting, and part of the left hand on one is missing. The old guy who used to play the fiddle isn't around any more. There's a young guy playing instead, with slicked-back hair. The cows and pigs and lambs of last year are—well, we'd rather not know. The boys with root beer barrels have grown up, and the teenager working the Tilt-a-Whirl is a new one. In fact, we realize, almost with a start, this fair isn't about sameness at all. It's celebrating the new harvest; it's depending on the constancy of change.

As we slide into autumn, we recognize that it is a season of change. If summertime seems to be unending sun and blue skies and swimming and late hot nights waiting for a cooling rain, autumn seems to be the season of inconstancy. It comes in warm, with leaves still green. But then there are the cooler nights, and the cold mornings. And suddenly there is the first thin white frost, and the leaves all hustling to put on their new finery. Then, just as it seems that the clouds are ready to start puffing out a few flakes of snow, there is another sudden warmth, another summer, so that we wonder if we haven't been wrong all along and autumn hasn't come at all. Then late October, and November, and the leaves huddle, shudder, and drop. And suddenly, unexpectedly, the branches are more bare than not, and we can see farther through the trees than we have been able to for a long time. And then it snows.

Autumn is a changeable season.

So it is in our lives. The long days of summer yield to the rituals of the new school year. The clothes in the store windows change, and suddenly it seems we must start thinking about coats again. In fact, there is much to think of: the school supplies must be laid in, the furnace should be cleaned, the snow tires checked, the jackets and hats and mittens brought down, the canner found again. With the onset of autumn we come into a whole new set of chores and delights, duties and joys. We are reminded that our world changes and that our lives change with it. The honking of geese flying south and school buses crossing an intersection both call us to this recognition.

In his poem "First Hesitations," the poet T. C. Avery captures this sense of change.

> *They begin late in August, those first hesitations:*
> *should you pull on long sleeves?*
> *If you breathe will the air swell,*
> *warm with ease and green, or will*
> *its edges flake—*
> *like rust or*
> *gold dust—*
> *away?*
> *And when, held in hand,*
> *a leaf seems to lose its last gleam,*
> *the passing is the ice-wreathed stillness*
> *along the edge of the far-pasture pond.*

The pieces in this section view autumn as a time of change. For some, this change is energizing and exciting, as for David James Duncan, who feels the tilting world beneath his feet, or for Esther Popel, who uses images of strength and power to depict autumn, or for Allen Young, who sees the season as a time of wondrous activity. For others, this change brings a meditative mood, as with Abram Van Engen, who sees in the falling leaves his own passing years, or Susan Fenimore Cooper, who sees change in the landscape as emblematic of an entire mindset. Others, such as Anne Lamott and E. B. White, find the changes represented in the season spiritually challenging, and they look for ways to cope with the knowledge and certainty of shifting landscapes and experiences.

Change brings with it anticipation; anticipation brings with it perhaps eagerness, perhaps anxiety—but surely uncertainty. It is these spiritual states that the season of autumn may evoke and represent. The task, autumn reminds us, is to approach the season with attentiveness and to approach the uncertainty with flexibility, patience, and endurance. For even as the air flakes "like rust or / gold dust," the season still seems to promise a "stillness / along the edge of the far-pasture pond."

FROM THE BOOK OF RUTH IN THE HEBREW BIBLE

In the Hebrew Bible, the book of Ruth is set among the Writings, the kethubim, *along with the praises and laments of the Psalms, the gnomic wisdom of the Proverbs, and the love poetry of the Song of Songs. Historically, however, the story is concurrent with the book of Judges, an autumnal season for the ancient Jewish people. After the glorious spring of redemption in the Exodus and the blazing summer of the wilderness wanderings, the people settle down to enjoy their land, their harvests, their milk and honey. But life is not that simple.*

Reverberating throughout the books of Judges and Ruth are the

But intertwined with the complex tones of lament, we also hear love and, with that love, the promise of a future.

Deuteronomic conditions for living a full and rich life: Remember the Lord your God who brought you out of Egypt, out of the house of bondage; keep his commandments; tenderly care for the land, for the stranger, for the widow and orphan. And all these reminders are summed up in the Shema, *to be recited daily: "Hear, O Israel, the Lord our God is One, and you shall love the Lord your God with all your heart and with all your soul and with all your might." The* Shema *reminded the ancient Jewish people, as it reminds us today, that life cannot be lived simply on our own terms. That there is covenant to keep, promises and obligations to fulfill. Indeed, the book of Judges records the anarchy that ensues when we neglect such duties, when we do only what is right in our own eyes.*

Naomi and her family are the victims of such anarchy, and the book of Ruth opens with a litany of swift and calamitous changes: famine, disloca-tion, loss, death ... and death again, and yet again. Life has not been kind to Naomi. A seemingly prudent decision to leave the land of the judges has left her bereft of husband, sons, and inheritance. Now faced with the pros-pect of returning to her former home and leaving behind her beloved daugh-ters-in-law, Naomi lingers in farewell. On the cusp of yet another decisive change, Naomi's words ring with fear, regret, sorrow, and, yes, anger. But intertwined with the complex tones of lament, we also hear love and, with that love, the promise of a future.

FROM THE BOOK OF RUTH

Many years ago, before kings ruled over the people of Israel and when the judges still judged, there was a famine in the land. Elimel-ech and his wife Naomi, and their two sons, Mahlon and Chilion, felt the pinch of hunger grow steadily into the dull weariness of starvation. Their inheritance, land in and around the small town of Bethlehem in the hill country of Ephrata, tired into worthlessness. What good are a few feet of soil that have turned to dust? Why stay in a land that God has deserted, that no longer flows with milk and honey? And what are the prospects for two young men on the brink of adulthood when raiders sweep down from the North and the judges predict only more famine, sword, and peril?

So Naomi and Elimelech and Mahlon and Chilion packed their few possessions, abandoned their inheritance, and set out for Moab. Moab was not, perhaps, their first choice, for it harbored the enemies of their own people. But it was nearby and it was green. Moab offered food, sanctuary, the promise of a future. Offered, but disappointed. True, there was food to eat, and Mahlon and Chilion soon found Moabite wives: Orpah and Ruth. But within ten years Elimelech died, then Mahlon, and then Chilion. Naomi was desolate. Bereft of her husband and her two sons, a widow in a strange country with two dependent daughters-in-law, she decided to return to Bethlehem, for she heard that the Lord had visited his people and given them bread.

As she traveled with Orpah and Ruth on the road toward the land of Judah, Naomi said to her two daughters-in-law, "Go back. Return to your mothers' houses. May the Lord bless you as you have blessed my sons and me. May the Lord give you another home, another husband, children for your inheritance."

Then she kissed them. But they lifted up their voices and wept. Orpah and Ruth said to Naomi, "No, we will go back with you to Bethlehem, to the land of Judah, to your own people."

But Naomi said, "Return, my daughters. Why will you come with me? Have I children in my womb whom I may give you as husbands? Return, my daughters, to your own country. For I am too old to find another husband and even if I did marry, would you wait for my embryo sons to grow up so that you could marry them? Would you grow old as widows? Oh, my daughters, for your dear sakes it is a bitter grief to me that the hand of the Lord is gone out against me."

A GATHERING OF POEMS
FROM THE HARLEM RENAISSANCE

In the poems collected here, some of the pride, confidence, and exuberant, joyous, raucous energy of the Harlem Renaissance flares out. These are poems of intense color—crimson, russet, rich brown, "deep pink blush"— and they are poems of richness—"swaying stalks," "hearts of gold."

But they are also poems of longing—"old songs of nomad days are in my mouth."

Esther Popel's "October Prayer" shouts to God, calling for a transformation from an autumn metaphor to a spiritual reality. Jean Toomer's "Cane: November Cotton Flower" speaks to suddenly

> In all these poems, there is a making sense of the powerful call of the season of autumn, a call made to our deepest lives.

unexpected grace and beauty in the middle of apparent waste. Isabel Neill's "October" seems to burst from the strong instincts within us that chime with the seasons—as David James Duncan will explore in "Tilt." And Marjorie Marshall's lovely, gentle evocation of autumn recalls Keats's own ode "To Autumn" in her harvesting of images.

In all these poems, there is a making sense of the powerful call of the season of autumn, a call made to our deepest lives. And that call is the in-drawn breath that is startled by the power and beauty in the autumn world.

October Prayer

ESTHER POPEL

Change me, oh God,
Into a tree in autumn
And let my dying
Be a blaze of glory!

Drape me in a
Crimson, leafy gown,
And deck my soul
In dancing flakes of gold!

And then when Death
Comes by, and with his hands
Strips off my rustling garment
Let me stand

Before him, proud and naked,
Unashamed, uncaring,
All the strength in me revealed
Against the sky!

Oh, God
Make me an autumn tree
If I must die!

Cane: November Cotton Flower

Jean Toomer

Boll-weevil's coming, and the winter's cold,
Made cotton-stalks look rusty, seasons old,
And cotton, scarce as any southern snow,
Was vanishing; the branch, so pinched and slow,
Failed in its function as the autumn rake;
Drought fighting soil had caused the birds to take
All water from the streams; dead birds were found
In wells a hundred feet below the ground—
Such was the season when the flower bloomed.
Old folks were startled, and it soon assumed
Significance. Superstition saw
Something it had never seen before:
Brown eyes that loved without a trace of fear,
Beauty so sudden for that time of year.

October

Isabel Neill

Now gypsy fires burn bright in every tree,
Now countless vagrant birds are winging south;
The white roads beckon and, unsought, yet sweet,
Old songs of nomad days are in my mouth.

I burn with every tree, I fly with every bird,
And know some gypsy witch, with mystic skill,
Has traced her crooked pattern across my heart.

Autumn

Marjorie Marshall

Mellow sunlight, soothing, warm,
Ripened grains which gaily bloom on the hills,
Swaying stalks like graceful arms
There beneath the sun at noon, rough and bright.

Maple leaves turned richly brown—
Save where deep pink blush is seen near the edge—
Wafted gently, softly down
To cool stones, moss-grown and green, nestled there.

Russet apples braving cold,
Sulking 'neath protecting leaves from the sun;
Burnished skins hid hearts of gold,
Such enticing loot for thieves, fit for gods!

Knoll and copse now redly tinged,
Quivering in the amber air, yield their fruit.
Autumn's almoner, the wind,
Scatters them like blessings rare on the earth.

E. B. White

FROM THE INTRODUCTION TO
ONWARD AND UPWARD IN THE GARDEN

The deceptive ease of his language, like honey on the tongue, often hides the shocking points he wishes to make about the way we live our lives.

In his writings, drawn across the lines of many genres, E. B. White brought to bear his wry and precise language to illuminate the unexpected in the observed. The deceptive ease of his language, like honey on the tongue, often hides the shocking points he wishes to make about the way we live our lives.

In the essay that introduces his wife Katharine's Onward and Upward in the Garden, *he pictures his wife old, sick, yet still—but we won't give away the last line. But notice how many meanings he encapsulates in the last three words.*

FROM THE INTRODUCTION TO *ONWARD AND UPWARD IN THE GARDEN*

When Miss Gertrude Jekyll, the famous English woman who opened up a whole new vista of gardening for Victorian England, prepared herself to work in her gardens, she pulled on a pair of Army boots and tied on an apron fitted with great pockets for her tools. Unlike Miss Jekyll, my wife had no garden clothes and never dressed for gardening. When she paid a call on her perennial borders or her cutting bed or her rose garden, she was not dressed for the part—she was simply a spur-of-the-moment escapee from the house and, in the early years, from the job of editing manuscripts. Her Army boots were likely to be Ferragamo shoes, and she wore no apron. I seldom saw her *prepare* for gardening, she merely wandered out into the cold and the wet, into the sun and the warmth, wearing whatever she had put on that morning. Once she was drawn into the fray, once involved in transplanting or weeding or thinning or pulling deadheads, she forgot all else; her clothes had to take things as they came. I, who was the animal husbandryman on the place, in blue jeans and an old shirt, used to marvel at how unhesitatingly she would kneel in the dirt and begin grubbing about, garbed in a spotless cotton dress or a handsome tweed skirt and jacket. She simply refused to dress *down* to a garden: she moved in elegantly and walked among her flowers as she walked among her friends—nicely dressed, perfectly poised. If when she arrived back indoors the Ferragamos were encased in muck, she kicked them off. If the tweed suit was a mess, she sent it to the cleaner's.

The only moment in the year when she actually got herself up for gardening was on the day in the fall that she had selected, in advance, for the laying out of the spring bulb garden—a crucial operation, carefully charted and full of witchcraft. The morning often turned out to be raw and overcast, with a searching wind off the water—an easterly that finds its way quickly to your bones. The bad weather did not deter Katharine: the hour had struck, the strategy of spring must be worked out according to plan. This particular bulb garden, with its many varieties of tulips, daffodils, narcissi, hyacinths, and other spring blooms, was a sort of double-duty affair. It must provide a bright mass of color in May, and it must also serve as a source of supply—flowers could be stolen from it for the building of experimental centerpieces.

Armed with a diagram and a clipboard, Katharine would get into a shabby old Brooks raincoat much too long for her, put on a little round wool hat, pull on a pair of overshoes, and proceed to the director's chair—a folding canvas thing—that had been placed for her at the edge of the plot. There she would sit, hour after hour, in the wind and the weather, while Henry Allen produced dozens of brown paper packages of new bulbs and a basketful of old ones, ready for the intricate interment. As the years went by and age overtook her, there was something comical yet touching in her bedraggled appearance on this awesome occasion—the small, hunched-over figure, her studied absorption in the implausible notion that there would be yet another spring, oblivious to the ending of her own days, which she knew perfectly well was near at hand, sitting there with her detailed chart under those dark skies in the dying October, calmly plotting the resurrection.

Anne Lamott

"Barn Raising," from
Traveling Mercies

If one were to describe Anne Lamott's journey toward faith, it might well be described as a journey through connectedness. This, in fact, is one of the major themes of Traveling Mercies. *It is this connectedness that brings Lamott closer to God, to faith, and to her church community. It is also this connectedness that brings her close to individuals—individuals such as Olivia and her parents.*

Lamott sets this account of Olivia's illness and her parents in the season of autumn. The summer has gone, and winter approaches. It is a time to think about barns, to think about storing up against the cold and preparing for what is coming. But as Lamott invokes this season, it becomes more than a metaphor. When the family descends into the horrors of a daughter's sickness, Lamott suggests that "the people who loved them could build a marvelous barn of sorts around the family." It is a barn made of concrete actions and more intangible gifts. There is money to be gathered and pain to be shared. Although the pain is real and inevitable, Lamott and others will have been building this barn all along, and there

> *If* one were to describe Anne Lamott's journey toward faith, it might well be described as a journey through connectedness.

will be shelter from winter's cold even as summer has ended and the "viral cloud of autumn" descends.

Autumn is a season of changes. So we build shelters, and wait.

"Barn Raising"

On an otherwise ordinary night at the end of September, some friends came over to watch the lunar eclipse, friends whose two-year-old daughter Olivia had been diagnosed nine months earlier with cystic fibrosis. Their seven-year-old daughter Ella is Sam's oldest friend: they met in day care and have been playing together for so long that I think of her as Sam's fiancée. Now out of the blue, the family has been plunged into an alternate world, a world where everyone's kid has a life-threatening illness. I know that sometimes these friends feel that they have been expelled from the ordinary world they lived in before and that they are now citizens of the Land of the Fucked. They must live with the fact that their younger daughter has this disease that fills its victims' lungs with thick sludge that harbors infections. Two-week hospital stays for nonstop IV antibiotics are common. Adulthood is rare.

Twice a day, every day, her parents must pound her between the shoulder blades for forty-five minutes to dislodge the mucus from her lungs. It amazes me that Sara, the mother—forty-ish, small-boned, highly accomplished—can still even dress herself, let alone remain so tender and strong.

The night of the lunar eclipse, some of our neighbors were making little cameo appearances on our street, coming outside periodically to check on the moon's progress, as if it were a patient: "How's his condition now?" But Sara and I stayed outside and watched the whole time. It was so mysterious, the earth's shadow crossing over the moon, red and black and silvery, like a veil, and then receding, like the tide.

Ella calls her little sister Livia; she stayed overnight with us the day Olivia was born, and we cooked pancakes in the shape of the letter O to celebrate the baby's arrival. From the beginning,

Olivia always got sicker than other babies; she caught colds that wouldn't leave, which led to coughs that sounded like those of an obese alcoholic smoker. But her doctor never found anything really wrong, and antibiotics always eventually cleared up the symptoms. Now she and I sit together in her room and eat chocolate, and I tell her that in a very long time when we both go to heaven, we should try to get chairs next to each other, close to the dessert table.

"Yes!" she agrees. She has round brown eyes and short yellow hair. What a dish! "More chocolate," she cries and throws me the ball she is holding—I tell you, this girl's got game. I taught her to love chocolate, which her parents still hold against me.

Whenever I'm out of town I worry that there will be bad news when I come home, that a friend will have come over to their house not knowing he or she was about to come down with a cold, and Olivia will end up back in the hospital on the two-week IV drip. She has a blue toy phone that she calls me on frequently. Sometimes when I am out of town, I imagine her calling me and chatting away on her phone. I was gone for a week of teaching at the end of summer this year, and I kept thinking of her. I almost called California to hear her voice. I was working too hard and staying up too late every night, and the people I was with were drinking a lot. I started to feel like a tired, wired little kid at a birthday party who has had way too much sugar, who is in all ways on overload, but still finds herself blindfolded and spun around for a game of pin-the-tail-on-the-donkey, and then pushed more or less in the direction of the wall with the donkey on it. But I was so turned around, so lost and overwhelmed and stressed that I couldn't even remember where the wall with the donkey was—or even in what direction it might be found. So I couldn't take one step forward without there being a chance that I was actually walking farther away from it. And it took me a while to remember that for me, the wall with the donkey on it is Jesus.

I didn't call Olivia, but I kept her in my prayers. I said to God, "Look, I'm sure you know what you're doing, but my patience is beginning to wear a *little* thin...."

A few days before the eclipse, I finally arrived home but only after Sam had gone to bed. I lay down next to him and watched him sleep. There was an ordinary full moon in the sky; I studied Sam by its light and felt entirely pointed in the right direction. But Olivia's mother had left a message on our machine, letting us know that Olivia had been sick again while I was gone. They had managed to keep Olivia out of the hospital, but it had been touch and go for days. Watching Sam sleep I kept wondering, how could you possibly find the wall with the donkey on it when your child is catastrophically sick? I don't know. I looked up at God, and thinking about Olivia, about how badly scarred her lungs are already, I said, "What on earth are you *thinking?*"

The eclipse moved in such peculiar time. Maybe it's that I'm so used to blips and sound bites, instant deadlines, e-mail. But the shadow of the earth moved across the moon in celestial time, somehow slowly and fleetingly at the same astronomical moment. It seemed like the moon was being consumed, and as if all the moons that ever had been were being consumed all at once. As if, in its last moments, you got to see the moon's whole life pass before your very eyes.

Watching Olivia watch the eclipse of the moon, I suddenly remembered New Year's Day, seven months ago, out at Stinson Beach with Sam and Olivia and her family. They have a huge German shepherd who is always with them; he hovers over Olivia looking very German. He was with us on the beach that day, chasing sticks Olivia's dad threw him. It was one of those perfect northern California days when dozens of children and dogs are running on the beach and pelicans are flying overhead, and the mountain and the green ridges rise up behind you, and it's so golden and balmy that you inevitably commit great acts of hubris. Olivia seemed fine—happy, blonde, tireless. Just a few days before, her parents had taken her to the doctor for lab work, because her colds were always so severe. But she didn't have a cold on New Year's Day.

Then two days later he called with the news that she had cystic fibrosis. Now, seeing her the night of the eclipse, her upward gaze of pure child wonder, I find it both hard to remember when she wasn't sick and harder to believe she is.

Olivia laughs at all my jokes. That night I kept pointing to our dog Sadie and saying, with concern, "Isn't that the ugliest cat you've ever seen?," and she would just lose her mind laughing.

At first, after the diagnosis, we were almost too stunned to cry. Olivia's family has a tribe of good friends around them, and everyone wanted to help, but at first people didn't know what to do; they were immobilized by shock and sadness.

By mid January, though, I had a vision of the disaster as a gigantic canvas on which had been painted an exquisitely beautiful picture. We all wanted to take up a corner or stand side by side and lift it together so that Olivia's parents didn't have to carry the whole thing themselves. But I saw that they did in fact have to carry almost the whole heartbreaking picture alone. Then the image of a canvas changed into one wall of a barn, and I saw that the people who loved them could build a marvelous barn of sorts around the family.

So we did. We raised a lot of money; catastrophes can be expensive. We showed up. Sometimes we cleaned, we listened, some of us took care of the children, we walked their dog, and we cried and then made them laugh; we gave them a lot of privacy, then we showed up and listened and let them cry and cry and cry, and then took them for hikes. We took Ella and Olivia to the park. We took the mother to the movies. I took Adam, the father, out for dinner one night right after the diagnosis. He was a mess. The first time the waiter came over, he was wracked with sobs, and the second time the waiter came over, he was laughing hysterically. "He's a little erratic, isn't he?" I smiled to the waiter, and he nodded gravely.

We kept on cooking and walking the dog, taking the kids to the park, cleaning the kitchen, and letting Sara and Adam hate what was going on when they needed to. Sometimes we let them resist finding any meaning or solace in anything that had to do with their daughter's diagnosis, and this was one of the hardest things to do—to stop trying to make things come out better than they were. We let them spew when they needed to; we offered the gift of no comfort when there being no comfort was where they had landed. Then we shopped for groceries. One friend gave them weekly massages, everyone gave lots of money. And that is how we built our Amish barn. Now, eight months later, things are sometimes pretty terrible for them in a lot of ways, but at the same time, they got a miracle. It wasn't the kind that comes in on a Macy's Thanksgiving Day float. And it wasn't the one they wanted, where God would reach down from the sky and touch their girl with a magic wand and restore her to perfect health. Maybe that will still happen—who knows? I wouldn't put anything past God, because he or she is one crafty mother. Still, they did get a miracle, one of those dusty little red-wagon miracles, and they understand this.

Sara was in a wonderful mood on the night of the eclipse. The viral cloud of autumn was about to descend, though, and this meant the family was about to find itself more exposed to danger, to cold germs, flu bugs, and well-meaning friends. There would be constant vigilance, fewer visits, endless hand washing, extra requests for prayer. There are a number of churches in the Bay Area and in fact around the country whose congregations pray for Olivia every week. And maybe it is helping. Still, the specter of the cold season hung above Olivia's parents that night like the mysterious shape-shifting moon. Sam and Ella stood off by themselves like teenagers, Olivia hung out with her mother and me. We all stared up into the sky for a long time, like millions and millions of people everywhere were doing, so we got to feel united under the strange beams of light. You could tell you were in the presence of the extraordinary, peering up at the radiance beneath the veil of shadow, the intensity of that rim of light struggling through its own darkness. Olivia kept clapping her hands against the sides of her face in wonder, as if she were about to exclaim, "¡Caramba!" or "Oy!" When the moon was bright and gold again, she ran up the stairs after her sister and Sam, who were cold and had gone inside to play.

Sara very calmly watched her girls go, and I could see that these days, her daughters were the wall with the donkey on it. We stood outside for a while longer, talking about this last flare-up, how frightened she'd felt, how tired. And I didn't know what to say at first, watching Olivia go chasing after the big kids, coughing. Except that we, their friends, all know the rains and the wind will come, and they will be cold—oh, God, will they be cold. But then we will come too, I said; we will have been building this barn all along, and so there will always be shelter.

Abram Van Engen

"THE DAY'S PEAK"

If there is a metaphor for a pilgrimage in modern North America, it must be a bus ride. The words conjure up images of long, tired hours; rolling wheels; hot pavement; grit; faces staring out windows at a landscape that seems unable—perhaps unwilling—to look back. It is a voyage through bleakness, but it is a voyage to awareness.

In this selection, Abram Van Engen steps onto a bus with no awareness of the pilgrimage that will begin. Though he will physically be traveling through space, the pilgrimage itself will be through time, augmented by the changing time of autumn. As the leaves fall around the bus, they change into paintbrushes; as Van Engen looks into his own reflection, it changes into his father's face—and he is afraid. It is a pilgrimage into an awareness of change, a change as inevitable but unpredictable as autumn itself.

In this selection, Abram Van Engen steps onto a bus with no awareness of the pilgrimage that will begin.

"The Day's Peak"

"Van Engen?"

The others pointed at me, sitting three-fourths of the way towards the back.

"You Van Engen?"

The bus driver's skinny finger leveled in my direction. Students backed away as he advanced down the aisle.

"Well, yes."

"John's boy?"

"That's me. Abram Van Engen."

"So."

The bus driver stopped his advance and leaned his body against the seat in front of me. He looked me up and down like a tailor fitting a suit.

"Name's Len," he said, extending his hand. "Len VanderKam. I grew up with your dad."

"You what?" I jerked his hand unexpectedly.

"I grew up with your dad."

"In little Doon, Iowa? That town's too small."

"Too small for what?"

"For anyone to come from it."

Len laughed. "Well, what can I say, Brommy? I'm from Doon."

I knew then Len was telling the truth. He used my Dutch name, a name that rolls up from the back of the throat, the name my grandmother—my oma—used in Doon. I could smell Iowa in the name.

Len received the immediate status of near divinity. He stood before me as a link, a man who knew my dad when he had been as old as me, a man who could tell me the stories that I had never heard. I could find out what my dad was like before Chronic Fatigue Syndrome, before the sapping of energy and the advent of depression—what he was like when he was young, like me.

"I met you before, but you were just a little thing. You wouldn't remember me. It's funny to see you grown up."

"It's funny to see you at all."

Len shrugged and grinned. "They handed me a list of the students who would be riding. I don't usually look at those things, but I'm glad I did this time."

"I'm glad you did too."

We faced each other in silence.

"Well," he said, "I probably shouldn't hold up the bus, you know. Folks will be wanting to leave." He turned toward the front. "Nice to see you," he tossed at me as students parted again.

I stood up. "Len, do you mind if I sit up front with you?"

"Sure. Sit wherever you like, Brommy."

"I want to hear stories from you, Len, stories about my dad."

"Stories? Oh, I don't know if I have any stories about your dad necessarily, but I'm always happy for the company."

I followed Len to the front and sat down beside him as the bus choked into drive and the wheels began to roll for a two-hour ride. I sat as the present before the past, waiting to see a man of time unfold the early features of a father I had known only in middle age. At home, I had discovered pieces of his childhood, but they always lay scattered around the house, disconnected from their stories. Once, in a closet in the basement, I discovered a box of photos, but little was written on the backs. In another corner, I found a box of trophies he had won—basketball, speeches, academic honors—all when he had been as old as me. Yet no one told me stories. No one brought to life the tokens that I found within my house.

"Tell me all you know."

"Your dad, oh, he was a crack-up. Big smile whenever he'd come by. And a laugh, well, you know his laugh. A kind of rollicking bellow is about the best way to describe it. He'd trip in the tongue till you'd think he was going to choke, and then he'd just explode, just burst right open, louder'n a cannon. We always knew him by his laugh. You know how it is."

I nodded as if I knew.

"'Happy Van' we called him. 'Hap' for short." Len chuckled and shook his head. I looked down at my shoes.

"What did you two do together?"

"What us? We painted. Painted in the summers and into the fall, making money. I was a little older, you know, so we didn't have the same circles from school and all, but we painted on the same crew, three years running."

"What'd you paint?"

"Barns, Brommy, we painted big, tall barns. Yeah, we dragged huge ladders out there and hoisted them up. Took our buckets and a fat brush and went to work. Three years running, summers into fall, like I said."

Len had his eyes on the road. He shouted the details of my father's past above the whirr of wheels, the bumps clunking beneath the bus, the noise of thirty students at our back. It was fall now. The leaves were turning bright against the sky, joining together in one great and final laugh before they fell, before fluttering beneath the grind of wheels on the pavement where they rolled between the lines that followed the contours of the road.

I watched the lines stretch into a point in the distance, a depth that kept receding as much as we advanced, like the lines Len shouted of a man who receded past my ability to meet.

"I paint in the summers too, Len. There must be stories."

"Painting stories, huh? Let me see." Len's brow furrowed on the lines. The bus rolled on in silence. "Well, Brommy," he said, "I don't remember much at all now. It was such a long time ago, you know? 'Bout all I remember is kind of what it was like. I mean, I remember sometimes little things, like the malts, but basically now it's all gone. Just the impression is left, you know?"

"The malts?"

"Yeah, see, we had this unwritten contract on the crew that if you dropped your brush, you had to buy all the others malts when we went to town. The rookies, they always had a little trouble right off. They would dip their brushes too deep in the buckets, see, not knowing any better or trying to do things too fast or something, I don't know. Anyway, they'd get too much paint on those suckers, and then it'd start to drip down the brush and all over the handle. You keep that up for the day and it's like trying to hold on to a snake. Damn thing squirms all over in your hand. Yeah," he chuckled, "we sure got a lot of malts out of the rookies."

Len laughed as he looked at the point ahead. I watched his face as his eyes narrowed and lines spread out around them, deep into his cheeks, meeting the lines of his upturned lips.

"And my dad?"

Len turned and looked at me, smiling wide. "Oh your dad couldn't hold on to a thing." He looked back. "At least he couldn't for the first summer, maybe all the way through, far as I can remember. I don't know how he made any money at all, he was always spending it on malts for us in town. Thing I remember, though, is that he'd never complain. He seemed to think it funnier than all the rest of us every time he dropped the brush. That much I remember because it was different, see. The other guys, they'd sometimes get all whiny or they'd beat themselves up about it or whatever else. But your dad, ha, he'd just smile and laugh, same as ever. We loved him for that."

Len looked over at me again with his smile. He reached out his hand and placed it on my head, as if I were a small child, as if he were blessing me for the laughter and the malts of my father's youth.

I turned away. Outside, the trees were laughing too, joining in a joke now thirty years old. I watched as the wind blew and the laughter bubbled over in the sun, twirling as it tumbled down.

"What was he like, Len?"

"Ah, Brommy, I've told you what he was like. As far as stories go, I'm afraid I don't have much to say."

"You remembered the malts."

"Yeah, but that's just who he was, 'Happy Van.'" Len was looking at me squarely as the lines of the road rolled under him. "That's how we all knew him. 'Hap' for short."

His eyes turned back to the road. Len was done. His memory had no more stories of my dad. They hadn't been that close, just painting companions. Just a piece of my father's youth, his life when he had been as old as me.

I stood, thanked Len, and turned. I wandered back down the aisle with a nickname, the taste of malts, and the sound of laughter as a paintbrush fell away.

Three-fourths of the way towards the back of the bus, I took my seat again and looked out the window. But I did not see through it. Instead, the darkness of the passing trees illuminated my face, a transparent face whose contours were traced by the falling leaves. I was scared and I could see that I was scared. I stared at myself as a nineteen-year-old, a face without wrinkles, without lines around the eyes, without furrows in the brow, and I saw in my features the features of a father I had never met—a man whose only lines were lines of laughter, spreading out from his lips, meeting the lines that encircled his eyes on a smooth cheek tanned by summer work.

In my face I saw Happy Van. I saw him in the slanting sun of a fall day—a grin and a bucket, a brush and a bellow on the Iowa plains, the few trees around beginning to crack, to turn, to join in the living joke of a boy whose laughter was his identity, a boy walking toward the mammoth barn that would occupy his week. And the ladder was there, and he was stepping up, and from his arm the bucket dangled with its thick, red paint.

But the scene beyond the window kept breaking through, interrupting my image. Sometimes the trees would disappear and open on the expanse of a wide field, erasing my face with the light that poured in. Sometimes the leaves of the trees would draw my eyes away, all the colors colliding behind the face through which I looked. And always the falling leaves were swirling in the wind.

But the dark brown of the tree trunks would return or the colors would blend into a background dark enough, and I would see again my face staring me in my face; I'd see my father's boyhood figure come again. High up on the ladder now, holding a bucket of paint, I saw him dip his brush too far, so far that when he pulled it up, the paint seeped through the bristles, flowing down the handle and over his hand, running the length of his arm. It gathered at his elbows, collecting in a pool, then dripping down in dark red spots that spattered on the green grass below.

And he smiled. High up on his ladder, nineteen years old, the day nearing its peak now when the shadows disappear and nothing reaches out, when the world becomes for a single moment instantly and only present. He was smiling then in the fullness of the day, smiling as he struggled to hold the handle of his brush, squirming like a snake. He reached to paint a spot and the snake went loose, freed itself from his grip, the whole brush plunging to the ground below. And my father's tongue would start to trip, gathering into a choke at the back of his throat, and then the explosion, a burst and a bellow at the height of his youth, the lines of laughter spreading out at his eyes as he checked his pocket for the change that would buy the others malts.

I saw him. I saw him in the middle of the window, the lines around his eyes filling in my own. But the lines around my eyes were lines of fear.

The images of my memory were stronger than the images of Len's stories, and they filled the face in the window with different forms. They etched an emptied man lying still behind the couch, a father napping after work to get the energy to eat. They etched a man whose laughter had choked, whose quiet form bent over books in the living room, working late into the night. They etched a man who I could not help imagining as me.

I was a painter. I was an academic, a scholar, geared for graduate school, for the professorate—for the same trajectory of life. Against the background of the trees, against the background of their falling leaves, I could not see who it was who looked at me, whether the youthful face of a father whose laughter earned a nickname in the town or the aging face of a man who fought fatigue—or me, just me, a nineteen-year-old on a two-hour ride, a boy or a man distinct from the boy or the man whose images kept filling in my face. The bus driver had asked for Van Engen. I told him my name was Abram. He called me Brommy, just like my oma did.

I squinted at the window, and the lines around my eyes spoke both the past and the future like the lines that Len had spoken, the lines that he now watched, converging on a point I could not avoid, a point I could not reach, a point I could not change.

I wish I could have met my father when he was nineteen. I wish I could have talked to him when the tongue still tripped, when the bellow was only inches from escape. I wish I could have been his friend, could have shared with him the joy of a day when the paint is so thick it drips from your elbows to the ground. I wish I could have laughed that final laugh with him, the laughter of a bright red leaf blown high into the air, caught in that brief moment when the sun has reached its peak and the shadows disappear, suspended, then descending, falling as slowly as the advance of age, its flared figure resisting the forces that pull it down to where it finally hits the pavement of a road where a bus goes rolling by.

The default of youth is joy. But what maintains that youthful joy as the season turns and the trees lose their tenuous grip?

I will not go tired to the grave, as if it were a bed. If I must go, let me be forced, someone struggling to keep me still as I squirm like a paintbrush with too much paint. And I will be smiling then, smiling with the grin of a nineteen-year-old boy high up on the side of a barn, lines of laughter spreading out from my eyes, lit by the sun at its peak, the shadows cleared away.

I looked out the window again. Through my transparent gaze, the leaves fluttered to the ground.

Susan Fenimore Cooper

"A DISSOLVING VIEW"

Susan Fenimore Cooper, the daughter of James Fenimore Cooper, was one of nineteenth-century America's most prominent nature writers; her "A Dissolving View" first appeared in The Home Book of the Picturesque: Or American Scenery, Art, and Literature *(1852). There the piece was published alongside landscape pieces by her father, by Washington Irving, and by William Cullen Bryant. In this piece, Cooper wishes to establish what is archetypically American in a landscape, and she chooses autumn as the season that mirrors that American-ness—in this, she is much like Henry David Thoreau in his "Autumnal Tints."*

> *We are natural to Eden, she suggests, but our presence must give "life and spirit to the garden."*

One of the attractions for her is autumn's changeableness, the fact that its colors shift from day to day and from season to season. It is therefore an "uncertain" and "fanciful" season. But that changeableness contributes to its sublime quality, lending it a kind of elusiveness that makes it all the more attractive. It is, she writes, a season of "festive gayety" and one that "fixes the attention anew." Such attentiveness must work itself out in a stewardly care for nature's bounty.

Cooper is not particularly interested in nature for nature's sake; she is very much interested in our presence in the world. We are natural to Eden, she suggests, but our presence must give "life and spirit to the garden." In the end, she envisions an autumnal world where humanity lives in ease and peace with nature, contributing to its beauty without exploiting its bounty.

"A Dissolving View"

Autumn is the season for day-dreams. Wherever, at least, an American landscape shows its wooded heights dyed with the glory of October, its lawns and meadows decked with colored groves, its broad and limpid waters reflecting the same bright hues, there the brilliant novelty of the scene, that strange beauty to which the eye never becomes wholly accustomed, would seem to arouse the fancy to unusual activity. Images, quaint and strange, rise unbidden and fill the mind, until we pause at length to make sure that, amid the novel aspect of the country, its inhabitants are still the same; we look again to convince ourselves that the pillared cottages, the wooden churches, the brick trading-houses, the long and many-windowed taverns, are still what they were a month earlier.

The softening haze of the Indian summer, so common at the same season, adds to the illusory character of the view. The mountains have grown higher; their massive forms have acquired a new dignity from the airy veil which enfolds them, just as the drapery of ancient marbles serves to give additional grace to the movement of a limb, or to mark more nobly the proportions of the form over which it is thrown. The different ridges, the lesser knolls, rise before us with new importance; the distances of the perspective are magnified; and yet, at the same time, the comparative relations which the different objects bear to each other, are revealed with a beautiful accuracy wanting in a clearer atmosphere, where the unaided eye is more apt to err.

There is always something of uncertainty, of caprice if you will, connected with our American autumn, which fixes the attention anew, every succeeding year, and adds to the fanciful character of the season. The beauty of spring is of a more assured nature; the same tints rise year after year in her verdure, and in her blossoms, but autumn is what our friends in France call *"une beauté journalière,"* variable, changeable, not alike twice in succession, gay and brilliant yesterday, more languid and pale to-day. The hill-sides, the different groves, the single trees, vary from year to year under the combined influences of clouds and sunshine, the soft haze, or the clear frost; the maple or oak, which last October was gorgeous crimson, may choose this season to wear the golden tint of the chestnut, or the pale yellow of duller trees; the ash, which was straw-color, may become dark purple. One never knows beforehand exactly what to expect; there is always some variation, occasionally a strange contrast. It is like awaiting the sunset of a brilliant day; we feel confident that the evening sky will be beautiful, but what gorgeous clouds or what pearly tints may appear to delight the eye, no one can foretell.

It was a soft hazy morning, early in October. The distant hills, with their rounded, dome-like heights, rising in every direction, had assumed on the surface of their crowning woods a rich tint of bronze, as though the swelling summits, gleaming in the sunlight, were wrought in fretted ornaments of that metal. Here and there a scarlet maple stood in full colored beauty, amid surrounding groves of green. A group of young oaks close at hand had also felt the influence of the frosty autumnal dews; their foliage, generally, was a lively green, worthy of June, wholly unlike decay, and yet each tree was touched here and there with vivid snatches of the brightest red; the smaller twigs close to the trunk forming brilliant crimson tufts, like knots of ribbon. One might have fancied them a band of young knights, wearing their ladies' colors over their hearts. A pretty flowering dogwood close at hand, with delicate shaft and airy branches, flushed with its own peculiar tint of richest lake, was perchance the lady of the grove, the beauty whose colors were fluttering on the breasts of the knightly oaks on either side. The tiny seedling maples, with their delicate leaflets, were also in color, in choice shades of scarlet, crimson, and pink, like a new race of flowers blooming about the roots of the autumnal forest.

We were sitting upon the trunk of a fallen pine, near a projecting cliff which overlooked the country for some fifteen miles or more; the lake, the rural town, and the farms in the valley beyond, lying at our feet like a beautiful map. A noisy flock of blue-jays were chattering among the oaks whose branches overshadowed our seat, and a busy squirrel was dropping his winter store of chestnuts from another tree close at hand. A gentle breeze from the south came rustling through the colored woods, and already there was an autumnal sound in their murmurs. There is a difference in the music of the woods as the seasons change. In winter, when the waving limbs are bare, there is more of unity in the deep wail of the winds as they sweep through the forests; in summer the rustling foliage gives some higher and more cheerful notes to the general harmony; and there is also a change of key from the softer murmurs of the fresh foliage of early summer, to the sharp tones of the dry and withering leaves in October.

There is something of a social spirit in the brilliancy of our American autumn. All the glory of the colored forest would seem displayed for human eyes to enjoy; there is, in its earlier stages, an air of festive gayety which accords well with the cheerful labors of the season, and there is a richness in the spectacle worthy of the harvest-home of a fruitful land. I should not care to pass the season in the wilderness which still covers large portions of the country; either winter or summer should be the time for roaming in those boundless woods; but with October let us return to a peopled region. A broad extent of forest is no doubt necessary to the magnificent spectacle, but there should also be broken woods, scattered groves, and isolated trees; and it strikes me that the quiet fields of man, and his cheerful dwellings, should also have a place in the gay picture. Yes; we felt convinced that an autumn view of the valley at our feet must be finer in its present varied aspect, than in past ages when wholly covered with wood.

The hand of man generally improves a landscape. The earth has been given to him, and his presence in Eden is natural; he gives life and spirit to the garden. It is only when he endeavors to rise above his true part of laborer and husbandman, when he assumes the character of creator, and piles you up hills, pumps you up a river, scatters stones, or sprinkles cascades, that he is apt to fail. Generally the grassy meadow in the valley, the winding road climbing the hill-side, the cheerful village on the bank of the stream, give a higher additional interest to the view; or where there is something amiss in the scene, it is when there is some evident want of judgment, or good sense, or perhaps some proof of selfish avarice, or wastefulness, as when a country is stripped of its wood to fill the pockets or feed the fires of one generation.

David James Duncan

"Tilt,"
FROM *MY STORY AS TOLD BY WATER*

Among the changes that autumn brings is a change in time—unless you live in Indiana, or certain parts of Arizona. We suddenly seem to gain an hour, and though it is a bit hard to see the sun set so early, it is a real pleasure to see the sunlight in the morning, as if somehow winter's advent has been forestalled.

In "Tilt," the essayist and novelist David James Duncan remarks on the change in seasonal time, but it is not just a practical, human-oriented time. Instead, he focuses on a celestial time change, as the earth tilts toward the solstice. He watches the life around him adjust to this change: the geese migrating overhead, the well-known and well-understood river quickly taking on entirely new and unexpected aspects.

David James Duncan remarks on the change in seasonal time, but it is not just a practical, human-oriented time. Instead, he focuses on a celestial time change, as the earth tilts toward the solstice.

But, like Susan Fenimore Cooper in her "A Dissolving View," Duncan is writing about more than mere change; he is writing about awareness. As he watches the geese overhead, it occurs to him that as they fly from winter, it is they who seem to stand still, and the earth itself that revolves away beneath them. The mountains, the rivers, he himself are quickly plunged toward the solstice, toward the Tilt. And surrounding him all the while are "intricacy and creativity" that are responding to this shift, this new plunging.

It is, concludes Duncan, a cause for enormous wonder—but wonder that comes only to those who are aware.

"TILT"

It was easy to forget, during the mere two seasons that constitute an Oregon coast year (seven months of wet, five of dry) that like a long-ago-injured woman who's learned to walk gracefully with a cane, Earth leans ever so slightly on her axis, inclining now toward the sun, now away from it as she orbits, thereby causing the angle at which sunlight strikes her to change constantly. It is impossible to forget this in Montana: Earth's "limp"—and the resulting shift of the landscape now toward, now away from, the sun—gives us four dramatically different seasons and all the migratory compensations of wildlife, the annual growth/deaths/dormancies of plant life, and the external and internal changes in human life—that occur in response.

It's impossible to forget equinoctial tilt in the Rockies because, when ignored, it silently slides healthy creatures into environs that suddenly fail to sustain life. I watched a solitary western bluebird, last December, try for an ineffectual quarter-hour to peck bugs, woodpecker-style, from the bark of a snow-covered, rime-blasted pine. This bleak drama took place a stone's throw from the nest box in which several bluebirds had hatched and fledged and thrived a few months before, yet the lone December blue was doomed by one small mistake: it had failed to respond to Tilt. Migration is a life-preserving path that animals *must* discover and trace as Earth's limp turns their homelands and homewaters inhospitable. The circumpolar seasonal journeys of terns and phalaropes, the marathon gauntlets run by wildebeest and caribou and swum by oceangoing tuna and salmon, the six-thousand-mile swims of the Alaska fur seal and humpback whale, are famous attempts to cancel the effects of Tilt. Watching the life of the Rockies, though, has led me to discover another form of migration about which I hadn't much thought: the equinoctial ride not of those who leave a given landscape, but of those who stay behind.

In the fly-fishing classic *The Habit of Rivers,* Ted Leeson glimpses this journey when he looks up from his home river at departing Canada geese. He writes,

> As the recognition of autumn comes suddenly, in a moment, so one day you first hear the geese.... Bound for the south, these birds seem to me a strange point of fixity...for in a sense they don't move at all. They take to altitudes to stay in one place, not migrating, but hovering, while the equinoctial tilting of the earth rocks the poles back and forth beneath them. The geese remain, an index of what used to be where, and of what will return again. Their seasonal appearance denotes your passing, not their own.

With this upside-downing of the word "migration," the so-called stasis of sedentary things becomes the illusion it in fact is. In relation to Earth's spectacular annual ticktock upon her axis, it is the so-called "migratory" mammals and birds that travel thousands of miles north and south who maintain their true solar place, and every geological and biological form that *fails* to respond to Tilt— every mountain, for instance, and we who remain in them—that does the traveling.

That the entire sedentary landscape migrates was never more clear to me than during my first Montana winter. I'd arrived in the Rockies in July and set about learning the new landscape in the best way I know: by befriending the trout stream that flows through my backyard. This friendship seemed to grow rapidly intimate. I memorized a two-mile beat of water, and was soon catching and releasing its inhabitants at will. I met the beavers, coyotes, deer, and elk. A cow moose one day stepped from the willows forty feet upstream of me, analyzed my flycasting for a moment, then responded with the most prolific and foamy urination I've ever seen, let alone been forced to stand in. I cleaned up the garbage and charted the flows of the creek. I made painstaking, hand-built improvements to its trout habitat, figuring I'd know these same riffles, pools, and improvements for years to come. In November, though, something unexpected happened: the entire watershed took off—mountains, trees, tributaries, animals, houses, humans, and all—on a journey into Tilt.

This migration began to grow perceptible on the day before Thanksgiving, when the temperature suddenly dropped fifty degrees and stayed there. Within a week, the fluid body I'd spent summer and fall befriending had become a motionless, silent solid. Because the skies stayed clear and there'd been no snow all fall, each subtle stage of transformation was perfectly visible.

On Day One, Thanksgiving Eve, when the air hit zero, a viscous ice that looked like fog began to slide down the creek's clear current, sheathing everything in the stream—submerged trees, water weeds, barbed wire, deer bones, car parts—in a soft cocoon of gray. On Day Two, Thanksgiving proper, at minus five, I found myself disconcertingly blessed with an ability to stand like Saint Peter on pools in which, just days before, I'd battled brown trout. Day Three, minus eight, the glides froze over thick but as clear as glass, and a prolific crop of geometric white roses sprang from that unlikely soil. I'd never seen such blossoms, or such terrain beneath: I'd stand in bright, heatless sunlight on what I still thought of as water, peering at white-petaled ice-roses sprung from clearest glass. Beneath glass and petals the fog-streams and galactic currents of the creek flowed in perfect silence, the bottom stones glowing sunlit beneath the viscous ice "fog-streams." Trout and whitefish finned above the glowing stones, dappled by geometric roseshadows as they calmly dodged the "fog."

On Day Four, even the fastest waters closed over, the last

little open rapid becoming a heap of smashed china plates. Beavers slipped in and out of the broken china through small, carefully maintained holes. Stripped willow twigs piled like fresh-hewn chopsticks at each hole. Standing by a pile of these artful sticks and china shards, I realized that, as surely as I have ever journeyed by boat, car, or plane, I had been carried into foreign country. The entire Earth had been my vessel. Though I walked the same few miles of trout stream daily, those miles and everything they contained had slid deeper and deeper into the foreign realms of Tilt.

I traded waders for skis, traversed the ever-changing glass plains, passed fresh-bloomed ice flowers, ever toothier icicles, ever-less-describable sculptures. Tiny hanging grottos of moving icicles tinkled, near each stilled rapid, like wind chimes. The wintry realm I'd entered grew so exotic my creek-skiings finally reminded me—no matter how cold the cold—of swimming through warm tropical reefs. Same complete immersion in intricacy and creativity. Same inexhaustible extravagance and style. Same inchoate gasps of thanks for all that I was seeing. Same no one listening, taking invisible bows.

Returning home from these soundings, I found that our house, too, sat differently upon the land. The log walls were no longer anchored to solid ground: they cut through the axial stream like a ship's prow. I'd step indoors with a sense of climbing aboard, make tea, sit at the window, watch the mountain world plunge, shiplike, through the slow equinoctial flow. Winter solstice became not a date on the calendar but a destination: something to sail toward, then *around,* the way schooners used to round Capes Horn and Good Hope. When my daughters climbed in my lap, I couldn't contain my wonder.

"We're moving!" I told them. "The house, the mountains, the whole world is sailing. Can you feel it?"

They gazed gravely at the mountains, then nodded with such serenity it seemed they'd always known. And on we glided, deep into winter, out around Cape Solstice, then straight on back toward spring.

"Autumn," from *Small Creatures and Ordinary Places*

Allen M. Young

Allen M. Young is curator of zoology at the Milwaukee Public Museum. In Small Creatures and Ordinary Places, *he invites us to see the wonders in our own backyards, close to the busy thoroughfares of urban development. In a move that gently corrects Susan Fenimore Cooper's vision of a cultivated garden, Young celebrates untidiness, the delightful messiness of nature's fecundity.*

> *Although autumn reminds us that nothing is "pristine," it prunes summer's luxuriant foliage, revealing the stark contours of mounds, crevices, and stream banks. It is difficult to hide in the fall.*

Autumn, in particular, with its dying flowers and lethargic insects brings a "welcome untidiness" that "marches along with the turn of the season." Young sees this turn, as does David James Duncan, as tied to earth's tilt. Autumn is the time when we momentarily lose our footing. Despite its yearly appearance, the first frost always surprises; despite an abundant harvest, we feel betrayed by the last dry stalks of corn. The memory of burning leaves is a memory of mortality.

Although autumn reminds us that nothing is "pristine," it prunes summer's luxuriant foliage, revealing the stark contours of mounds, crevices, and stream banks. It is difficult to hide in the fall. Yet, in the dry crunch of dead leaves, on the fallen logs quietly rotting beneath a filmy white crust, at the bottom of a mulched pond, life quietly simmers. And if we still ourselves into quietness, we too will smell the fresh, tart piquancy of a new day.

"Autumn"

Less than a month ago I sat out here on the deck in the backyard with the morning summer air steaming with the pulse of life. I remember spotting, just for a moment, a striking pair of cardinals flitting through the thick brambles at the rear of the yard. Bumblebees noisily plundered rich payloads of russet and yellow pollen from that tall patch of purple coneflowers and black-eyed Susans bordering the garage. Small heaps of shavings from walnut shells piled up on the fence posts, the persistent handiwork of squirrels, caught my attention. As dawn evaporated away into high noon like the disappearing dew, the big silver maple in the middle of the yard sprang to life with the whine of unseen cicadas clinging to its drooping branches. And of course, tenacious yellowjackets tried to chase me off the deck and, on occasion, almost succeeded. Life from the deck by late summer was a richly textured scene, more so than in some other recent summers. I could feel the drumming of life's bigger design in the drone of bees, buzz of cicadas, splashes of butterfly colors, and soft nighttime melodies of snowy tree crickets. For a place close to the city, this yard was well blessed with full cast of characters.

I'd like to think this condition had something to do with my refusal to keep a fastidious, tidy yard. For by summer's close, the borders were fuzzy and frazzled with bent weeds of many kinds, great breeding grounds for insects and spiders. All of this I did not mind and, in fact, had hoped would be the end product of my unabashed lack of attention. I view my backyard as a natural experiment of sorts—a place where I freely encourage the struggle between traditional yard care and letting things be. In short, I urge my yard to act as my summer entertainment. Indeed, by summer's end this year, my backyard was a grand success, delightfully messy.

This kind of untidiness says something very good about the land. No matter if it is a backyard or field or patch of forest. This was a great summer, with just the right mix of warm temperatures and rainfall to shape bumper crops of plants and insects. It was a good season too for my little vegetable garden. Now, on the verge of a cold snap, there are a few green tomatoes left on the vines, but over the past two months we gorged ourselves over and over on fresh salads using those tomatoes. The corn this year did its usual thing. What few tender ears there were went quickly to the squirrels. Nevertheless we enjoyed planting the garden and making the earth produce. And anyway, I don't mind not eating all of the harvest from the garden. I get great pleasure from seeing things sprout out of the dark earth, reach toward the sky, and bear fruit. My garden serves all that live in the yard and all that pass through it. No mind that my vegetable patch was invaded by creeping Charlie and other weeds, native and exotic. Again, ecological messiness, no matter the players and game plan, does not bother me. In the backyard as everywhere else, nature is messy.

Nor is there any such thing as pristine, since every place is a mix of native species and outside invaders. These situations, of course, engender awesome distress in preservationists, but it should be less of an issue for ecologists and conservationists. All of the land is one big experiment. The rules and steps change all of the time, as do the players. I like to think of my yard, at the end of the growing season and when autumn begins to show its personality, as part of this messiness. This welcome untidiness in the yard marches along with the turn of the season. Great celestial events, unfolding with the elegance of an immense timepiece, have changed the complexion of the backyard. The grass and weed patches are littered with golden dead leaves cascading from the silver maple as the cooling breezes of autumn push off the dense, steamy air of summer's last hurrah. By this time, it is almost impossible to find, upon close inspection, a single leaf still on a tree or bush that is not riddled with holes made by legions of beetles, grasshoppers, and caterpillars. Stems and leaves are now tough and pithy, a far cry from their soft tenderness in spring and early summer. My garden tools are stored away in the garage already, and soon the push mower will follow them. Change rings through the air as skies leaden by day become crystalline clear at night with a crisp light show of a million stars. Now when I go for a walk in the neighborhood, it is downright cold and feels raw to the bone on some nights.

But the cold mornings of light frost have not stopped me from sitting on the deck at dawn, even though everything now is parched, browned, and withered. What leaves still remain on the bushes and the grass are crusted in a trace of white icing. They resemble large frosted cereal flakes. The view is clear, clean, and crisp, not the soft blurred mosaic of summer's impressionist portrait that filled this place the past several months. But the mode and tempo of this cleansing of the landscape does not always follow a definitive rhythm one year to the next. A first killing frost of the season always sneaks up on me. I really don't know when it will come, only that it surely will. In fact, in these parts, there can be as much as a 30-day variance in the first killing frost date from one year to the next. This presents a tricky, teasing dilemma for many creatures.

The arriving cold of autumn is good in a special way. With summer's ebullient finale behind, I must look hard and with great patience into the fields, woods, gardens, and parks to sense autumn's message. Born of the sun's glow and captured by the remarkable food-making chemistry of plants in months past are the waning stragglers left over from a crop of insects. Field crickets, often heard but seldom seen sentinels in a Lilliputian world where time is measured by clocks genetically blueprinted in creatures, chirp with a slowed beat from hidden lairs beneath old rock piles, logs, and rock gardens. The season silences the blasts of summertime rock concerts and loud human music that robbed the night air of its soft chants of katydids, crickets, and frogs. Even we quiet down in the fall.

I must struggle now to hear the faint, melodic purrings of the snowy tree cricket, an ethereal, pale-green creature haunting garden bushes, above the remaining noises of society's technological over-kill. Senescing, sunburst tufts of tall grasses in fields at night hold only an occasional "zip-zip-zip" dirge of a cone-headed grasshop-per, not the full symphony that ringed the air here before. Wooded lots proliferate autumn's batches of tiny moths, a smorgasbord of diverse, intricately patterned wing-color designs, a virtual multitude of little understood species clinging to cold, lighted window screens.

For some, there is confusion about when summer ends and autumn begins. But true autumn is always abundantly clear to me. The signs of that season reign supreme. When true autumn sweeps across the land, its cooling brush repaints the canvas of foliage from greens to bright colors at the other end of the light spectrum. The process is irreversible, even if temperatures rise again. The fields turn reedy and brittle and their once ebullient insects and spiders fall away, burying themselves in the dense thatch or dying off. This is true autumn. It is a season, however, of betrayal. Life does not go away quickly. The march is clearly into deathly cold and pro-grammed senescence.

But dying is always an individual matter, or should be. Some grasshoppers die off more quickly than others in the same field. When the weather turns cold, I look to the sun-drenched spots in the yard or field near noon to find clues that life struggles to hold on, even though it is doomed. Insects and their close relatives among the arthropods, such as spiders, remember, are generally unable to maintain a warm internal body temperature at a level allowing them to stay active. When it gets cold, the solution is to move into warm spots and out of the shade to warm up. This is what these creatures do all of the time, no matter the season. But in autumn, the behavior takes on special meaning as life winds down. Call it a last-ditch effort, one that gives a final, passing glimpse of life that will not grace the land until next summer.

Autumn seasons nowadays do not necessarily have the same feel to them they had many years ago. Burning leaves along the roadsides, whether one agrees with the practice or not, gave the air a special incense seeping through the cold. Shifting eddies of breeze fanned the stacked and packed embers of the pile's core, casting a warm orange glow as the sun disappeared. Red-hot, wind-whipped ashes crackled, giving those late Saturday afternoons in October a ritualistic feel that seemed as ancient as druid celebrations. In some manner, this was a neighborhood happening, playing out against the descending frost. Somehow that practice added a patina of finality to the end of warmth and the promise of much colder days and weeks ahead. That event is mostly gone now; yet the debut of autumn, with its persistent chill, still comes to mark the exodus of summer.

Now and then, there are occasional warm days wedged into the descending curtain of cold. On days like this, I am out on the deck or taking a walk, sensing that life struggles to hold on, to get in one last hurrah before hard frost and, after that, winter will shut it down. When airspaces are still golden and warm, life suddenly reappears, if ever so briefly, in the middle of autumn. An occasional magnificent, immense green and blue dragonfly now flies slowly over the garden. Just a few months ago, many fattened themselves on thousands of mosquitoes, gnats, and flies. Ornery, high-strung yellowjackets, their ranks now well thinned by frosts, frantically search for the sweets of mashed apples on the driveway. Near the fence line at the rear of the yard, a few hardy workers of thatching ants are roaming across the high mound of their nest. But not all insect life surges back for another moment in the sun. I can no longer find metallic green beetles skirting a sandy path down to the lake. Indeed, all that is left now are remnants of the breeding populations that flourished in summer.

We are now in the season of a few loose ends, but for the most part, the lines are sharper on the landscape, the air less dense, and autumn's message is to the point, clean and definite. Features of the land, once hidden by foliage, now become boldly obvious. When the weather conditions are right, very few, if any, sojourns

47

along a wooded path compare to the inspirational magnificence and celebratory mood of autumn colors. The seemingly simple beauty of these trees uplifts the spirit in spite of summer's passing and energizes you to walk briskly on. Living close to a city makes the "nature" experience even more treasured. These are the best days for gazing at the portrait autumn has splashed on nature's canvas. Sunlight cascades down through the branches or brightens a distant slope of forest with a vibrancy that is impossible to describe. Being in the woods on such days cleanses the spirit and mind, bringing joy and a welcome respite from life's ups and downs.

Consider thinking of this cycle of seasons the following way. In spring, life sprouts from the eggs and seeds sown last summer, well before the first frost and autumn's descent over the land. In summer, life reaches a full bloom, not just among plants but among animals too. Then in autumn, life literally falls off its pedestal of prolific glory. But while autumn may feel and behave as an ending, it is really a new beginning. For all that we enjoyed in the yard or meadow this summer has its living fate now sealed away beneath the leaf mulch, in the soil below the frost line, even in the middle of rotting logs in the forest. Life has gone underground only to be saved from winter's wrath and to bloom once again to great heights next summer. In autumn, the drama of life switches for most creatures from branches, leaves, and stems to the mulch below, and in winter to the deep recesses of pond-bottom mud and sand. Life flourishes but it is temporarily more subdued than exuberant. It is also put to the ultimate test of its versatility and fortitude, challenging some numbers of each species, be it arthropod or plant, to survive the rigors of winter seasons at the western edge of this great lake.

Life is very seasoned at sowing its eggs and seeds well in advance of the hard frost. Reedy stems in the meadow bear the bulbous galls of flies and an occasional egg case of a praying mantis.

A new generation of some 40 species of this region's wild bees are sealed away as pupae in earthen cells. Those that survive will hatch in spring to be the new season's first wave of pollinators that will allow many of our native species of plants to propagate. Grasshoppers are hunkered down under the tall grass thatch of the meadow. And very soon, all of those colors and sounds of summer will be but memories for another year. Things are fading out fast. But I can still see in my mind those puffs of yellow butterflies swirling around a roadside mud puddle on a steamy afternoon after a thunderstorm.

The woods now going threadbare shows us the forest's inner strength. We see the strong profile of the trees, blurred and softened over summer by dense foliage and the pleasantly distracting rustle of small animals, often heard but not seen. As the leaves turn and fall, the woods takes on a new personality, exposing its core. Time is tilting, branches are creaky, and squirrels scamper through the undergrowth. Here and there an evergreen still stands as a reminder of what was, but this is the time when deciduousness paints the land with new tones and messages.

But for sure, as I sit on the deck in the cool air or stroll through the woods nearby, autumn exudes an illusion, one of completeness and finality. Life is unquestionably present, just wisely concealed. Butterflies are chrysalises sheltered from the wind or partly grown caterpillars wrapped in silken sheaths and plant debris. Crickets, grasshoppers, and katydids are knots of eggs in the earth and twigs. Moths are tough cocoons and sticky masses on branches. Dragonflies, diving beetles, and tadpoles are nestled in mud. Squirrels and chipmunks are holing up with hoards of nuts and seeds. Mated, fattened queen wasps are wedged in tight crevices in log and rocks, ready to build new colonies next summer. When the dried leaves of autumn crunch beneath our feet, all is not dead, but rather transformed into a different state to cope with winter's impending wrath.

So we must not let autumn fool us into believing that life, so aptly expressed in many different creatures big and small, drab and gaudy, is on the verge of being snuffed out by its frosts. Look to the gaudy colors of autumn leaves to signal the eventual presence of renewed life. In autumn's vibrant colors there are reminders of summer's fullness of life, of winter's impending bleakness, and the prospect of spring not far beyond. Autumn compels us to think about life's transience and continuity all in one. What perishes come the descending cold and frosty nights are the leftovers, the tired individuals that have passed their breeding cycle and fulfilled their roles or those caught off guard by the cold. But for the most part, other members of these species are well ensconced by this time for winter.

I know that the killing frost is close at hand. The land still simmers with the final ebbing of summer's harvests, but soon it will be over. When I sense these transitions, from warmth to cold, from insects abounding everywhere to their crescendo and exit, I am pulled up short by the realization that very soon hard frost will clear the landscape of insect sounds and colors for another year. But life is not gone. Life is never gone. An optimistic, strong message prevails.

Beyond the killer ice and later the bitter winds and deep snows, life flourishes. As with the bald-faced hornet, all creatures prepare for survival through frost and winter well before the frost sets in. Beneath the ice and snow, the hardened soil holds the numbed but living capsules of new life. The soil is a tomb now of spores, seeds, and roots—not a dead, but a living tomb—that will sprout a fresh, new verdancy when spring softens and warms the earth and all it holds. When the mornings are much colder and the view from the deck is one of silence and snowy whiteness, I will think about the cricket's eggs in the soil, the butterfly chrysalises and moth cocoons in the brambles, the dragonfly nymphs ensconced in mud beneath the ice of the pond.

So, in the hard frost I sense that is not far off now, there will be not just the cleansing of the landscape of mosquitoes, flies, and yellowjackets, but a reinscription of the promise of life yet to be. I am sure that out there, in the now brittle and naked brush, under a rock or log, lies a living new mother bald-faced hornet. I would be honored if she would appear in my yard next year, but this is unlikely. Nature is that way, a shifting, whimsical cacophony of changing scenes and players, a guarantee that nothing stays the same one year to the next.

In the meantime, I will pay close attention to the sentinels of this season. There is still time to celebrate what summer has given, simple yet complex and exquisite living graces, high in the treetops or close to the ground. As the weather turns and the nights become frosty rather than steamy, life still clings to the branches above my head as I walk along, and as more and more falling leaves create an amazing portrait of colors on grass, pavement, and forest floor. Life struggles to hold on, to give us those now fading, weakening sounds—acoustical shadows of summer—as the cold closes in.

PART TWO

Endings

INTRODUCTION

There is a midsummer and a midwinter, says Edwin Way Teale, but "no midspring or midautumn. These are the seasons of constant change." True enough. Yet, autumn, unlike spring, is marked not only by change but also by endings, as the medieval poets knew well: "Now fade rose and lily-flower / That for a while bore that sweet savor / in summer, that sweet time...."

Sweet summer, we know, lasts only "for a while," and so autumn becomes the season to say goodbye. Goodbye to the lake as we shake ourselves dry and climb back onto land. Goodbye to loosened schedules and lazy days as we winterize the well, pull in the boats. The long, slender dock retreats section by section into a squat tower of heavy wood, hunkered down for the winter, land-locked for another year.

We may not anticipate autumn's endings, but we do expect them, for they are the rituals we enact year after year. We close the cottage, wave farewell to college students, bed down the plants, hang the storm windows, rake up the dead leaves, put away the shorts and swimsuits and cotton tees, and haul out sweaters and socks. There is a whiff of mortality about these ordinary, homey chores. "The bustle in a house / The morning after death / Is solemnest of indus-tries / Enacted upon earth," Emily Dickinson reminds us, drawing together familiar domestic rituals with the finality of death. Falling leaves, in particular, tug us toward melancholy. William Shakespeare, looking at the frost-stripped trees, is moved to contemplate his own declining strength:

> *That time of year thou mayst in me behold*
> *When yellow leaves, or none, or few do hang*
> *Upon those boughs which shake against the cold,*
> *Bare ruined choirs, where late the sweet birds sang.*

And nearly three centuries later, Gerard Manley Hopkins sees even in a child the specter of imminent death:

> *Márgarét, are you gríeving*
> *Over Goldengrove unleaving?*
> *Leáves, líke the things of man, you*
> *With your fresh thoughts care for, can you?*
> *Áh! ás the heart grows older*
> *It will come to such sights colder*
> *By and by, nor spare a sigh*
> *Though worlds of wanwood leafmeal lie;*
> *And yet you will weep and know why.*
> *Now no matter, child, the name:*
> *Sórrows spríngs áre the same.*
> *Nor mouth had, no nor mind, expressed*
> *What heart heard of, ghost guessed:*
> *It ís the blight man was born for,*
> *It is Margaret you mourn for.*

But what strange creatures we are. Although autumn's endings are inevitable, as stylized as ritual, they still catch us unawares. The "first killing frost of the season always sneaks up on me,"

Allen Young writes. "I really don't know when it will come, only that it surely will." And it is not just the first frost that sneaks up on us, but all the other harbingers of autumn. We're startled one morning not to see the bird feeders crowded with quarrelsome nuthatches and finches, the sticky red nectar untouched by a hummingbird. Or, as A. Bartlett Giamatti notes, the baseball season ends abruptly and with it the last warm promise of summer's delights. So autumn's endings are heralded both by things that are suddenly present—frost, scarlet leaves, chilly nights—and things that are suddenly absent. The autumn woods, writes Alice Meynell, yield "to their last sunset."

Yet, we are never quite certain when we will be left bereft. Was yesterday the last warm day, or will we be surprised by another week of Indian summer, that "resurrection that has no root in the past, nor steady hold upon the future, like the lambent and fitful gleams from an expiring lamp." We hold our hands to the warm bricks on the flower planters and our faces up to the sun, grasping this moment, a bit of eternity crystallized in time. One of those perfect fall days will be the last, though known only in retrospect; the prospect of death, if not death itself, hangs in the air in the fall. So November, as Kent Gramm reminds us, becomes nature's "elegy."

Indeed, not just November, but the entire season is crowded with elegiac remembrances: September 11, Veterans' Day, Remembrance Day, All Hallows' Eve, the Day of the Dead. The grief of deaths past, the gray skies, the shortened hours of sunlight, the brown grass and crumpled leaves threaten to overwhelm us. Which is why we need not just elegies in autumn but also the somber and glorious rituals of the great liturgies. Liturgies do not sentimentalize death—"ashes to ashes and dust to dust"—but they do remind us that without endings we cannot have a new beginning. They stir us to action.

The high holy days of the Jewish autumnal calendar include Rosh Hashanah, the new year, which commemorates both the creation of the world and its ultimate judgment—first and last things brought together in a single celebration of life's completed cycle. But Rosh Hashanah is preceded by the month of Elul, when we are enjoined to take inventory of our lives, and followed by Yom Kippur, the day of atonement, when our sincere repentance is met with forgiveness. The Christian liturgy recognizes the beginning of fall with ember days, a time for fasting and repentance. Although ember days occur at the beginning of each of the four seasons, they are perhaps most poignant in the autumn, when willful abstinence takes its proper role—not as a life-denying force but as a cleansing of body and soul that prepares us for the harvest feasts. As a thirteenth-century writer noted, we fast during the autumnal ember days so that we might "repress the drought of pride" and become ripe with the "fruit of good works." Ramadan, a central month in the Islamic liturgical year that is frequently, though not always, observed in autumn, also recognizes human imperfections and failures by imposing a stringent fast during the daylight hours. Yet here, too, fasting opens up each evening into renewed commitment, energy, and feasting.

These autumnal rites of fasting and repentance announce the blessing of endings, for they clear away the clutter of our lives, sweep out the barns, and make room for the fresh, ripe fruit of the harvest. Autumn juggles the blazing opposites of elegy and liturgy, the finality of farewell and the promise that goodbyes are only for a season. There will be another winter, another spring, another summer in which we accumulate the glory and muck of daily life. And there will be another autumn when we shed our dry leaves and open our hearts to a new harvest.

FROM THE BOOK OF RUTH IN THE HEBREW BIBLE

In this second selection from the book of Ruth, we encounter the harshness of endings. Naomi has known other farewells—to family and friends, to her home in Bethlehem, to her husband and sons, but none, perhaps, as poignant as this farewell to her daughters-in-law. They are the last connection to her children, her last hope for grandchildren, but more than that they are her friends, her comforters, her beloved daughters. It is not without reason that Naomi refuses her given name, "pleasantness," to take up that of Mara, "bitterness." I went away full, she says; I have come back empty.

> *Without laying down the tried and true, there cannot be the taking up of love's light burden.*

And yet here we have also another ending—Ruth's ending. For Ruth, too, says goodbye. Goodbye to her family, to familiar haunts, to security, to her own language, customs, and people. But without this ending, there cannot be a new beginning. Without laying down the tried and true, there cannot be the taking up of love's light burden. The sojourn in Moab has indeed come to an end, but in Bethlehem it is just the beginning of barley harvest.

FROM THE BOOK OF RUTH

Then Orpah and Ruth lifted up their voices and wept, and Orpah kissed her mother-in-law goodbye. But Ruth clung to Naomi.

Then Naomi said to Ruth, "Orpah, your sister-in-law, is going back to her people, her land, and her gods. Follow her and return with her."

But Ruth said, "Do not entreat me to leave you or to turn away from you; for where you go I will go, and where you dwell I will dwell; your people shall be my people and your God my God; where you die I will die and there will I also be buried. May the Lord judge me if anything, even death, parts me from you."

When Naomi saw that Ruth could not be dissuaded, she ceased arguing, and they set off down the road to Bethlehem. When they came to Bethlehem, the rumors soon flew about the city. "Is this not Naomi?" the women whispered.

"Do not call me Naomi, the beautiful one," replied Elimelech's widow. "Call me Mara, the bitter one, for the Almighty has made me bitter indeed. I went away full, replete with husband and sons, but the Lord has brought me back empty. Why should you call me Naomi when the Lord has humbled me, and the Almighty has brought me nothing but adversity?"

So Naomi and Ruth, her Moabite daughter-in-law, returned from the country of Moab to the city of Bethlehem. And it was the beginning of the barley harvest.

A Gathering of Poems
and an Essay from World War I

The poems that came out of the trenches and the home front during World War I were not infrequently set during autumn. That setting was deliberate. The common motif here is that of a harvest, but an ironic harvest replete with death and endings. Thus, the scenes of rural plenitude and falling leaves and full fields that are sometimes evoked bear a bitter weight; they seem to mock the harvest of dead bodies that travel in carts along the same roads that once bore bright fruit to market.

Henry Major Tomlinson's essay brings that ironic harvest to the city. As he rides the train or walks the streets of London, he is caught between the brisk autumnal optimism of his fellow citizens and the barren lethargy of his own heart. Yet, in the quiet, almost forgotten sanctuary of an old bookshop, he senses—if only for a moment—the sweet odor of harvests past and the fleeting hope that they may, perhaps, come once again.

> The common motif here is that of a harvest, but an ironic harvest replete with death and endings.

Break of Day

Siegfried Sassoon

There seemed a smell of autumn in the air
At the bleak end of night; he shivered there
In a dank, musty dug-out where he lay,
Legs wrapped in sand-bags,—lumps of chalk and clay
Spattering his face. Dry-mouthed, he thought, "To-day
We start the damned attack; and Lord knows why,
Zero's at nine; how bloody if I'm done in
Under the freedom of that morning sky!"
And then he coughed and dozed, cursing the din.

Was it the ghost of autumn in that smell
Of underground, or God's blank heart grown kind,
That sent a happy dream to him in hell?—
Where men are crushed like clods, and crawl to find
Some crater for their wretchedness; who lie
In outcast immolation, doomed to die
Far from clean things or any hope of cheer,
Cowed anger in their eyes, till darkness brims
And roars into their heads, and they can hear
Old childish talk, and tags of foolish hymns.

He sniffs the chilly air; (his dreaming starts).
He's riding in a dusty Sussex lane
In quiet September; slowly night departs;
And he's a living soul, absolved from pain.
Beyond the brambled fences where he goes
Are glimmering fields with harvest piled in sheaves,
And tree-tops dark against the stars grown pale;
Then, clear and shrill, a distant farm-cock crows;

And there's a wall of mist along the vale
Where willows shake their watery-sounding leaves.
He gazes on it all, and scarce believes
The earth is telling its old peaceful tale;
He thanks the blessed world that he was born ...
Then, far away, a lonely note of the horn.

They're drawing the Big Wood! Unlatch the gate,
And set Golumpas going on the grass:
He knows the corner where it's best to wait
And hear the crashing woodland chorus pass;
The corner where old foxes make their track
To the Long Spinney; that's the place to be.
The bracken shakes below an ivied tree,
And then a cub looks out; and "Tally-o-back!"
He bawls, and swings his thong with volleying crack,—
All the clean thrill of autumn in his blood,
And hunting surging through him like a flood
In joyous welcome from the untroubled past;
While the war drifts away, forgotten at last.

Now a red, sleepy sun above the rim
Of twilight stares along the quiet weald,
And the kind, simple country shines revealed
In solitudes of peace, no longer dim.
The old horse lifts his face and thanks the light,
Then stretches down his head to crop the green.
All things that he has loved are in his sight;
The places where his happiness has been
Are in his eyes, his heart, and they are good.
Hark! there's the horn: they're drawing the Big Wood.

October

SIEGFRIED SASSOON

Across the land a faint blue veil of mist
Seems hung; the woods wear yet arrayment sober,
Till frost shall make them flame; silent and whist
The dropping cherry orchards of October
Like mournful pennons hang their shrivelling leaves
Russet and orange: all things now decay;
Long since ye garnered in your autumn sheaves,
And sad the robins pipe at set of day.

Now do ye dream of Spring when greening shaws
Confer with the shrewd breezes, and of slopes
Flower-kirtled, and of April, sweetling guest;
Days that ye love, despite their windy flaws,
Since they are woven with all joys and hopes
Whereof ye nevermore shall be possessed.

There's Nothing Like the Sun

EDWARD THOMAS

There's nothing like the sun as the year dies,
Kind as it can be, this world being made so,
To stones and men and beasts and birds and flies,
To all things that it touches except snow,
Whether on mountain side or street of town.
The south wall warms me: November has begun,
Yet never shone the sun as fair as now
While the sweet last-left damsons from the bough
With spangles of the morning's storm drop down

Because the starling shakes it, whistling what
Once swallows sang. But I have not forgot
That there is nothing, too, like March's sun,
Like April's, or July's, or June's, or May's,
Or January's, or February's, great days:
August, September, October, and December
Have equal days, all different from November.
No day of any month but I have said—
Or, if I could live long enough, should say—
"There's nothing like the sun that shines today."
There's nothing like the sun till we are dead.

The Falling Leaves

Margaret Postgate Cole

November 1915

Today, as I rode by,
I saw the brown leaves dropping from their tree
In a still afternoon,
When no wind whirled them whistling to the sky,
But thickly, silently,
They fell, like snowflakes wiping out the noon;
And wandered slowly thence
For thinking of a gallant multitude
Which now all withering lay,
Slain by no wind of age or pestilence,
But in their beauty strewed
Like snowflakes falling on the Flemish clay.

"An Autumn Morning"

Henry Major Tomlinson

The way to my suburban station and the morning train admonishes me sadly with its stream of season-ticket holders carrying dispatch-cases, and all of them anxious, their resolute pace makes it evident, for work. This morning two aeroplanes were over us in the blue, in mimic combat; they were, of course, getting into trim for the raid to-night, because the barometer is beautifully high and steady. But the people on their way to the 9.30 did not look up at the flight. Life is real, life is earnest. When I doubt that humanity knows what it is doing, I get comfort from watching our local brigadiers and Whitehall ladies on their way these tranquil Autumn mornings to give our planet another good shove towards the millennium. Progress, progress! I hear their feet overtaking me, brisk and resolute, as though a revelation had come to them overnight, and so now they know what to do, undiverted by any doubt. There is a brief glimpse of a downcast face looking as though it had just chanted the *Dies Irae* through the mouthfuls of a hurried breakfast; and once more this laggard is passed in the day's race towards the higher peak. The reproof goes home. It justly humiliates. But the weather is only a little west of south for one of the last fair days of the year; and the gloom of the yew in the churchyard—which stands over the obscure headstone of a man named Puplett—that yew which seems the residue of the dark past, has its antiquity full of little smouldering embers of new life again; and so a lazy man has reasons to doubt whether the millennium is worth all this hurry. As it is, we seem to have as much trouble as there is time to classify before supper; by which time, from the look of the weather, there will be more. Then why hurry over it? The tombstone says Puplett was a "thrifty and industrious parent," and I can see what happened to him in 1727. What would I not give, I ask myself, as I pause by the yew, and listen to the aeroplanes overhead, for a few words from this Puplett on thrift, industry, and progress! Does he now know more than brigadiers?

It may be that what Europe is suffering from in our time is the consequence of having worked too hard, since that unlucky day when Watt gave too much thought to a boiling kettle. We have worked too hard without knowing why we were doing it, or what our work would do with us. We were never wise enough to loaf properly, to stop and glance casually around for our bearings. We went blindly on.

There is a street which turns abruptly from my straight road to the station. It goes like a sudden resolution to get out of this daily hurry and excitement. It is a pre-war street. It is an ancient thoroughfare of ours, a rambling and unfrequented by-way. It is more than four years since it was a habit of mine to loiter through it, with a man with whom I shall do no more pleasant idling. We enjoyed its old and ruinous shops and its stalls, where all things could be bought at second-hand, excepting young doves, ferrets, and dogs. I saw it again this morning, and felt, somehow, that it was the first time I had noticed it since the world suddenly changed. Where had it been in the meantime? It was empty this morning, it was still, it was luminous. It might have been waiting, a place that was, for the return of what can never return. Its sunlight was different from the glare in the hurrying road to the station. It was the apparition of a light which has gone out. I stopped, and was a little fearful. Was that street really there? I thought its illumination might be a ghostly sunlight haunting an avenue leading only to the nowhere of the memory. Did the others who were passing see that by-way? I do not think so. They never paused. They did not glance sideways in surprise, stare in an expectancy which changed almost at once into regret for what was good, but is not.

Who would not retire into the near past, and stay there, if it were possible? (What a weakness!) Retrospection was once a way of escape for those who had not the vitality to face their own fine day with its exacting demands. Yet who now can look squarely at the present, except officials, armament shareholders, and those in perambulators? This side-turning offered me a chance to dodge the calendar and enter the light of day not ours. The morning train of the day I saw in that street went before the War. I decided to lose it, and visit the shop at the top of the street, where once you could buy anything from a toddy glass to an emu's egg having a cameo on it of a ship in full sail. It was also a second-hand bookshop. Most lovers of such books would have despised it. It was of little use to go there for valuable editions, or even for such works as Sowerby's *Botany*. But when last the other man and myself rummaged in it we found the first volume of the *Boy's Own Paper*, and an excellent lens for our landscape camera. An alligator, sadly in need of upholstering, stood at the door, holding old umbrellas and walking-sticks in its arms. The proprietor, with a sombre nature and a black beard so like the established shadows of his lumbered premises that he could have been overlooked for part of the unsalable stock, read Swedenborg, Plato, Plutarch, and Young's *Night Thoughts*—the latter an edition of the eighteenth century in which an Edinburgh parson had made frail marginal comments, yellow and barely discernible, such as: "How True!" This dealer in lumber read through large goggles, and when he had decided to admit he knew you were in his shop he bent his head, and questioned you steadily but without a word over the top of his spectacles. If you showed no real interest in what you proposed to buy he would refuse to sell it.

There I found him again, still reading—Swedenborg this time—with most of the old things about him, including the Duck-billed Platypus; for nobody, apparently, had shown sufficient interest in them. The shop, therefore, was as I have always known it. There was a spark of a summer's day of 1914 still burning in the heart of a necromancer's crystal ball on the upper shelf by the window.

The curio there, which was really animated, put down his book after I had been in the shop for some minutes, regarded me deliberately as though looking to see what change had come to me in four such years, and then glanced up and nodded to the soothsayer's crystal. "It's a pity," he said, "that those things won't really work." He asked no questions. He did not inquire after my friend. He did not refer to those problems which the crowds in the morning trains were eagerly discussing at that moment. He sat on a heap of forgotten magazines, and remained apart with Swedenborg. I loafed in the fertile dust and quiet among old prints, geological specimens, antlers, pewter, bed-warmers, amphorae, and books. The proprietor presided over the dim litter of his world, bowed, pensive, and silent, suggesting in his aloofness not indifference but a retired sadness for those for whom the mysteries could be made plain, but who are willful in their blindness, and so cannot be helped.

I came upon a copy of *Walden,* in its earliest Camelot dress (price sixpence), and remembered that one who was not there had once said he was looking for it in that edition. I turned to the last page and read: "Only that day dawns to which we are awake ..."

I reserved the book for him at once, though knowing I could not give it to him. But what is the good of cold reason? Are we awake in such dawns as we now witness? Or has there been no dawn yet because we are only restless in our sleep? It might be either way, and in such a perplexity reason cannot help us. I thought that perhaps I might now be stirring, on the point of actually rousing. There, in any case, was the evidence of that fugitive spark of the early summer of 1914 still imprisoned in its crystal, proof that the world had experienced a dawn or two. An entirely unreasonable serenity possessed me—perhaps because I was not fully roused—because of the indestructibility of those few voiceless hopes we cherish that seem as fugitive as the glint in the crystal ball, hopes without which our existence would have no meaning, for if we lost them we should know the universe was a witless jest, with nobody to laugh at it.

"I want this book," I said to the shopman.

"I know," he answered, without looking up. "I've kept it for you."

Alix Kates Shulman

"The Island," from
Drinking the Rain

*At age fifty, Alix Kates Shulman decided to leave New York City, with its
enormous political, family, and literary demands, and travel north to Maine,
where she would live in a cabin with no electricity, plumbing, or telephone—*

*The summer may be
ending, and the vital life
that she has known may be
threatened by her return
to the city, but suddenly,
all around her, she senses
and witnesses a shocking
fecundity, which gives her
a new resolve.*

*and no grocery store. She would
live independently as much as possible, even foraging for much of her
food.* Drinking the Rain *is her
reflective chronicle of that period in
her life and of the ways in which
she grew in understanding of her
own self, her own abilities.*

*In the following selection,
Shulman finds autumn upon her.
She has gathered many of the
apples, and she has been watching the geese fly south. The air
is colder, and she recognizes that soon she will have to leave. (The cabin,
after all, is not insulated, and the woodstoves uncertain.) But she puts off
the movement back to the city for as long as she can, and finds something
remarkable in the days before she leaves: a surprising and powerful abun-*

dance. The summer may be ending, and the vital life that she has known may be threatened by her return to the city, but suddenly, all around her, she senses and witnesses a shocking fecundity, which gives her a new resolve.

"The Island"

It's October 18—later than I've ever been on the island. Dense foggy mornings, frosty nights, a lucent crown of brilliant red and golden leaves on the distant ridge. A stately great blue heron arrives at dusk to fish the cove; hundreds of ducks mass offshore in a huge black armada; two cedar waxwings with their masked faces and jaunty crests swing on the ripened goldenrod burning across the nubble in the cool October light; honking geese V southward overhead—all preparing for winter. Soon, I fear, I too, succumbing to the cold, will have to pack and leave.

A storm rages that night, bringing heavy winds and choppy seas. When it clears, the normally white beach is littered with masses of dark seaweed thrown up from the deep and other interesting debris that cause bathers to think post-storm beaches "dirty." (One summer, in fact, the city of Portland hired teams of teenagers to rake up and burn all the seaweed, driftwood, and refuse that had accumulated on South Beach during the previous winter, only to see much of it replaced during the next big storm. The one lasting result I could see of all that fruitless effort was the pitiful waste of the driftwood fuel I'd come to count on.) According to a booklet on seaweeds Jerry has kindly mailed up to me, many species of seaweed are exposed only after a storm; so at the next low tide I go down to the beach in my poncho to investigate.

The shore is strewn with balls of Irish moss, immense blades of smooth long-stemmed kelp, similar to the Japanese kombu, and several long whips of the rare sea plant I'd longed to find, alaria. This brown seaweed, sometimes called honey kelp, winged kelp, or, in Japanese, wakame, looks very like ordinary long-stemmed kelp but for the delicious hollow rib which is actually a continuation of the stem, or stipe, running from the holdfast all along the blade to the very tip and which, when sliced into a salad or stew, adds a sweet tasty crunch, something like water chestnuts.

When I've gathered all the alaria I can find, I crisscross the beach several times more looking for tangle and dulse, but without success, and pass up two more left-handed fisherman's gloves at their historic spot. Heading up the beach toward the nubble, I notice what looks like a giant quahog, the largest I've ever seen, lying alone like a rock in the midst of a great expanse of white sand at the top of the beach, far from the water.

I stoop to examine it. Its shell is open about half an inch, revealing the firm plump flesh of a living clam. I pick it up. Measuring eight or nine inches across, it lies in my hand like a stone weighing several pounds—equivalent in size to perhaps a dozen of my ordinary, laboriously procured clams. As soon as I poke the flesh the quahog snaps closed its shells, clamming up tight. I drop it into the bucket.

For years I've seen only ashtrays in those largest of all empty clam shells strewn along the shore, have passed them in ignorance, like most beachcombers, oblivious of their species or how they got there. I suppose I assumed they'd been snatched from the ocean by gulls and dropped from the sky—even though their smooth shells offer no purchase for a beak and seem far too heavy for a gull to lift. Now, remembering that storms can toss entire armadas onto shore, I wonder if perhaps the ocean itself hasn't somehow hurled it here.

Can it be safe to eat? With plants the trick is to avoid harmful species; but with shellfish it's the tainted individual one must guard against by making sure each specimen is alive and healthy when caught. This is not always as easy as it appears; it takes some practice to discover each species' telltale vital motions. Most creatures naturally retreat or flee when they sense danger: clams clam up, periwinkles slam shut their opercula, crabs scram; but (as humans have sometimes observed closer to home) some live creatures act dead and some dead ones look alive. Crustaceans that have just shed their shell go limp and simulate corpses, while lifeless empty bivalve shells are sometimes misleadingly glued shut by a cement of water and sand. To guard against these traps, I've learned to cook my bivalves separately; then, if an individual fails to open, or if a sand-filled one finds its way into the pot, I can remove the duds, let the sand sink, and skim off the good broth. Ordinarily I wouldn't consider eating a creature lacking any means of surface locomotion found so far from its underwater habitat; but this particular clam is so clearly alive and so loaded with meat—big enough for an entire meal—that I decide to risk it.

That evening I turn my catch into the sweetest chowder I've ever had. In the pot, it gives up a rich aromatic broth and yields over a cupful of nutty meat. I thicken the strained broth with gelatinous Irish moss (the same agent used commercially to thicken ice cream), add the chopped meat, flavor it with sea rocket, garlic, and angelica, and garnish it with six inches of crisp stipe of fresh alaria that I sliver with a paring knife. To the accompaniment of foghorns and buoy bells, beside a crackling fire, I slowly eat my dinner.

The next day I'm down at the shore hunting again. I find three more specimens of the giant clam, and the following day, two. I scrub them, steam them open, and anatomize them, examining each intricate organ before I eat them. I'm so absorbed that not till the third day do I turn to my books to see what I can find out about this newest and easiest catch. Gibbons, in an entire brief chapter devoted to its praises, tells me I have found not a quahog but a surf clam, the largest clam species on the Atlantic seaboard. Like so many wild foods, the surf clam is widely scorned by all but a few initiates—including Gibbons, and now myself. I'm pleased to find I've been chopping into my chowders parts of the clam that even Gibbons disdains as tough. From him I learn to sauté and savor unadorned the large tender cylindrical abductor muscles, the very part of the scallop we consume and prized by Gibbons in the surf clam as sweeter than the sweetest scallop's.

Tomorrow, according to the forecast, begins another week of cold with intermittent rain. Having already felt the first premonitory chill of winter, I'm resigned to boarding up and leaving for the city in at most a week. In the few remaining days I concentrate exclusively on surf clams, snatching them from cresting waves before the undertow can rush them out again. As I toss the empty shells out to sea, I wonder if and where they'll wash ashore to be collected for ashtrays by day-trippers ignorant of what they've found—like me until just this week. It troubles me that though I read Gibbons's book straight through, I never before noticed a surf clam. What other edible species may be lying unrecognized at my feet?

On Friday the sea turns calm, and there are no more clams.

Bundled up on the deck in parka, muffler, and gloves to capture the few precious hours of remaining light, I seem to have entered a new mode. I glance up from my book to notice the apple tree heavy with ripe fruit. But instead of being small and green, the apples are yellow, some tinted with delicate pale-pink stripes, some as large as market fruit. My surprise registers more as a feeling than as a thought. I reproach myself for having made no more than half a dozen apple pies this year, as many batches of applesauce, two apple cakes, only three jars of apple chutney, a few experimental savory dishes—and all mainly from windfalls, since I couldn't bear to pluck a fruit before its prime. And now the most perfect apples will go uneaten. (If I had a family to feed we could store our apples for the winter in bins, or dried, or preserved in chutneys, jams, and sauces. But alone I'm able to eat just so many apples.)

Seeing this vast casual waste, I feel a pang of regret—fleeting and dismissible, since I've had all the fruit I want. I let it go and return to my book. But glancing up to reflect on a passage, I see again the groaning tree and the pang returns, this time closer to a thought. Each time I look up it nags at me, expanding bit by bit into the space between my other thoughts, until finally I put down my book and try to grasp it. I focus on the feeling as I fill in one small gap after another, connecting what have hitherto been disparate, even contrary, takes, until at last it's there before me, full-blown as the apple tree itself: a long thought that lengthens and spreads like the sun's rays at day's end till it tints the entire sky— surely the kind of thought Ouspensky means by "long":

This island, which has been my refuge from the waste that is the other side of glut, produces excess of its own. There are all those apples, finally ripened to perfection, and they will not be eaten. Everywhere I look I see a world of astonishing abundance, wild extravagance, glorious waste. Hundreds of thousands of dock seeds, my muffin enricher, fringe the bluff. Touch-me-nots (or jewelweed) fling their edible seeds into the air at the merest touch of a bird or breeze. Brilliant red rose hips, my staple tea, my daily hit of Vitamin C, now entirely surround the cabin. They're already perfectly preserved, and though birds will feed on them all winter there'll still be plenty for me when I return in spring. Countless sea-weeds, naturally dried and salted, line the shore; blackberry leaves, goldenrod, bay all beckon me to harvest and dry them for winter infusions. Everywhere I turn I see abundance and overflow—as excessive as the glut I deplore in the city, but with the crucial dif-ference that here it's all biodegradable. Whatever I leave behind far from being wasted will nourish the soil and grow again.

From a few isolated tentative flashes, my thought has length-ened into an awareness of abundance that replaces the pang of regret with a purr of joy. And still, as long as I concentrate, it has plenty of room to grow—and will continue to grow and stretch until, after many more meals and years, it will eventually encompass a great cornucopia of edibles in perfect ecological balance spiraling in circles downward to the sea within a ten-minute radius of my hearth. Before I'm done I will have found and eaten: elderberries, raspberries, blackberries, huckleberries, currants, shadberries, rose hips, jewelweed, fiddleheads, goldenrod, sheep sorrel, charlock, bay leaves, all from the brush surrounding the cabin; then just down the stairs above the beach: angelica (for parsley), Scotch lovage, dandelion, chicory, beach peas, red clover, orach, lamb's-quarters, strawberry goosefoot, goosetongue, sea rocket, strand wheat, yellow dock, apples; in the tidal flats and among the rocks: steamer clams, quahogs, surf clams, green crabs, blue mussels, horse mussels, periwinkles, dog whelks, moon shells, sea urchins, lobsters, eels; in the tidal pools that form my seaweed garden: sea lettuce, tiger moss, Irish moss, tangle, bullwhip kelp, long-stemmed kelp; and strewn across the beach after a storm: alaria, purple dulse, laver or nori, and colonies of arame; then venturing across the beach, up the path, onto the dirt road: a dozen other varieties of apples, as well as pears, cattails, pineapple weed, juniper berries, serviceberries, cranberries, chokecherries, strawberries, staghorn sumac, Jerusalem artichokes, acorns, chestnuts; and in the woods: wild ginger, blueberries, mint, ground nut, wood sorrel, and various edible fungi. All are part of the living cohort I first glimpsed on the subway in its human manifestation and now see daily in myriad forms everywhere I look.

Not only on the nubble but everywhere, once I've learned how to see. In the cracks of city sidewalks, on the Colorado Rocky mountainsides, in the lawns of Cleveland Heights and the yards of Santa Fe, in the gutters of Honolulu, on the trails of Oahu, sprinkling the desert and lining the riverbanks, I see endless offerings of discarded or unharvested food: pigweed, nasturtiums, laurel, mint, watercress, prickly pears, plums, apricots, avocados, guavas, cherries, crab apples, oranges, lemons, pomegranates—a garden of delectables unrecognized, snubbed, forgotten by a world that goes to the store.

I decide to fill a garbage bag with a selection of dried seaweeds and a few small bags with dock seeds, rose hips, and bay leaves to take back to the city as a reminder of the difference between abundance and glut, between a long thought and a short one.

Now the wild spinach has all gone to seed and the nights have turned so cold that I fear the water will freeze and crack the cistern. I drain it, pack my bags, close off the propane, and before dusk falls reluctantly board up the cabin.

As I look back at the nubble from the end of the road where I wait for Lucy Chaplain to pick me up in the island taxi to take me and my gear to the ferry, I see the great blue heron light again at the base of the Shmoos. I unpack the binoculars to watch him fish. How majestically he stands on one foot in the roiling surf as the tide flows in. He wades through the water so slowly that his movement is almost imperceptible, though once I see him swat at something in the air with his great wing, then snatch it with his beak. Mostly he just waits and watches, patient and still, until the moment comes to plunge his head into the water to grab his prey and then, throwing back his head, consume it in a few snaps of his long beak. I watch his darkening silhouette with its stilt legs and slender throat until there's barely light to see by.

I want my thoughts to be as patient and slow as the heron standing at the water's edge fishing the incoming tide for as long as it takes to catch the treasures swimming by. Or I want them, like the barnacles opening up to feed when the tide comes in, to filter the plankton newly streaming around me, so rich and abundant that what I can't find here hardly seems worth wanting.

A. Bartlett Giamatti

"THE GREEN FIELDS OF THE MIND"

A. Bartlett Giamatti wrote only a few works dealing with baseball, though he was, after leaving the presidency of Yale University, president of baseball's National League for three years and commissioner of baseball for five months before his untimely death. Yet, each of those writings exhibits his poignant suggestion that there is more to baseball than the mere game, even more than the mere statistics—a claim that might verge on heresy for the devout. There is, his writings suggest, a way in which the game serves as a kind of icon of the human experience, showing in its fads and excesses, in its passion and drama, something of the rhythms that make us truly human.

And one part of this icon-like quality is its ability to remind us of our endings. In his short essay "The Green Fields of the Mind," Giamatti speaks to mortality: "There comes a time when every summer will have something of autumn about it." As baseball comes into autumn it comes toward its ending, and "Dame Mutability never loses."

> *As baseball comes into autumn it comes toward its ending, and "Dame Mutability never loses."*

The poignant quality of this knowledge is one to be either embraced or resisted, and Giamatti dwells on both possibilities. But he knows that this is autumn, and autumn, if it does nothing else, dispels illusion.

"The Green Fields of the Mind"

It breaks your heart. It is designed to break your heart. The game begins in the spring, when everything else begins again, and it blossoms in the summer, filling the afternoons and evenings, and then as soon as the chill rains come, it stops and leaves you to face the fall alone. You count on it, rely on it to buffer the passage of time, to keep the memory of sunshine and high skies alive, and then just when the days are all twilight, when you need it most, it stops. Today, October 2, a Sunday of rain and broken branches and leaf-clogged drains and slick streets, it stopped, and summer was gone.

Somehow, the summer seemed to slip by faster this time. Maybe it wasn't this summer, but all the summers that, in this my fortieth summer, slipped by so fast. There comes a time when every summer will have something of autumn about it. Whatever the reason, it seemed to me that I was investing more and more in baseball, making the game do more of the work that keeps time fat and slow and lazy. I was counting on the game's deep patterns, three strikes, three outs, three times three innings, and its deepest impulse, to go out and back, to leave and to return home, to set the order of the day and to organize the daylight. I wrote a few things this last summer, this summer that did not last, nothing grand but some things, and yet that work was just camouflage. The real activity was done with the radio—not the all-seeing, all-falsifying television—and was the playing of the game in the only place it will last, the enclosed green field of the mind. There, in that warm, bright place, what the old poet called Mutability does not so quickly come.

But out here, on Sunday, October 2, where it rains all day, Dame Mutability never loses. She was in the crowd at Fenway yesterday, a gray day full of bluster and contradiction, when the Red Sox came up in the last of the ninth trailing Baltimore 8–5, while the Yankees, rain-delayed against Detroit, only needing to win one or have Boston lose one to win it all, sat in New York washing down cold cuts with beer and watching the Boston game. Boston had won two, the Yankees had lost two, and suddenly it seemed as if the whole season might go to the last day, or beyond, except here was Boston losing 8–5, while New York sat in its family room and put its feet up. Lynn, both ankles hurting now as they had in July, hits a single down the right-field line. The crowd stirs. It is on its feet. Hobson, third baseman, former Bear Bryant quarterback, strong, quiet, over 100 RBIs, goes for three breaking balls and is out. The goddess smiles and encourages her agent, a canny journeyman named Nelson Briles.

Now comes a pinch hitter, Bernie Carbo, onetime Rookie of the Year, erratic, quick, a shade too handsome, so laidback he is always, in his soul, stretched out in the tall grass, one arm under his head, watching the clouds and laughing; now he looks over some low stuff unworthy of him and then, uncoiling, sends one out, straight on a rising line, over the center-field wall, no cheap Fenway shot, but all of it, the physics as elegant as the arc the ball describes.

New England is on its feet, roaring. The summer will not pass. Roaring, they recall the evening, late and cold, in 1975, the sixth game of the World Series, perhaps the greatest baseball game played in the last fifty years, when Carbo, loose and easy, had uncoiled to tie the game that Fisk would win. It is 8-7, one out, and school will never start, rain will never come, sun will warm the back of your neck forever. Now Bailey, picked up from the National League recently, big arms, heavy gut, experienced, new to the league and the club; he fouls off two and then, checking, tentative, a big man off balance, he pops a soft liner to the first baseman. It is suddenly darker and later, and the announcer doing the game coast to coast, a New Yorker who works for a New York television station, sounds relieved. His little world, well-lit, hot-combed, split-second-timed, had no capacity to absorb this much gritty, grainy, contrary reality.

Cox swings a bat, stretches his long arms, bends his back, the rookie from Pawtucket who broke in two weeks earlier with a record six straight hits, the kid drafted ahead of Fred Lynn, rangy, smooth, cool. The count runs two and two, Brides is cagey, nothing too good, and Cox swings, the ball beginning toward the mound and then, in a jaunty, wayward dance, skipping past Briles, feinting to the right, skimming the last of the grass, finding the dirt, moving now like some small, purposeful marine creature negotiating the green deep, easily avoiding the jagged rock of second base, traveling steady and straight now out into the dark, silent recesses of center field.

The aisles are jammed, the place is on its feet, the wrappers, the programs, the Coke cups and peanut shells, the doctrines of an afternoon; the anxieties, the things that have to be done tomorrow, the regrets about yesterday, the accumulation of a summer: all forgotten, while hope, the anchor, bites and takes hold where a moment before it seemed we would be swept out with the tide. Rice is up. Rice whom Aaron had said was the only one he'd seen with the ability to break his records. Rice the best clutch hitter on the club, with the best slugging percentage in the league. Rice, so quick and strong he once checked his swing halfway through and snapped the bat in two. Rice the Hammer of God sent to scourge the Yankees, the sound was overwhelming, fathers pounded their sons on the back, cars pulled off the road, households froze, New England exulted in its blessedness, and roared its thanks for all good things, for Rice and for a summer stretching halfway through October. Briles threw, Rice swung, and it was over. One pitch, a fly to center, and it stopped. Summer died in New England and like rain sliding off a roof, the crowd slipped out of Fenway, quickly, with only a steady murmur of concern for the drive ahead remaining of the roar. Mutability had turned the seasons and translated hope to memory once again. And, once again, she had used baseball, our best invention to stay change, to bring change on. That is why it breaks my heart, that game—not because in New York they could win because Boston lost; in that, there is a rough justice, and a reminder to the Yankees of how slight and fragile are the circumstances that exalt one group of human beings over another. It breaks my heart because it was meant to, because it was meant to foster in me again the illusion that there was something abiding, some pattern and some impulse that could come together to make a reality that would resist the corrosion; and because, after it had fostered again that most hungered-for illusion, the game was meant to stop, and betray precisely what it promised.

Of course, there are those who learn after the first few times. They grow out of sports. And there are others who were born with the wisdom to know that nothing lasts. These are the truly tough among us, the ones who can live without illusion, or without even the hope of illusion. I am not that grown-up or up-to-date. I am a simpler creature, tied to more primitive patterns and cycles. I need to think something lasts forever, and it might as well be that state of being that is a game; it might as well be that, in a green field, in the sun.

Kent Gramm

FROM *NOVEMBER:* *LINCOLN'S ELEGY AT GETTYSBURG*

"There are two kinds of elegies," writes Kent Gramm. "One is a melancholy contemplation, such as Gray's 'Elegy Written in a Country Church-Yard'; and the other is lament and praise for the dead, ending with comfort and hope—such as Milton's 'Lycidas' or Lincoln's Gettysburg Address. Both kinds are conceived in the fragile, passing beauty of time and dedicated to the mystery of eternity. Each kind of elegy blooms in sorrow from the soil of the past; its beauty remains for tomorrow."

> *H*eroes, he reminds us, are not perfect, merely persistent.

In the book from which the following selections are taken, Gramm weaves together a sustained elegy for losses both public and personal, including the deaths of his father Len (L. L.) and mother Ruth in the month of November. Writing for his children, he burrows into the sorrowful soil of the past—the young victims of many wars; his own fraught relationships with his parents; their disappointments and griefs; the early death of his grandmother, Ingeborg—to find words from which beauty can blossom. But it is a beauty hard-worn. Heroes, he reminds us, are not perfect, merely persistent. Duty, sacrifices, inconsistencies, the petty indignities of illness and age—these are the fragments from which the endings of autumn, and also its hopes, are made.

FROM *NOVEMBER:*
LINCOLN'S ELEGY AT GETTYSBURG

November 2: Our Fathers (L. L.)

All Soul's day—a day for commemorating the unknown men, women, and children who died in the faith.

On November 2, 1863, President Lincoln received a letter from Judge David Wills of Gettysburg, Pennsylvania, chairman of the committee for the establishment of the Soldiers' National Cemetery. Though the address for the occasion would be delivered by the distinguished orator Edward Everett, Wills and the committee wished the president to have a symbolic role in the ceremony: "It is the desire that, after the oration, you, as chief Executive of the nation, formally set apart these grounds to their sacred use by a few appropriate remarks." But Abraham Lincoln saw his role differently. Gettysburg would be the place to tell the people why.

Lincoln had never been in any doubt as to the reason; he did not have to search his imagination or measure public opinion. He had said it years ago: the American experiment in government by the people was "the last, best hope of earth." This time, he must say it better than he ever had before.

That hope must be more than comfort for people who are suffering, for mothers and wives who are grieving. Like the expectation behind the religion Abraham Lincoln grew up with, *that hope* transfers deed to deed. In saying the speech, Lincoln must make word and hope and deed *one*—which is to say, he must make them *faith*. He must define the American faith.

So the message, on this solemn occasion, this dark November day, must be one of hope. Not false hope, not something manufactured. Real hope must be based on something real. As Juergen Moltmann wrote in the 1960s, hope "can overstep the bounds of life, with their closed wall of suffering, guilt, and death, only at the point where they have in actual fact been broken through." So where in actual fact, have the boundaries of tyranny been broken through? By whom? Is it humanly possible, as the modern world believed, at all? If not, does the postmodern awareness we have gained at the cost of ghastly wars convince us, with Camus, that we can only "think clearly, and hope no more"?

Sometimes Americans might forget to care whether representative democracy lives or dies; but here is one tyranny most of us do care about: Death. Our own. A little hope would be a good thing in this matter.

On an anniversary of the letter Abraham Lincoln received from the judge, in a larger sense a similar letter was sent to my father. On a November 2, he died.

On the morning of his stroke, he had been shaving. Shaving was very difficult for him because he was afflicted with Parkinson's disease. His whole right side was crippled. He used his left hand to guide his right, and so the shaving process was as fragile as trying to roll a BB around the edge of a glass. The stroke must have hit like a sledgehammer inside his head. *"Massive cerebral hemorrhage" is written as cause of death on your grandfather's death certificate.* But that was not what finally did it. He actually died of pneumonia. That was brought on by three months of lying in the hospital unable to move. He could never fill his lungs with air and clear them. Then they carried him out into thirty-degree weather to move him from the hospital to a nursing home.

On a Friday, L. L. was carried out into the cold air, put into an ambulance, transported to the north side of town, carried out into the cold again, and put into a private room. Cold was not his friend.

He was susceptible to "The Chills." One late fall night when I was a child, my father came in from the bus stop, shaking uncontrollably. Doubled over in agony, he was nearly helpless, unable to get a heating pad for himself, barely able to sip a cup of hot water. The exquisite torture of those Chills struck at any time, cause unknown, like a stroke of fate, not necessarily in frigid weather, no matter what Len tried to do to prevent them. I get them myself now and I know that they make one virtually surrender the will to live. The Chills hit my father every few years. That final November, Len was too weak to shiver; instead he got pneumonia. On Saturday the prognosis was plain.

November in Wisconsin is gray, cold, and wet. It offers neither the stupendous colors and clear blue sky of October, nor the snow and festivity of December. It is a month to be endured. On Sunday morning we got the telephone call. Arriving at the nursing home we found a Hawaiian luau going on in the large lounge, leis draped over fragile aged people propped in wheelchairs, loud cheap music from the speakers—a schlocky setting for Len, and for his death. In his younger days, L. L. had been a musician.

He lay on his bed, eyes—gray like Lincoln's—not completely closed. He had been propped upon pillows, his arms partly outspread. Now he belongs to the ages.

Or rather, once again the ages might belong to him. He believed that we live many lives, moving like a glimmer from one body to another, down through time, building our own futures, creating the Karma that names us. Truly, in this scheme, the only investment that never fails is goodness.

My father's Lutherans believe in salvation by grace through faith, and he would not have disagreed with them. No, no. It is by grace that we are given chance after chance. But what for? Certainly not simply for one's own salvation.

I believe that L. L.'s sense of duty and his compassion did not guarantee for him an escape from the wheel of birth and death—not without help, anyway. A hero is not perfect. One who heals others cannot always heal himself. Len's good works were countered by the futility of his labor for wealth and security; his faith was constrained by his despair.

He would not have opted for salvation anyway. Sit in heaven, fishing all day? No, no. Got to step right along. There's a lot to do; many more people need help. The world has to be straightened out; there's work to be done.

You can't find the living among the dead.

November 26: Shall Not Perish (Beautiful and Brave)

Len had spoken of fear in the last hours; Ruth would not. Wishing to comfort me, she denied her fear, like an officer in battle. A good soldier learns to accept fear, knowing that fear can be managed. To deny fear in such circumstances is not evasion but courage. But Ruth had plenty of plain, raw bravery, too. It was not the ignorant, youthful kind of the new recruit; she had looked death in the eye many, many times. When the doctor told her that kidney failure is fatal, she simply nodded that she understood. When I told her, a few weeks later, that without dialysis she would lapse into a coma in a few days, she did not blink.

Perhaps soon I can stop writing about war. I have wanted to know how people act under pressure, and why they do what they do. Walt Whitman wrote that he had visited tens of thousands of soldiers wounded and dying in Washington hospitals, and that not one of them had cried out in fear or failed to face the end steadily. I no longer need to read about Civil War soldiers, those young men whom Ruth had seen as old men parading on Decoration Day. I have seen what I was looking for in my own mother. We are a pampered and self-indulgent generation, but our parents were a heroic generation and they have taught us enough to pass to our own children.

John Keats wrote a line that brings us as close as we can come by our own efforts to goodness, to truth, and to God: "A thing of beauty is a joy for ever." Those words of another tuberculosis sufferer—a young man as marked for death as Wilfred Owen—do not mean merely that we ought to act like ladies and gentlemen, despite our natures, instead of like louts. It means that we can decide that the dead shall not have died in vain, and that some things shall not perish from the earth. Ruth decided that Ingeborg would not perish. That decision was a brave one. To make it might have been necessary for survival, but to keep it converted original bravery into daily courage. Her kind and beautiful mother did live on, despite Ruth's anger, confusion, poverty, and fear: Ingeborg's graciousness and generosity with imperishables lived on in someone who had decided to make those virtues her own. Character is a work as well as a gift, and hope is an achievement of faith.

A hero is excellent, though not perfect. "If thou, Lord, shouldest mark iniquities, who shall stand?" Now, especially, when we are conscious of our flaws and inadequacies and perfidies to the point of boredom, it is well to remember by looking at our forebears that heroes conquer their venality. It is not enough merely to be excellent and reprehensible at the same time.... A hero conquers weakness. Each of us fights a war, and it is of practical and eternal value never to surrender. "I know who I am, and who I may be if I choose." Courage is the way to beauty. Beauty is the best we have; it is the image of God.

Ruth's mind remained clear until she lapsed into a coma. A few hours from the end, as I sat near the bed in the old wing chair, a nurse came in and asked "Are you all right?" I nodded. I looked at my mother. I can never lose her. A thing of beauty is a joy forever.

Alice Meynell

FROM "DRY AUTUMN"

Alice Meynell, an English essayist and poet twice nominated as Britain's Poet Laureate, here reflects on an unexpected autumn, one no novelist could describe by rote. Rather than the "crimson woods and yellow," she celebrates the long dry grasses softened into a "hundred exquisite browns." For this is a dry autumn, not one of moldering leaves or "gaudy decay" but one burned crisp by the unfaltering sun. Meynell exults in this strange landscape, a splendid autumnal demise "without pathos." If we must come to an end—and indeed we must—then let it be the "vital fires" of autumn that consume us as we yield gracefully to our last sunset.

> If we must come to an end—and indeed we must—then let it be the "vital fires" of autumn that consume us as we yield gracefully to our last sunset.

FROM "DRY AUTUMN"

Autumn had borne herself with a heroism of sunny weather. Where we had been wont to see signals of distress, and to hear the voluble outpouring of an excitable temperament, with the extremity of scattered leaves and desperate damp, we beheld an aspect of golden drought. Nothing mouldered—everything was consumed by vital fires. The gardens were strewn with smouldering soft ashes of late roses, late honeysuckle, honey-sweet clematis. The silver seeds of rows of riverside flowers took sail on their random journey with a light wind. Leaves set forth, a few at a time, with a little volley of birds—a buoyant caravel. Or, in the stiller weather, the infrequent fall of leaves took place quietly, with no proclamation of ruin, in the privacy within the branches. While nearly all the woods were still fresh as streams, you might see that here or there was one, with an invincible summer smile, slowly consuming, in defiance of decay. Life destroyed that autumn, not death.

The novelist would be at a loss had we a number of such years. He would lose the easiest landscape—for the autumn has among her facile ways the way of allowing herself to be described by rote. But there were no regions of crimson woods and yellow—only the grave, cool, and cheerful green of the health of summer, and now and then that deep bronzing of the leaves that the sun brought to pass. Never did apples look better than in those still vigorous orchards. They shone so that lamps would hardly be brighter. The apple-gathering, under such a sun, was nearly as warm and brilliant as a vintage; and indeed it was of the Italian autumn that you were reminded. There were the same sunburnt tones, the same brown health. There was the dark smile of chestnut woods as among the Apennines.

For it was chiefly within the woods that the splendid autumn without pathos gave delight. The autumn *with* pathos has a way there of overwhelming her many fragrances in the general odour of dead leaves generalized. That year you could breathe all the several sweet scents, as discriminated and distinct as those of flowers on the tops of mountains—warm pine and beech as different as thyme and broom, unconfused. Even the Spring, with her little divided breezes of hawthorn, rose, and lilac, was not more various.

Moreover, while some of the woods were green, none of the fields were so. In their sunburnt colours were to be seen "autumn tints" of a far different beauty from that of a gaudy decay. Dry autumn is a general lover of simplicity, and she sweeps a landscape with long plain colours that take their variations from the light. When the country looks "burnt up," as they say who are ungrateful for the sun, then are these colours most tender. Grass, that had lost its delicacy in the day when the last hay was carried, gets it again. For a little time it was—new-reaped—of something too hard a green; then came dry autumn along, and softened it into a hundred exquisite browns. Dry autumn does beautiful things in sepia, as the water-colour artist did in the early days, and draws divine brown Turners of the first manner.

The fields and hedgerows must needs fade, and the sun made the fading quick with the bloom of brown. For one great meadow so softly gilded, I would give all the scarlet and yellow trees that ever made a steaming autumn gorgeous—all the crimson of the Rhine valleys, all the patched and spotted walnut-leaves of the *mühl-thal* by Boppard, and the little trees that change so suddenly to their yellow of decay in groups at the foot of the ruins of Sternberg and Liebenstein, every one of their branches disguised in the same bright, insignificant, unhopeful colour.

An autumn so rare should not close without a recorded "hail and farewell!" Spring was not braver, summer was not sweeter. That year's great sun called upon a great spirit in all the riverside woods. Those woods did not grow cold; they yielded to their last sunset.

Leo Dangel

FROM OLD MAN BRUNNER COUNTRY

In Old Man Brunner Country, *the Midwestern poet Leo Dangel evokes the life of the Dakotan farmer. In the first two poems in this grouping, Dangel presents a land with very prescribed codes. If you are insulted, you fight. If you take a walk, it's purposeful. Here, in autumn, a schoolyard is for fighting, and a walk is for hunting. Ends are prescribed for means.*

But in the third selection, Dangel shows that human experience is never so predictable. In the hilarity of a Halloween night, he sees what he least expects, as the sight of an orange passing down a line becomes a kind of sacrament.

Dangel shows that human experience is never so predictable. In the hilarity of a Halloween night, he sees what he least expects, as the sight of an orange passing down a line becomes a kind of sacrament.

No Question

There was no question,
I had to fight Arnold Gertz
behind the high school that Friday.
All fall he kept throwing pool balls
at me in the rec room.

There was no question,
I was scared spitless at the mere sight
of his grimy fists and bull neck.
When we rolled on the cinders
and grappled and thumped each other,

there was no question,
I was actually winning
when the principal broke us up.
And when Arnold went hunting pheasants
on Sunday, everybody said

there was no question,
he was a damn fool to climb through
a barbed wire fence with a loaded shotgun.
There were exactly eight of us guys
who were classmates of Arnold so

there was no question,
I had to be one of the pall bearers,
even though I never liked Arnold,
never would have, but I was sorry
the accident happened,

there was no question,
and if he hadn't got himself shot,
I wonder if he finally would have let me alone.
There is no question,
I wonder about that.

How to Take a Walk

This is farming country.
The neighbors will believe
you are crazy
if you take a walk
just to think and be alone.
So carry a shotgun
and walk the fence line.
Pretend you are hunting
and your walking will not
arouse suspicion.
But don't forget
to load the shotgun.
They will know
if your gun is empty.
Stop occasionally.
Cock your head and listen
to the doves you never see.
Part the tall weeds
with your hand and inspect
the ground.
Sniff the air as a hunter would.
(That wonderful smell

of sweet clover is a bonus.)
Soon you will forget
the gun in your hands,
but remember, someone
may be watching.
If you hear beating wings
and see the bronze flash
of something flying up,
you will have to shoot it.

Passing the Orange

On Halloween night
the new teacher gave a party
for the parents.
She lined up the women
on one side of the schoolroom,
the men on the other,
and they had a race,
passing an orange
under their chins along each line.
The women giggled like girls
and dropped their orange
before it got halfway,
but it was the men's line
that we watched.
Who would have thought
that anyone could get them
to do such a thing?
Farmers in flannel shirts,

in blue overalls and striped overalls.
Stout men embracing one another.
Our fathers passing the orange,
passing the embrace—the kiss
of peace—complaining
about each other's whiskers,
becoming a team, winning the race.

A GATHERING OF POEMS
AFTER SEPTEMBER 11, 2001

In the initial aftershock of September 11, it seemed that the world had undergone an apocalyptic fissure as irreparable as the terrors of World War I, with which this section began. The poems gathered here were written by New Yorkers still shocked by their vulnerability. There is no easy comfort in their words. Nor are words them-selves easy to come by. Meena Alexander longs to write poetry of the season, to see and describe the linden tree by the river. But what comfort does nature hold when "Sweet and bitter smoke stains the sky"? In a similar vein, Kimiko Hahn's terse lines sketch out the colliding worlds of the ordinary and the surreal. In the end, she and her daughter can only "look for something more than disbelief."

> *W*hat comfort does nature hold when "Sweet and bitter smoke stains the sky"?

Aftermath

MEENA ALEXANDER

There is an uncommon light in the sky
Pale petals are scored into stone.

I want to write of the linden tree
That stoops at the edge of the river

But its leaves are filled with insects
With wings the color of dry blood.

At the far side of the river Hudson
By the southern tip of our island

A mountain soars, a torrent of sentences
Syllables of flame stitch the rubble

An eye, a lip, a cut hand blooms
Sweet and bitter smoke stains the sky.
(New York City, September 13–18, 2001)

Boerum Hill Tanka

KIMIKO HAHN

1

Overtaking the crisp air, from across the Bay blow
pages of documents and ashes of terror.

3

A neighbor hoses down her small front garden: snap
peas, zinnias, morning glory vines, grief. So
much grief.

5

Trying to make a daughter's lunch. Trying to
find the other's transit pass. Trying to find a
moment to collapse.

6

At a midnight clap of lightning I sit bolt upright—
more terror? This time across the street?

8

From the Promenade—where my daughter and I saw
Tower Two collapse—we look for something
more than disbelief.

PART THREE

Work

INTRODUCTION

Sowing in the sunshine, sowing in the shadows,
Fearing neither clouds nor winter's chilling breeze;
By and by the harvest, and the labor ended,
We shall come rejoicing, bringing in the sheaves.

Bringing in the sheaves, bringing in the sheaves,
We shall come rejoicing, bringing in the sheaves,
Bringing in the sheaves, bringing in the sheaves,
We shall come rejoicing, bringing in the sheaves.

One of the most familiar of the nineteenth-century harvest hymns proclaims with glad shouts that autumn is a time for work. It is work that stems from that burst of energy the cool weather evokes from bodies finally tired of the summer sun, and it is work that is propelled by necessity. Winter will be bitter indeed if we do not lay up provisions and work until our labor is ended.

The northern wind is a brisk taskmaster, writes H. W. Shepheard-Walwyn in one of those personifications beloved by earlier nature writers: "Prepare for Winter!" the wind bawls at us in icy blasts. And the author continues, "It is only necessary to glance around to discover upon every side fresh confirmation of his relentless mandate. Nature is preparing for Winter on all hands. The Swallow has prepared for Winter by funking it altogether. The major portion of Nature's 'star' soloists have prepared for it, either by following hastily in his tracks, or by making arrangements for a temporary retirement from active service. Down in the dingle, the Dormouse, being for obvious reasons hardly in a position to emulate the example of Philomel, has already crammed himself to bursting point with food, and is now making to 'veil the winter of his discontent' in the mists of a cowardly oblivion. Various other bright-eyed beasties are still bustling about, full of importance, amassing pathetic little hoards of nuts and acorns which, only too often, some other fellow will contrive to steal."

Such determined busyness reminds us that autumn tasks call us to pick up the routines we laid down during the summer sabbath. "Six days you shall labor and do all your work" is a commandment with particular resonance in the fall. Whereas daylight hours steadily diminish in the inexorable march toward the winter solstice, work hours increase. The old metaphors speak of responsibility and routine—to get back into harness, to put your hand to the plough—and conjure images of smooth leather, worn supple with age, and chapped hands, grown rough with work. Harness and hand speak too of the delicate balance between discipline and drudgery we feel as deadlines loom and demands increase. "I'm troubled about the book, tired, and these beautiful autumn days feel wasted because I am only half there," writes May Sarton as she struggles to write *The House by the Sea.* "The only thing is to work along day by day and try to concentrate on making one page, one paragraph, better." To write with that intensity and integrity is, as another writer and teacher notes, a "deliberate, word-by-word crawl" across the page. "It's agonizingly slow, has none of the thrill of a rushy-headlong write," Barbara Hurd says, "and my students hate it. It's too much like work."

But school is the place where most of us first learn the routine of work, and school, for North Americans, is inextricably linked to the smells and sounds of autumn. For many, the arrival of September demands the purchase of notebooks, new pens and pencils, and a fresh box of crayons—even if you are fifty-two. For others, the memories are more quiet: It is the distilled aroma of tansy "on the quiet dusty airs of autumn afternoons," remembers Donald Culross Peattie, "that will remind me, wherever I breathe it, of New England walls, of autumn days at college when new friends were made, new thoughts encountered, and the prospect of another year of loved and chosen study stretched ahead." For yet others the memories are more ambiguous or even painful. Lauren Springer admits that "It took a while for negative associations with the beginning of the school year to wane, for the golden sunlight and foliage to stop conjuring up the intestinal butterflies that went along with similarly toned school buses lurching down the street."

Springer's comments remind us that where there is work, there is also sorrow. The "laborious landscape" that Verlyn Klinkenborg evokes in central Iowa produces abundant corn and rising anxiety over falling prices. Ruth gleaning in the field is romantic only when painted in oils; migrant children juggling apples and ABCs defy the serenity of a pastoral scene. It is sometimes difficult, as Tracy Kidder writes, "to believe that all fifth graders' futures lay before them out of sight, and not in plain view behind."

Yet, just here lies the challenge to our spirits: to pursue routine with hope and to transform labor into dancing joy. Walt Whitman tries to capture these nuances in his image of the industrious spider:

> *A noiseless patient spider,*
> *I mark'd where, on a little promontory, it stood iso-*
> > *lated,*
> *Mark'd how, to explore the vacant, vast surrounding,*
> *It launch'd forth filament, filament, filament out of*
> > *itself,*
> *Ever unreeling them, ever tirelessly speeding them.*

Yet, Whitman's American singularity—"It launch'd forth filament, filament, filament out of itself"—misses the profound truth of this simple Vietnamese work song:

> *Husband, wife and even child*
>> Ro khoan ro khoan ro khuay!
> *All try to catch the fish;*
>> Ro khoan ro khoan ro khuay!
>
> *The river now is so immense,*
>> Ro khoan ro khoan ro khuay!
> *We cannot see the wharf.*
>> Ro khoan ro khoan ro khuay!

The rhythmic call of this *Hò,* or work song, serves a practical end: It coordinates rowers in their small working boats. But their hard physical labor is lightened by melody and communal response. Everyone—"husband, wife and even child"—catches the fish, and all chant the nonsense syllables of the refrain, *"Ro khoan ro khoan ro khuay!"* lifting voice and body into the joy of common effort. In the immensity of the river that carries the boats far from the wharf, there is comfort in the "we" who cannot see the shore.

The great work rituals of autumn—harvest, school, raking the leaves, preparing the Thanksgiving feast—all call us to work together, to accept our dependence on others as a wondrous sign of our humanity. It is in autumn that we learn to work—and to sing—in a chorus that binds us together with love and hope.

FROM THE BOOK OF RUTH IN THE HEBREW BIBLE

This middle section from the book of Ruth begins and ends with work. No sooner have Naomi and Ruth arrived in Bethlehem than Ruth announces that she will go out into the fields to glean the grain. And work she does, not only during the barley harvest but also through the wheat harvest that follows. As we follow Ruth out into the fields, we recognize her courage. It is no small thing for an unaccompanied woman to venture outside the city gates, and an alien woman is more vulnerable than most to the suggestive leers and groping hands of rough farm laborers. The work is hard and unromantic. To be a gleaner is to enter into the fellowship of the poor. Yet, love demands the yoke of routine.

Today Ruth gleans, and tomorrow … and tomorrow.

But love is never dreary, and this selection, bounded by work and routine, fairly sparkles with delicious surprises: Boaz's tender generosity: Stay here to glean, drink my water, work with my servants, eat this lunch; Ruth's scrupulous care: here, Naomi, three bushels of grain and food from my noontime meal; Naomi's amazement: This Boaz is our kins-

It is within this daily cycle of work and routine that we find the greatest surprise of all. God is not our adversary.

man. *For it is within this daily cycle of work and routine that we find the greatest surprise of all. God is not our adversary, the one who brings calamity upon us, but our loving protector under whose wings we find our refuge.*

FROM THE BOOK OF RUTH

Naomi's husband had a wealthy kinsman named Boaz. And Ruth, the Moabite woman, said to Naomi, "Let me go out to the fields and glean the grain that the reapers leave behind. Perhaps I will find a landowner in whose sight I will find grace."

And Naomi said to her, "Go, my daughter."

So Ruth went out and came to a field and gleaned after the reapers. By chance she came to the field of Boaz, kinsman to Elimelech. And on just that day Boaz himself came out from Bethlehem to look on his field. Boaz said to the reapers, "The Lord be with you."

And they answered him, "And also with you."

Then Boaz asked the overseer, "Who is that young woman?"

The overseer replied, "That is the Moabite woman who came with Naomi from the country of Moab. She arrived this morning and asked, 'Oh please, let me glean after your reapers.' And she has been working since the early morning, with only a brief rest."

Then Boaz approached Ruth and said to her, "My daughter, do not go into another field to glean, but stay here with my women workers. Watch and follow them. I have told the young men to leave you alone, and when you are thirsty, drink from the water jugs they have filled for my field hands."

Ruth fell on her face and bowed to the ground and said to Boaz, "How is it that I have found grace in your sight and that you have chosen to favor me, since I am a stranger and an alien?"

But Boaz said to Ruth, "I have heard of all the kindness you have shown toward your mother-in-law since the death of your own husband. You have left your father and your mother and the land where you were born, and you have come to a nation that was strange and alien to you. The Lord will reward you, the Almighty God of Israel under whose wings you have come for refuge."

And Ruth said, "Let me find grace in your sight, my lord, for you have comforted me and spoken kindly to me, even though I am not one of your servants."

At the mealtime, Boaz said to Ruth, "Come, eat bread and dip it into the wine."

Ruth sat down among the reapers, and Boaz handed her parched grain. She ate until she was satisfied but still she had food left over. When she got up to return to her gleaning, Boaz commanded his young men, "Let her gather not just among the remnant barley, but also among the grain that is heaped up, ready to be put into sheaves. And leave a few sheaves out for her to take without shame. Don't taunt, tease, or rebuke her in any way."

So Ruth gleaned in the field until evening. Then she threshed the grain—nearly three bushels full—took it up, and returned to the city. She gave Naomi not only the threshed grain but also the food she had reserved from her own lunch.

And Naomi said, "Where have you gleaned today? In whose field did you work? Blessed be the owner in whose sight you found grace."

Ruth said, "The man's name for whom I worked is Boaz."

"Blessed be Boaz of the Lord," Naomi replied, "for he is doing good both for us and for our dead loved ones. This Boaz is our kinsman."

Then Ruth said, "Boaz also said to me, 'Stay with my young women until the harvest is ended.'"

And Naomi told Ruth, her daughter-in-law, "It is best, my daughter, that you stay in his fields and close to his women workers, so that the young men in the other fields will not take advantage of you."

So Ruth gleaned in the field of Boaz, close to his women workers. She gathered grain throughout the barley harvest and also the following wheat harvest, and she lived with Naomi in Bethlehem.

Lauren Springer

"THE ARRIVAL OF FALL," FROM
THE UNDAUNTED GARDEN

Lauren Springer, who lives and gardens in Colorado, welcomes the onset of fall as a time of reinvigoration rather than a time of loss. In fact, she refers to autumn as the season of "reprisal." While the days are less hectic, the relentless demands of summer subdued by cooling nights, the gardener can watch with a kind of mellow glee as the plants slowly fall into themselves to create mulch for next year's beauty. The season is also one in which extravagant new textures and colors emerge. As she combines the eye of the gardener as technician, and the eye of the gardener as artist, and the eye of the gardener as philosopher, Springer finds in her garden a kind of inspiration for the human soul, where autumn brings both a tempered realism and renewed exertion.

> *W*hile the days are less hectic, the relentless demands of summer subdued by cooling nights, the gardener can watch with a kind of mellow glee as the plants slowly fall into themselves to create mulch for next year's beauty.

"The Arrival of Fall"

Fresh, vibrant June passes to a languid, slow July. Then comes a turning point, when summer suddenly feels utterly tiresome. Some years, late summer weather is kind and merciful, indulging the gardener in a quick turn to cool nights and days filled with a mellow, amber sunlight that actually feels good on the face, totally unlike the prickling and piercing rays of high summer. Other years, the wait is interminable, summer's heat oozing on well into months traditionally autumnal.

Autumn has become my favorite time of the year. It took a while for negative associations with the beginning of the school year to wane, for the golden sunlight and foliage to stop conjuring up the intestinal butterflies that went along with similarly toned school buses lurching down the street. While some find spring with all its optimistic beginnings the finest season in the garden, I much prefer the unfrenzied pace of fall. In the spring, it is easy to feel overwhelmed by the sudden demands of the garden. A long winter has a way of creating such great yearnings and high expectations that I could almost say I feel a bit pressured by the new season, not to mention out of shape after a lazy winter spent fattening up by the fire. By autumn, I'm synchronized with the garden, lean and mean, realistic about my expectations. The garden requires much less of me—weeds are well under control and careful deadheading has long been abandoned. As a friend once described so well, the autumn garden is a machete garden. Anyone still trying to control or tame it in September is either hopelessly deluded or has a strange need to use large cutting tools from the jungle. The season transforms the garden and the gardener. While a similar scene in June might send one scrambling for stakes and twine, come September it is a wonderful sense of release to watch plants collapse slowly on each other, soft and heavy with the weight of a full season's growth. Leaves begin to yellow and brown. Flowers become seeds. Everything is soft, large, ripe. As I walk among the plants, they reflect my mood—placid and self-satisfied.

Fall isn't all retrospective mellowness. It is also a time for renewed activity. As the oppressive heat wanes, rediscovered energy can be put to great use, and not just for the traditional autumnal rite of bulb planting. Seed collecting kicks into high gear. Autumn is also the best time to assess the garden and decide which plants need to be moved, divided or tossed out altogether. Plants are at their largest, and crowding is painfully evident. A plant from which one waited patiently for some sign of beauty can now be given the old heave-ho without reservations if it has failed to perform. Integrating new plants is easier than ever; a full, live picture lies before the gardener, helping inspire good combinations as compared to the spring, when tiny, barely awakened leaf rosettes require calling upon strong imaging powers to visualize what may develop later. Most plants relish the chance to put out good roots without the competition of top growth and moisture-sapping heat. The soil stays warm much longer than the air, giving fall-planted individuals a long season of underground growth and establishment. If it weren't for the fact that some plants are not available in the fall, I would probably stop almost all my spring planting. Even small transplanted seedlings, given the benefit of some mulch around their base, have done remarkably well when planted in the fall.

Autumn is a time when warm color and rustling sounds resonate throughout the plant world. In the deciduous woodlands of the East and Midwest, winter spreads down the land from north to south, from highland to lowland, rolling a carpet of foliage color over the landscape before it. The land, so serenely green for all those months, suddenly looks like an infrared photograph. On the grasslands of the prairie and plains, the tired gray-green and buff of late summer take on richer amber, sienna and rust tones as the foliage and seedheads of the grasses ripen. Late-blooming wildflowers, predominantly deep golds and purples, attract sleepy butterflies and bees, while more energetic birds frenetically gorge themselves on seeds before the first snow cover blankets the land.

The sun arcs lower in the sky, softening and burnishing the light. All colors seem to emanate an inner warmth as if the heat of the summer were stored within them. The most mundane scenes—an empty concrete basketball court alive with whirling, wind-blown leaves, a chocolate-brown field spiked with tawny corn stubble—take on the qualities of gold leaf, the light of a Venetian Renaissance painting.

The lower sun also creates lovely lighting effects in the garden. While in summer it would be suppertime before any similar effect might be possible, now mid- and late afternoon becomes a time for backlit drama. Grass panicles glisten and shimmer when touched by the slanted light; foliage reds and golds are intensified as the sun passes through them; fragile petals resemble halos given this autumnal spotlight.

Just as fall is a time for letting go, for riding with the slow, melancholy yet beautiful decline toward the inevitability of winter, it is also a time for loosening up rigid color rules. What may jar in the May and June garden is a welcome sight in October. Colors have richened and deepened with the cooler temperatures and golden light. The sunlight of autumn softens the boundaries that in spring and summer define orange, red, magenta and purple. The gardener should soften as well. Just as a person living out his or her last years should be indulged some special extravagances and not judged too harshly for them, so should an autumnal garden be allowed a grand finale of wild color fireworks without too many "tasteful" restraints. Nature combines cobalt skies, red and yellow leaves and purple asters; the gardener does well to take inspiration from these stunning scenes.

Form and texture take on their most important roles this time of the year—seedheads, flower stalks and the mature size of the plants create a sense of fullness, of tactile and visual abundance. Grasses hiss and rattle in the breezes like so many whispering crones. I chuckle thinking of the overexcited Halloweeners soon to pass by the ravenna grass and miscanthus clumps. Not only are the grasses large enough to hide a menacing creature, their wind-borne voices are sure to strike fear in the more imaginative and suggestible trick-or-treaters. The sweet civility of Christmas, with its parade of guests to kiss and horrible velvet jumpers to wear, scored a distant second on my childhood holiday rankings, far behind the front-runner, Halloween. Those seemingly interminable dark walks between houses, long before street-lit safety became an issue, were more adrenalizing than the mountains of candy filling the sack. Sadly Halloween, with our good-natured attempts to protect the little ones from the increasingly dangerous traffic and increasingly sick adults, has become an utter bore. Children show up listlessly at the door with parents in tow. Well-lit malls and gymnasiums filled with high-tech scary props that now often host the event will never equal those unchaperoned nights spent running from whispering, chattering, cackling plant life.

Back in the garden, a frosty morning transforms all things hairy, spiny, silver. Prickly pear, snowball and claret-cup cactus are caught in a crystalline net of hoary spines. Lambs ears, santolina and *Salvia argentea* glisten in the weak early sunlight. The artemisias, a frosty sight even in the heat of summer, take on an ethereal quality. *Artemisia caucasica,* a four-inch shrublet, and huge four-foot *A.* x "Power Castle" are the laciest. Whitest are groundhugging *A. stellerana* and 18-inch *A.* x "Valerie Finnis." Prettiest of all, though, is the sparkling silver skeleton of "Silver King" artemisia's flower panicles. The foliage of this plant is nice, but I can find silver in many other plants less inclined to bossiness in the garden. The only reason I tolerate this spreading garden thug (and only in one small, isolated spot) is for those delicate flower stalks that appear late in the summer and remain until the first heavy snow flattens them. Their airy effect is intensified on those mornings when hoarfrost transforms the landscape and they look like white plumes of chilled breath from the garden.

Two very distinct autumn scenes dominate my garden. The east-facing rose garden offers lingering pastel perennials and frost-tolerant annuals among the last cabbagy heads of various peach, pink, yellow and white ever-blooming David Austen roses. On the other side of the house, in the warm western sun, grasses, late-blooming perennials and tough annuals in hot colors—indigo-blue, red, orange, gold, purple—burn brightly until well into November when a pummeling of successive hard frosts and snowy dustings finally extinguish them. The two areas couldn't be any more different in mood.

Color in the autumn garden is more than blossoms, however. While many perennials and annuals continue bravely late into the season, it is the combination of these flowers with the complex tapestry of changing foliage color, both in woody plants and in the herbaceous, that gives autumn its richness. Fresh green becomes the exception rather than the norm, evergreen plants suddenly leap forth with emerald intensity after a spring and summer of blending shyly into the background. Somber black-green firs and pines pair beautifully with gold and russet ash and plum trees planted among them. Icy blue Colorado spruces and junipers vie for attention with crimson burning bush and orange-red sumacs.

On a smaller scale, many perennials are also touched by autumn's colorful kiss. The leaves of bergenia and the carmine-flowered forms of *Dianthus deltoids,* the maiden pinks, both take on garnet tones still framed by a froth of white alyssum. Hints of plum appear in the tips of aggressive blue *Sedum reflexum,* fighting it out with the equally ambitious hardy iceplants, *Delosperma nubigenum.* The latter's succulent chartreuse mats are showing touches of the ripe raspberry color they become in the depths of winter. Blues and silvers shimmer all the more intensely with the interjection of straw yellow, amber and red. A steely fountain of blue avena grass becomes a principal player as balloon flower goes gold next to it; a blue juniper shimmers with orange-red *Zauschneria* flowers as a partner. Small naked autumn crocus flowers, a cool lavender hue, poke up in front of a sculptural mass of maroon sempervivums. Some peonies join the foliage party, while others are more modest, preferring to remain a dull green to the last. A shocking pink anemone-flowered one I have no name for is the finest—it seems to have the need for attention, both in its brilliant spring display and now, as it glows apricot near the huge, sprawling blue leaves of sea kale, *Crambe maritima.* A tuft of tawny Siberian iris foliage completes this scene. Magenta colchicums raise their leafless blossoms through a cloak of scarlet leadwort foliage; the last few of leadwort's brilliant flowers stud the picture like blue sequins.

Many shrubs also turn fiery come autumn. Every year at this time I marvel at the surreal scarlet of burning bush, *Euonymus alata,* and think perhaps I should break down and plant one. But the bush is just too nondescript for the other fifty weeks of the year for me to give it precious garden space, so I continue to enjoy the plants vicariously elsewhere. The shrubs in my private infrared landscape must also hold their own at other times of the season. Crimson pygmy barberry changes from its summer color of muted maroon to flaming russet, enhancing the tawny daisies of hardy mum "Mary Stoker." Short days and cooler nights transform the glossy, narrow leaves of low-growing, drought-tolerant sand cherry, *Prunus besseyi,* to burgundy. A must with these rich red foliage tones is some ice blue foliage—perhaps a few tufts of blue sheep's fescue or blue avena grass, a petite "Blue Star" juniper or a squat, four-foot dwarf blue spruce variety like "Globosa" or "R. H. Montgomery." Both the purple-leaved forms and plain blue-green species of drought-tolerant smoke bush, *Cotinus coggygria,* have fabulous foliage through the growing season. Plumes of flower panicles, turning from peach in midsummer to buff to almost white in autumn, give the shrub its common name. In the autumn, the "smoke" is joined by fire as the foliage turns a smoldering orange.

The most beautiful fall planting I have ever seen included no annuals, perennials, trees or shrubs. It was a gathering of rambunctious vines on a ten-foot cyclone fence. The fire-engine red, palmate foliage of Virginia creeper (*Parthenocissus quinquefolia*) formed the back-drop, like royal tapestry. *Clematis paniculata* was still in bloom, wafting its sweet scent from cascading creamy flowers. Lace fine (*Polygonum aubertii*) contributed a froth of just barely over-the-hill, translucently white flowers. Entwined throughout were the seedheads of three clematis vines—those of yellowed-flower lemon-peel clematis, *Clematis tangutica,* and *C. orientalis,* a silky silver, and native *C. ligusticifolia,* a parade of cottony puffballs. The colors and textures of this casual vertical garden, which I doubt was planted with much thought aside from wanting to cover the ugly fence with some tough, fast vines, can match the most well-or-chestrated herbaceous border in early summer. The image, in all its loose, ripe abundance, speaks more eloquently than any prose for the garden in autumn.

May Sarton

from *The House by the Sea*

Though May Sarton developed an impressive career as a poet and novelist, she herself suffered from enormous self-doubt and debilitating depression, which left her questioning her writing skills and even her sense of vocation. Nonetheless, she continued to write, often finding inspiration from the places in which she lived. In 1973, she left her home in Nelson, New Hampshire, where she had written Journal of a Solitude, *and moved to York, Maine. There she found renewed creative energy, and within four years she had written another journal-memoir,* The House by the Sea.

Autumn is a time for work, for gathering flowers and words, for tending garden and book.

In the two months that Sarton describes in this selection, she weaves together the brilliant autumn landscape by her coastal house and the duties and craft of the writer. Hardly a paragraph goes by without reference to the flowers, the work of the garden, the changing trees, the sea. But intermingled with those references are descriptions of her work on a manuscript, her readings on college campuses, her contacts with other artists for mutual encouragement. Even as she waits for the first hard frost to kill the last of the flowers, she waits for the right words to finish her book. In this intermingling, Sarton creates a unity of work and season. "I'm troubled about the book, tired, and these beautiful autumn days feel wasted because I am only half there," she writes. Only later, as the frost comes and the season ends with a fear of cancer, does she conclude that she "can finish the book." Autumn is a time for work, for gathering flowers and words, for tending garden and book. It is a time for good work that looks toward a harvest—and the winter.

FROM THE HOUSE BY THE SEA

Saturday, September 6th

Where to begin? I ask myself each day. I do the chores slowly, try to start out at least on a good steady slow rhythm.... Susan Garrett called yesterday to ask whether I would like to see some gardens that afternoon, and off we went at half past three with two young women who had kindly wanted to do this for me because they liked my books. It *was* a delightful expedition, to three gardens, each very different from the other. Mrs. Howells at Kittery Point gave us two night-blooming cereus to watch open after we got home (and they did open at precisely nine—a poignant glory because it comes and goes so fast). I enjoyed the gardens and the delightful women who created them, but my hackles rise always at the attitudes of garden club members. I fear I am unregenerate, or perhaps simply old-fashioned, for I do not really like "arrangements" where too often a kind of ingenuity (using strange leaves or lettuce or a cabbage to be "interesting") replaces the simple joys of just plain old-fashioned bunches of flowers, which is what I love. I was pleased to note that nowhere did I see such a variety of annuals as I have in my wild, untidy, weedful picking garden here.

Tuesday, September 16th

I was woken at six by the gentle ripple of what I think must have been an owl's cry as it flew past. It is quite unlike any other bird sound. It is wonderful to wake up now knowing I have a clear day ahead and can walk to my own rhythm, not hurrying. This afternoon

I intend to put up tomatoes.... I simply couldn't bear the rich accumulations yesterday lying in a flat basket on the kitchen counter; so I went to Lesswings and found the wire stand for boiling. I can use the lobster pot. I've never done this before, so it is an adventure.

Anne and Barbara came for supper ... a great reunion, as we haven't seen each other for two months, and there was so much to talk about, to hear and tell, the time simply fled.... Of course, we walked all around the garden first. Anne is one person who comes here who always notices everything I have done. Luckily the gentians are still beautiful in a little corner which has a heather and a heath in it too, and later on will have lavendar colchicum. We went to take a look at the single closed gentian Raymond noticed near the apple orchard—such a thrill! Mary-Leigh in an orange jacket came slowly creeping along on her huge mower, trying it out. It is bright orange, and she looked extremely decorative sitting on it.

But the best was after we came in and stood for minutes watching the birds at the feeder from the porch window ... such a flurry of wings coming and going, and so many birds these days! We saw the two pairs of nuthatches, white- and rose-breasted, chickadees, house finches, goldfinches, a towhee on the ground, a thrush in one of the cherry trees, a vireo and a migrating warbler, greenish-yellow, jays, of course. This morning I caught a glimpse of an immature rose-breasted grosbeak in the pine tree, trying to get up courage to join the other birds at the feeder.

After supper we sat by the fire and talked about the farm they hope to buy in two years when Anne's children have left home. How lovely it will be if they are near by!

Saturday, September 27th

There does seem to be some Fate—gremlins? furies?—at work whenever I have to read poems. In April there was a blizzard and I entered Lewiston to read at Bates in two feet of unploughed snow, visibility nil; in late July when I read at Ogunquit it was almost as hot as the day a million hens died in Maine; and now I have been away for five days of torrential rain at Cornell University and then Massapequa, Long Island—terrifying return yesterday, as our plane had to turn back to Hartford and dump us there. After a long wait and no luggage turning up, we went by bus to Boston. The rain was a deluge and there were sudden claps of thunder and lightning so at one point I thought someone had thrown a bomb! I must say that bed, at midnight with a cup of cocoa on a tray, and Tamas by my side, was Heaven!

Monday, September 29th

Henry Guerlac had kindly arranged a dinner party in my honor at the Society of the Humanities. I so rarely attend a dinner party these days (have I ever, in fact, been part of society?) that I found it all delightful, especially as I sat beside Ammons, the poet, and felt at home with him at once. He is very shy, a sandy-haired, middle-aged man, who is recovering from winning all the prizes last year.... I was quite amused to hear that he feels *silenced* at this point. Alison Lurie was two chairs away on my left. I really had no chance to talk with her. She looks like a gentle perceptive witch. Part of the charm of the evening was the great paneled room with romantic friezes painted along the ceiling, the formal scene itself, and such a splendid dinner, starting (curiously) with raspberries. I had had lunch with James McConkey and young McCall.... I felt quite deprived that Jim was far away at the other end of the table. But for once I went to bed after a social occasion having no remorse for some faux-pas or madness of over-enthusiasm or rage.

The contrast to all this could not have been greater than the cellar room in the Massapequa, Long Island, library where I read poems the next day ... but what a delightful audience it was! I do love reading the poems. It's like hearing music again ... you can hear it in your head, but it is not the same thing as a concert, and poetry only lives and breathes when it is spoken aloud....

Tuesday, October 7ᵗʰ

Yesterday at two p.m., when I was fast asleep, trying to quiet down after a harrowing morning of work and be ready for David Michaud, who was coming at three for a short visit, the front door bell pinged. I got up and staggered down in my stocking feet, thinking it must be a delivery. Instead, an elegant middle-aged woman stood there and said, "I'm from La Jolla and couldn't resist coming to see you to tell you how much I admire … et cetera." I was cold with anger, flurried, and said, "Please give me a moment to put on some shoes … I was resting." It's strange how very perturbed and jangled I felt, but so far no one has arrived here unannounced, and I hoped it would never happen. I couldn't shake the anger, and told her and her daughter whom she went to fetch (the daughter had stayed in the car) that I felt it was an imposition, and would they knock on Anne Lindbergh's door unannounced? "I should have written her a note to ask," said the woman, "but there was no time, since we are just passing through." All summer I have been badgered by people who have to come to see me at *their* convenience, because they are in the region, and I've done hardly any good work as a result. I suppose that is why I felt outraged. These last days have been or felt like "my real life" again … the autumn so beautiful, the dark blue sea, and time to myself … it all got ripped to pieces by "a person from Porlock" yesterday.

I slept badly, a night of flotsam and jetsam moving around in my head. At one point I had such a clear vision of Rosalind that it is still vivid. I was really too tired after David left … all I could manage was to pick a few flowers (any night now we'll have the killing frost).

It is not that I work all day; it is that the work needs space around it. Hurry and flurry break into the deep still place where I can remember and sort out what I want to say about my mother. And this is a rather hard time, because it is still hard to write about her, so I was more than usually vulnerable and exposed.

Tuesday evening, October 7ᵗʰ

A marvelous day here…and now the most perfect Fra Angelico blue sea, no wind, the sunset just touching the end of the field. Perfectly still, except for the cry of a jay far off.

I must try to note exactly what happened, for it was such a great day. First I finished the portrait of my mother. On my walk with Tamas we ran into Mary-Leigh and Bev mowing the far field in the woods … and Bev pointed out to me a huge owl, sitting on a dead branch, looking down at us. The owl was wide awake—unusual for an owl in daylight and turned dark eyes on us … and then, much to my dismay, on Bramble! (Bramble had not seen this awful presence over her head!) We made our escape, and Bramble is now home, thank goodness. I think I have seen the owl once before, not really seen, but have been aware of the silent passage of great wings just above my head in the woods. I have always dreamed of seeing an owl here; this one was a barred owl, I think.

The mail brought plants—twelve primroses, three Shasta daisies, three stokesia, and six of the small blue campanula. They looked rather dwindled and sad after their journey, but I got them all in and covered the primroses with plastic pots, as frost is announced for tonight. I had it in mind not only to pick the last flowers, just in case, and that I did too, but also (madness!) to make jam from green cherry tomatoes … there are dozens of them, so I picked four cupfuls and have just now got them all ready under a layer of lemon, cinnamon, and ginger, mixed with two cups of sugar, and shall cook them before I go off on my expedition tomorrow.

Thursday, October 16ᵗʰ

I'm troubled about the book, tired, and these beautiful autumn days feel wasted because I am only half there. The only thing is to work along day by day and try to concentrate on making one page, one paragraph, better.

I have been meaning to note something Charlotte Zolotov

said in a letter the other day. When we met in New York I mentioned that I have it in mind to write a cookbook for the solitary person someday. She says, "A lot of poetry of living, especially alone, takes place in the kitchen." I thought of this yesterday when I was cutting up green cherry tomatoes to make a second try at jam (the first turned out too runny because I was rushed). I looked down on Raymond far below cutting out brush to frame the dogwood we had just put in (and lovely they look ... their red leaves catching the evening light!) and felt calmed by the domesticity, cutting up, finding cinnamon and ginger, enjoying the smells of the kitchen, and looking out into the autumn woods. It was, as Charlotte said, a moment full of poetry. The poetry, perhaps, is in making something quietly without the anguish and tension of real creation. Often I am very tired when I have to cook my dinner, especially on these days of fierce work in the garden. But always, once I get started, I feel peace flow in, and am happy.

Wednesday, October 22nd

Amazing that we have had no hard frost yet! Last evening I picked more large pink dahlias, three of the annual lupine, scabiosa, and marigolds ... so there are still bunches of flowers in the house. That was after I put in more than two hundred small bulbs. It was so warm I was pursued by mosquitoes under the bushes.

The pressure mounts these days, and, as always when I need to concentrate on my own work, more and more demands pour in—this week recommendations to do two batches of mss which I am obliged for different reasons to read carefully and comment on. The result is that I feel ill and have nervous indigestion. I would give almost anything not to have to respond to anyone or anything for three weeks—impossible dream!

The beech leaves are still glowing in a great arch over the road at one interval of a hundred yards or so. I look forward to arriving there each day when I walk Tamas. Because of the rain, the brooks and little ponds are full, and the startling beauty now is brilliant leaves floating on their shiny black surface, and at last yesterday reflecting a blue sky.

The journal will have to wait, I guess, till I am through this tunnel.

Monday, October 27th

The marvelous weather goes on, and still no hard frost. I came back from a reading at Dartmouth, two nights away, yesterday afternoon and was able to pick some last bunches of flowers for the house … such joys! Now it is a windless day, a glittering ocean, so brilliant one cannot see the blue for the dazzle….

Lotte is just back from a show of her photographs in Philadelphia and must have been tired, but as always we had a long good talk. She always manages to set everything in proportion for me again.

I'm dreadfully anxious about the book and must get to work now. The reward will be planting lily bulbs this afternoon.

Thursday, November 13th

Yesterday I picked a few marigolds, a tiny blue primrose, and some bachelor's buttons—the very last of the garden. I don't remember an autumn when hard frost held off so long, but now we are in for it. In a way I am glad, as I was afraid the tulips would think it was spring.

I have been in limbo because of a scare about possible cancer. I was in the hospital for three days for a biopsy, and yesterday, home again, heard that all is well….

I realized that I am not afraid of dying, but what made me feel awful was what a mess it will be when I do, and what a lot of work involved for those who will have to take care of things here. I felt, "I simply cannot die and leave all this to be taken care of!"

It was wonderful to come back here day before yesterday to the shining dark blue sea, to the wide arc of the ocean, now that the leaves have gone.

Verlyn Klinkenborg

"OCTOBER," FROM *THE RURAL LIFE*

Autumn brings some very specific tasks to bear, particularly on those who are not city dwellers. There are the leaves to rake, the harvest to be brought in, the woodpile to finish, the canning, the gathering of apples—all manner of provision for the coming season. The work comes with a sense of both gathering in what has been sown, and also guarding and sheltering against coming hardships. In The Rural Life, *Verlyn Klinkenborg, a writer for the* New York Times *whose columns have extolled life in the rural Midwest, focuses on the small but piercing details of ordinary life.*

In "October," Klinkenborg examines the tasks of autumn, beginning with the farm harvest and with the firing up of the woodstove—an act, he notes, that calls all the dogs in the house. These tasks are neither certain nor unalloyed. The woodstove begins to burn what has been collected over a season or two, but each piece burned recalls the fact that another will have to be split for the next season. Even more poignant is the harvesting of the corn in the Iowa fields. While the fields are abundant and the harvest good, the farmer also recognizes falling prices and

> In The Rural Life, Verlyn Klinkenborg, a writer for the *New York Times* whose columns have extolled life in the rural Midwest, focuses on the small but piercing details of ordinary life.

sees a legislature so deadlocked by party disagreement that no real help will be forthcoming. Even the harvest of his own garden is uncertain, leading Klinkenborg to conclude that gardens are "full of cheap sermons." And yet, the work is not hopeless; around him is evidence of something beyond the self: large cycles of movement, migration, ecology, and time itself. These give him a real hope, indeed a swelling hope that he finds echoed in John Keats's "To Autumn."

"OCTOBER"

The weather has been unseasonably hot in central Iowa, and farmers who are used to worrying about getting crops out of the fields before the weather turns wintry are harvesting with the air-conditioning turned up full in the cabs of their combines. The Midwest is never more beautiful than at this season, even though the air is dull with humidity. The ditches have ripened into pale ocherous colors, shades of russet intermixed, and in the fields where soybeans have already been harvested, the stubble lies slicked back like an old man's crew cut. The corn hasn't stood in shocks for sixty years and more, but even as it stands—still in rows, dry, skeletal ruins of the plant it was in mid-August—it suggests cool weather, sharp nights, and the plumage of that most autumnal bird, the pheasant.

Because of the dry, warm weather, harvest is running ahead of schedule, and the fields are full of machinery. All-devouring combines run down the rows cutting twenty-foot swaths well into the night, moving across the landscape in the darkness, their lights suggesting earthgoing yachts or mobile oil refineries. Grain wagons pull alongside, offloading beans or corn from the combines' hoppers. In the stubble rows, trucks with red boxes wait to be loaded, and then one after another they make their way to grain elevators and storage bins, where grain dryers work ceaselessly. The local news programs report uneven crop maturity, and when they're asked, farmers say they hope for a freeze.

It's a laborious landscape, and that's part of its beauty. But even as farmers stare ahead at the rows of uncut corn in the headlights, their minds are on the grain glut, which has dropped prices below the cost of production, and on the decline in the value of farmland. The fields are enormous, the yields are remarkable, the machinery is gargantuan, and so is the level of agricultural debt. The margin on which the enterprise operates this year is nearly nonexistent, which is why, as farmers watch the harvest progress, their minds are also on Washington, where year after year Democrats and Republicans debate the terms of relief.

One day last spring the fire in the kitchen woodstove went out and was never relit. I didn't record the date, because some endings are lost in a crowd of beginnings, passing unnoticed until months later, when the oversight seems almost melancholy. So I note here the first fire of the new season: October 4, thermometer lodged in the midforties, a chill in the bones of the house, rain falling hard through dwindling yellow hickory leaves. When the kindling caught the first dry log—a length of honey locust—in its flames, the stove called all the dogs. They sprawled across the warm tiles, mouths agape. Not a half hour had ticked away, and there we were, back on the night before the fire went out for the last time last spring.

A kind of accounting has been going on here for the past few weeks, how many pounds of honey gathered, how many bales of hay laid up in the loft, how many cords of wood stacked and under cover. This is such an ancestral satisfaction—the antithesis of the city's constant abundance—that it feels almost embarrassing to acknowledge it, the sign of the hayseed. The manure pile, steaming in the cool drizzle, looks like simple wealth, and so do the hickory nuts that crack beneath my feet as I walk to the barn and the milkweed pods that crowd against the fence line, ready to burst. The mice are fattening up in the woodshed. There's a fine crop of horsehair coming in on the mares and the gelding. It will go to make bird nests in spring.

In April what you see are your own intentions. In October you see their unexpected wreck and fulfillment. All summer potato vines spread across a corner of the garden. But when I lifted a plant, hoping to rob new potatoes, I saw that the vines, every one, had rotted right at the soil. Meanwhile two peach trees—planted vainly, I thought, by previous owners—blossomed heavily and set fruit. When September came, the peaches turned as red as the Virginia creeper is turning now. I finally picked one, just to savor my doubts. But it was the very promise of a peach. A garden is so full of cheap sermons.

I found myself Monday on a stretch of rural highway in eastern Colorado at the time of morning when round bales lying in the hay fields look like cattle grazing, and vice versa. I was driving toward the sunrise, which was still only a premonition in the distance. The horizon in that direction was a long, low ridgeline dotted either with trees that resembled a band of clouds or clouds that had rooted themselves with stems to earth or possibly very large sheep moving single file with a grim and stately purpose.

Over the ridge and into the next swale rode the pickup, and there I saw a small corral with four horses, all of them looking intently—wishfully, I suspect—at the kitchen light that had just been switched on in a dark ranch house across the barnyard. On a fence post near the road sat a bulbous red-tailed hawk. The rising light caught in his eye, and to me he looked dour, hungry for a diet less rich in rodents, a palate-cleansing carrot perhaps or a plate of watercress.

I've always loved the crescendo Monday brings, but I've always thought of it in strictly urban terms. By the time darkness has begun to wear away on a New York Monday morning, the city has rumbled to life, shaking off Sunday like a distant childhood. Soon the streets are filled with people, some of whom look as though their coattails had caught in the city's gears and dragged them headlong from their beds. Millions of weekday morning habits iterate themselves anew, yet even the familiarity of it all seems somehow fresh.

But in deep country, near, say, Last Chance, Colorado, the week evolves more slowly. Monday's chores look much like Sunday's. The headlong rush to get kids off to school is no different on the Colorado plains than anywhere else. But once the school bus has come and gone, once the high school kids have driven themselves off to class in a neighboring town, silence falls over the highway again. The low angle of the sun seems to give every object it strikes a higher profile. Its light throws the long shadow of a pickup and horse trailer into the far ditch, where the driver waves to himself.

On yet another fence post another hawk preens, and on the unplowed side of the road antelope move stiffly up a ridge and out of sight. Then the highway is still, except for the wind. What day of the week it is is anybody's guess until the next vehicle passes, when, for a moment—in the presence of a service truck or a postal carrier or a delivery van—Monday reappears.

When fall comes to the Southwest, the chamisa blooms, and suddenly a shrub that is inconspicuous most of the year seems to dominate the landscape. An old chamisa plant grows upright out of a weir of downswept dead boughs, and its whiplike pale green branches terminate in clumps of yellow florets, which brush against one's hips. When rain falls—and Santa Fe recently got half an inch—the scent of chamisa seems almost too heavy for the wind to carry. The odor is opaque, insidious. It infiltrates. It loiters. Even with nostrils buried deep in the plant, you end up asking, What does chamisa smell like?

The common name of chamisa is rabbitbrush, and the scientific name is *Chrysothamnus nauseosus,* which says something about the olfactory impression chamisa makes on botanists. But *nauseosus* is a pretty vague descriptor. If you went about giving binomial names to the artifacts of modern life, how many of them might deserve *nauseosus* as their specific term? Coming upon a stand of chamisa, trying again to decipher its scent, you wonder, *Nauseosus* how? "It smells like a rank little fox," said one Santa Fe resident. "It smells like being four years old," said another, an answer that hints at the profound association between odor and memory. To use the perfumer's language, the scent of chamisa is at once woody, green, and animalic, with several miscellaneous notes thrown in. It smells like a kitchen full of fresh herbs where a mouse has died behind the stove. It smells like a sachet in a drawer full of rubber gloves. It smells like the Southwest in autumn.

Talking about scent is like speaking a foreign tongue badly: you're always searching for a word that lies just out of reach, uncertain, finally, of your own meaning. It's easier to describe a complex emotion than a complex odor. What do the dogs of Santa Fe think when the chamisa comes into bloom? Perhaps an entire spectrum of scent goes into eclipse, concealed beneath the weight of rabbitbrush. Or perhaps in the unending orchestration of smell in their world, the blossoming of chamisa is like the sudden entrance of the cello section, playing slightly out of tune and out of tempo. In the end, you're brought up hard against the circularity of scent. Chamisa smells like chamisa. And vice versa.

On a warm October afternoon, high in a sugar maple, a crow tore apart a hornet's nest, discarding shreds of gray hornetpaper like leaves in a monochrome fall. A hail of ladybugs rose and then fell against the south side of the house. They were hapless fliers burdened by ungainly wing-covers, clattering almost inaudibly against the parched siding, seeking cracks and lifted clapboards to winter under. The sight of so many ladybugs in flight, each one armed with a faint acrid stench, looked like the threat of a hard season coming. When that many creatures take shelter at once, you wonder what they're sheltering from. Soon we'll know.

The woods are bright, brighter where the maples stand against a backdrop of unchanging hemlock. Even as light leaks out of the month, the woods seem to compensate, opening again to the western horizon. The sun has made its way southward like the fox that crosses the pasture most evenings. The air wears the tannic acidity of decaying leaves. The suppleness of light just when it fades in late afternoon seems almost mocking. It's a humiliating display of color, towering out of the treetops and into the backlit clouds overhead. At twilight Lindy found a newly killed male cardinal lying in the grass, its head severed by one of our cats. There was nothing in the day as sharply defined as the line where the black around its bill met the red of its crest.

That morning I had lit a brush pile on fire. There was a raucous half hour when the flames seemed to catch at something inside me. Then the fire settled down to business, smoldering steadily, adding its own taint to the air. Crab apple leaves on boughs cut a day earlier shriveled like a time-lapse glimpse of late autumn. The fruit sizzled and dropped into the flames. A couple of hours later the pile was nothing more than a small mound of ash.

After twilight had come and gone and the temperature had dropped, I walked down again to where the bonfire had been. I turned the ashes with a manure fork. A night breeze blew across the coals and reddened them. They seemed to ripple in the darkness, their light refracted by their heat. For a moment I stood beside them, taking in their warmth. The unsteady lights in the ashes looked like the fires of some ancient city seen from high above, a place described by Goethe long ago, when he wrote, "The king is out hunting, the queen is expecting a child, and so things could not be better."

At noon today, local apparent sidereal time will be approximately 1:29. The Julian Day will be 2450384, which is the number of days since high noon on the first of January 4713 B.C.E. That was the last time the twenty-eight-year solar and nineteen-year lunar cycles began on the same day as a fifteen-year Roman tax cycle, a coincidence first noticed in 1582 by the percipient Joseph Justus Scaliger, who invented the Julian calendar. Exactly 7,980 years will have passed before these cycles resume in unison and a new Julian Period begins, in the year 3267. (That will be some celebration.) If you probe a little deeper into the subject of time, you discover leap seconds and negative leap seconds and International Seconds. There's a Modified Julian Date and a Truncated Julian Date. There are ideal clocks generating proper time. Greenwich Mean Time has a familiar, prime meridian ring to it, but alas it's been replaced by Coordinated Universal Time, which sounds as though Earth presumed to control the clockwork in the distant cosmos.

But what do we call the hour we gained when we set our clocks back last night? It has no name. You make a pilgrimage to all the appliances—the alarm clocks, the wall clocks, the coffeemaker, the telephone, the VCR, the PC—and it seems for a moment as though time were a utility that got pumped into the house with the alternating current. Daylight Saving Time is the ultimate flat tax. Everybody pays up when it begins on the first Sunday in April, and on the last Sunday in October everybody reaps a one hundred percent refund of their hour, not a second of it lost to overhead. There are a few confusing exceptions. The Hopi Reservation doesn't observe Daylight Saving Time. The Navajo Nation, which surrounds the Hopi Reservation, does. The state of Arizona, which surrounds Navajos and Hopis alike, doesn't. All three entities returned to synchronicity with the rest of the country, and their neighbors, last night. So did Indiana.

There's a geographical equivalent to this temporal leap. Imagine driving north through the open prairie, along the edge of one township after another. (A township is a surveyed square six miles to a side.) The farther north you go, the more the lines of longitude converge, which means the township grid is steadily being compressed by the longitudinal grid. To adjust for this, the road north makes a lateral jog every twenty-four miles. We have just made the big jog east (the sun rises earlier now) on the northward road into winter. We keep going this direction for another fifty-five days until the road ends and the tundra begins. Out there the caribou and musk ox are grazing, a sign that it will be time to turn around and head back south toward summer.

When snow began falling on Sunday, I realized that a line from Keats—"until they think warm days will never cease"—had been running through my head for weeks. The line is from "To Autumn," one of the loveliest poems in the language, and "they" are the bees, whose "clammy cells," as Keats calls their comb, have been "o'erbrimm'd" by summer. Jonathan Bate, author of a book called *The Song of the Earth,* observes that the late summer of 1819, the season leading up to the completion of Keats's ode on September 19, "was clear and sunny on thirty-eight out of the forty-seven days from 7 August to 22 September" and that temperatures were milder in the final week of that period than they had been in three years.

This wasn't merely a spate of beautiful weather. It was weather of a kind, Bate notes, that would actually make breath come easier for a consumptive like Keats. There could be nothing more personal than the question of Keats's lung capacity, and yet "To Autumn" doesn't read as a personal poem. There's something deceptively long-winded in the syntax of the first stanza, and some critics have seen a consumptive's hectic flush in the stubble plains touched with "rosy hue." But Bate reminds us, too, how broad the boundaries of "personal" experience really are. For Keats those boundaries include the season as a whole. The fine weather o'erbrimm'd him, and in doing so gave voice to itself.

Until the past few days, it was a Keatsian autumn, full of what the poet calls, in a letter from those same weeks, "chaste weather—Dian skies." Never mind that the leaves are now almost gone, or that the skies are now unchaste, gray, and dousing us with snow showers. Somehow the brightness of the trees created the illusion that the periphery of my awareness had expanded.

When Lindy and I walked the dogs, it felt as though we were all walking with eyebrows raised, though for the dogs that would be with nostrils distended.

Keats personified autumn, imagining her by a cider press or fast asleep in a "half-reap'd furrow." Personifying the natural world is so fundamental and so limitless that it seems sometimes like the foundation of all poetry. To some, I suppose, personifying nature is an act of hubris, a refusal to accept the otherness of the world around us. But in a fall like this one—dry after a long wet, warm after unusual coolness—personifying nature seems like a means of meeting nature halfway. In the ghostliness of Keats's autumn, "sitting careless on a granary floor," what we really see is the way the season swells within us.

John Keats

"To Autumn"

John Keats wrote his autumn ode while living in Winchester, England, in 1819. It was a time when the evenings were growing earlier and colder, and when Keats himself was aware that his young life was coming to an end. Each day, before dinner, he walked through the cathedral yard and along a tree-lined, paved path, through the old city gates and into country alleys and gardens, and finally out to St. Cross meadows along the River Itchen. What he saw on these walks became the stuff of "To Autumn." Keats distills into this single poem the entire sense of what autumn is: the fruit, the gourds, the harvest and granary floor, the mossy cottage trees, full-grown lambs, and gathering swallows—*the adjective* gathering *a perfect choice for the whole of what he is doing in this poem of celebration in the tasks and seasonal routines of autumn.*

> $\mathcal{K}$eats distills into this single poem the entire sense of what autumn is: the fruit, the gourds, the harvest and granary floor, the mossy cottage trees, full-grown lambs, and gathering swallows.

To Autumn

1

Season of mists and mellow fruitfulness,
Close bosom-friend of the maturing sun;
Conspiring with him how to load and bless
With fruit the vines that round the thatch-eves run;
To bend with apples the moss'd cottage-trees,
And fill all fruit with ripeness to the core;
To swell the gourd, and plump the hazel shells
With a sweet kernel; to set budding more,
And still more, later flowers for the bees,
Until they think warm days will never cease,
For summer has o'er-brimm'd their clammy cells.

2

Who hath not seen thee oft amid thy store?
Sometimes whoever seeks abroad may find
Thee sitting careless on a granary floor,
Thy hair soft-lifted by the winnowing wind;
Or on a half-reap'd furrow sound asleep,
Dows'd with the fume of poppies, while thy hook
Spares the next swath and all its twined flowers:
And sometimes like a gleaner thou dost keep
Steady thy laden head across a brook;
Or by a cider-press, with patient look,
Thou watchest the last oozings hours by hours.

3

Where are the songs of spring? Ay, where are they?
Think not of them, thou hast thy music too,—

While barred clouds bloom the soft-dying day,
And touch the stubble-plains with rosy hue;
Then in a wailful choir the small gnats mourn
Among the river sallows, borne aloft
Or sinking as the light wind lives or dies;
And full-grown lambs loud bleat from hilly bourn;
Hedge-crickets sing; and now with treble soft
The red-breast whistles from a garden-croft;
And gathering swallows twitter in the skies.

Stephen Dobyns

"THE MUSIC ONE LOOKS BACK ON," FROM *BODY TRAFFIC*

The novelist and poet Stephen Dobyns began writing as a police reporter for the Detroit News, *but in "The Music One Looks Back On," he pulls back from the drama of the crime calendar to reflect on "the sort of day that builds a life." He recalls one day in early fall, when there is a guest in the house, and children outside playing, and everyone waking up to a day remembered as yellow. It is a day "without rancor or angry words," the sort of day that plays a gentle concerto.*

Autumn's high holiday celebrates with all the fuss and wondrous confusion and joy of big

> *But autumn's ordinary days murmur quietly of the small, the expected, the familiar.*

dinners with pies and turkeys. But autumn's ordinary days murmur quietly of the small, the expected, the familiar. Here too is cause for thanksgiving, in the small round of eating and sleeping and washing up that measures out our true contentment.

The Music One Looks Back On

In early autumn, there's a concerto
possible when there's a guest in the house
and the guest is taking a shower and the host
is washing up from the night before.
With each turn of the tap in the kitchen,
the water temperature increases or drops
upstairs and the guest responds with little groans—
cold water for low notes, hot water for high.
His hair is soapy, the tub slippery
and with his groaning he becomes the concerto's
primary instrument. Then let's say the night
was particularly frosty and now the radiators
are knocking, filling the house with warmth,
and the children are rushing around outside
in the leaves before breakfast, calling after
their Irish setter whose name is Cleveland.
And still asleep, the host's wife is making
those little sighs one makes before waking,
as she turns and resettles and the bed creaks.
Standing at the sink, the host hums to himself
as he thinks of the eggs he'll soon fry up,
while already there's the crackle of bacon
from the stove and a smell of coffee. The mild groans
of the guest, the radiator's percussion,
children's high voices, the barking of a dog,
even the wife's small sighs and resettlings
combine into this autumn concerto of which
not one of the musicians is aware as they drift
toward breakfast and then a leisurely walk

through the fields near the house—two friends
who haven't seen each other for over a year.
Much later they will remember only a color,
a golden yellow, and the sound of their feet
scuffling the leaves. A day without rancor
or angry words, the sort of day that builds a life,
becoming a soft place to look back on,
and geese, geese flying south out of winter.

Wendell Berry

FROM "A NATIVE HILL"

When Wendell Berry decided to return to his ancestral farm in the Kentucky mountains, the choice was neither sentimental nor slovenly. He knew he was returning to a working farm, as a working farmer. Yet—or rather because of this decision—he was also strengthening his vocation as a writer. Here Berry takes a hard-headed look at the complicated intersection of violence and craft that defines so much of North American work. He begins by reflecting on an episode from the American frontier told by a Methodist circuit minister, Jacob Young. As Young describes the process of building a road in Henry County, Kentucky, one cold November day, he appreciates his "good-natured and civil" fellow-laborers and the bountiful landscape in which they work. Yet, this work is tinged with violence. In Berry's hands, the images of road and path, and the contrasting ways in which they bisect the land, become metaphors for the choices we face to enrich the world through our work or to rape it. The path, writes Berry, adapts itself to the land; it is a "ritual of familiarity." The road, however, resists the land, rushing across the countryside without thought or intimate physical contact.

Autumn, too, figures in contrasting ways throughout the essay. In

> *I see myself "growing out of the earth," Berry writes, and then falling back into it "like leaves in the autumn."*

Berry's younger days, it seemed like the season of restlessness, change, desire. But when he returns to the family farm, autumn itself returns to a rhythmic cycle: I see myself "growing out of the earth," Berry writes, and then falling back into it "like leaves in the autumn." It is in autumn that we pause to consider whether and how our work enriches the world. And these questions, as Berry suggests, are profoundly human and profoundly religious.

FROM *AUTOBIOGRAPHY OF A PIONEER* BY JACOB YOUNG

[The] costume [of the Kentuckians] was a hunting-shirt, buck-skin pantaloons, a leathern belt around their middle, a scabbard and a big knife fastened to their belt; some of them wore hats, and some caps. Their feet were covered with moccasins, made of dressed deer-skins. They did not think themselves dressed without their powder-horn and shot-pouch, or the gun and tomahawk. They were ready, then, for all alarms. They knew but little. They could clear ground, raise corn, kill turkeys, deer, bears, buffalo, and, when it became necessary, they understood the art of fighting the Indians as well as any men in the United States. Here I will give the reader a specimen of their manners and customs, which will convey some knowledge of their real character.

Shortly after we had taken up our residence, I was called upon to assist in opening a road from the place where Newcastle now stands, to the mouth of Kentucky river. That country, then, was an unbroken forest. There was nothing but an Indian trail passing the wilderness.... Pursuant to previous notice, I met the company early in the morning, with my ax, three days' provisions and my knapsack. Here I found a captain, with about one hundred men, all prepared to labor—about as jovial a company as I ever saw, all good-natured and civil. Had a man been there who had ever read the history of Greece, he would have thought of the Spartans in their palmy days. This was about the last of November, 1797. The day was cold and clear. The country through which the company passed was delightful. It was not a flat country, but, what the Kentuckians called, rolling ground. It was quite well stored with lofty timber, and the undergrowth was very pretty. The beautiful canebrakes gave it a peculiar charm. What rendered it most interesting was the great abundance of wild turkeys, deer, bears, and other wild animals. The company worked hard all day—were very quiet, and every man obeyed the captain's orders punctually.

Just about sundown the captain called us to leave our labor, and, after a short address, he told us the night was going to be very cold, and we must make very large fires. We felled the hickory-trees, in great abundance, and made great log-heaps, mixing the dry wood with the green hickory. And, laying down a kind of sleepers under the pile, we elevated the heap and caused it to burn rapidly. Every man had a water-vessel in his knapsack. We searched, and found a stream of water, and, by this time, the fires were showing to great advantage. So we warmed our cold victuals, ate our suppers, and spent the evening in hearing the hunter's story relative to the bloody scenes of the Indian war. We then heard some pretty fine singing, considering the circumstances.

Thus far, I enjoyed myself well, but a change began to take place. They became very rude, and raised the war-whoop. Their shrill shrieks made me tremble. They chose two captains—divided the men into two companies, and commenced fighting with the fire-brands—the log-heaps having burned down. The only law that I can recollect for their government was, that no man should throw a brand without fire on it, so that they might know how to dodge. They fought for two or three hours in perfect good nature, till brands became scarce, and they began to violate the law. Some were severely wounded, blood began to flow freely, and they were in a fair way of commencing a fight in earnest.

At this moment, we heard the loud voice of the captain ordering every man to retire to rest. They dropped their weapons of warfare, rekindled the fires, and laid themselves down to sleep. Suffice it to say, we finished our road according to directions, and returned home in health and peace.

From "A Native Hill" by Wendell Berry

The significance of this bit of history is in its utter violence. The work of clearing the road was itself violent. And from the orderly violence of that labor, these men turned for amusement to disorderly violence. They were men whose element was violence; the only alternatives they were aware of were those within the comprehension of main strength. And let us acknowledge that these were the truly influential men in the history of Kentucky, as well as in the history of most of the rest of America. In comparison to the fatherhood of such as these, the so-called "founding fathers" who established our political ideals are but distant cousins. It is not John Adams or Thomas Jefferson whom we see night after night in the magic mirror of the television set; we see these builders of the road from New Castle to the mouth of the Kentucky River. Their reckless violence has glamorized all our trivialities and evils. Their aggressions have simplified our complexities and problems. They have cut all our Gordian knots. They have appeared in all our disguises and costumes. They have worn all our uniforms. Their war whoop has sanctified our inhumanity and ratified our blunders of policy.

But my understanding of this curiously parabolic fragment of history will not be complete until I have considered more directly that the occasion of this particular violence was the building of a road. It is obvious that one who values the idea of community cannot speak against roads without risking all sorts of absurdity. It must be noticed, nevertheless, that the predecessor to this first road was "nothing but an Indian trail passing the wilderness"—a path. The Indians, then, who had the wisdom and the grace to live in this country for perhaps ten thousand years without destroying or damaging any of it, needed for their travels no more than a footpath; but their successors, who in a century and a half plundered the area of at least half its topsoil and virtually all of its forest, felt immediately that they had to have a road. My interest is not in the question of whether or not they *needed* the road, but in the fact that the road was then, and is now, the most characteristic form of their relation to the country.

The difference between a path and a road is not only the obvious one. A path is little more than a habit that comes with knowledge of a place. It is a sort of ritual of familiarity. As a form, it is a form of contact with a known landscape. It is not destructive. It is the perfect adaptation, through experience and familiarity, of movement to place; it obeys the natural contours; such obstacles as it meets it goes around. A road, on the other hand, even the most primitive road, embodies a resistance against the landscape. Its reason is not simply the necessity for movement, but haste. Its wish is to *avoid* contact with the landscape; it seeks so far as possible to go over the country, rather than through it; its aspiration, as we see clearly in the example of our modern freeways, is to be a bridge; its tendency is to translate place into space in order to traverse it with the least effort. It is destructive, seeking to remove or destroy all obstacles in its way. The primitive road advanced by the destruction of the forest; modern roads advance by the destruction of topography.

We have lived by the assumption that what was good for us would be good for the world. And this has been based on the even flimsier assumption that we could know with any certainty what was good even for us. We have fulfilled the danger of this by making our personal pride and greed the standard of our behavior toward the world—to the incalculable disadvantage of the world and every living thing in it. And now, perhaps very close to too late, our great error has become clear. It is not only our own creativity—our own capacity for life—that is stifled by our arrogant assumption; the creation itself is stifled.

We have been wrong. We must change our lives, so that it will be possible to live by the contrary assumption that what is good for the world will be good for us. And that requires that we make the effort to know the world and to learn what is good for it. We must learn to cooperate in its processes, and to yield to its limits. But even more important, we must learn to acknowledge that the creation is full of mystery; we will never entirely understand it. We must abandon arrogance and stand in awe. We must recover the sense of the majesty of creation, and the ability to be worshipful in its presence. For I do not doubt that it is only on the condition of humility and reverence before the world that our species will be able to remain in it.

Standing in the presence of these worn and abandoned fields, where the creation has begun its healing without the hindrance or the help of man, with the voice of the stream in the air and the woods standing in silence on all the slopes around me, I am deep in the interior not only of my place in the world, but of my own life, its sources and searches and concerns. I first came into these places following the men to work when I was a child. I knew the men who took their lives from such fields as these, and their lives to a considerable extent made my life what it is. In what came to me from them there was both wealth and poverty, and I have been a long time discovering which was which.

The most exemplary nature is that of the topsoil. It is very Christlike in its passivity and beneficence, and in the penetrating energy that issues out of its peaceableness. It increases by experience, by the passage of seasons over it, growth rising out of it and returning to it, not by ambition or aggressiveness. It is enriched by all things that die and enter into it. It keeps the past, not as history or as memory, but as richness, new possibility. Its fertility is always building up out of death into promise. Death is the bridge or the tunnel by which its past enters its future.

I have been walking in the woods, and have lain down on the ground to rest. It is the middle of October, and around me, all through the woods, the leaves are quietly sifting down. The newly fallen leaves make a dry, comfortable bed, and I lie easy, coming to rest within myself as I seem to do nowadays only when I am in the woods.

And now a leaf, spiraling down in wild flight, lands on my shirt at about the third button below the collar. At first I am bemused and mystified by the coincidence—that the leaf should have been so hung, weighted and shaped, so ready to fall, so nudged loose and slanted by the breeze, as to fall where I, by the same delicacy of circumstance, happened to be lying. The event, among all its ramifying causes and considerations, and finally its mysteries, begins to take on the magnitude of history. Portent begins to dwell in it.

And suddenly I apprehend in it the dark proposal of the ground. Under the fallen leaf my breastbone burns with imminent decay. Other leaves fall. My body begins its long shudder into humus. I feel my substance escape me, carried into the mold by beetles and worms. Days, winds, seasons pass over me as I sink under the leaves. For a time only sight is left me, a passive awareness of the sky overhead, birds crossing, the mazed interreaching of the treetops, the leaves falling—and then that, too, sinks away. It is acceptable to me, and I am at peace.

When I move to go, it is as though I rise up out of the world.

Tracy Kidder

"September,"
from *Among Schoolchildren*

Certainly one of the great autumn rituals is the return to school. Here are the school bus routines to learn, the anxiety over the new teacher, the joy over seeing old friends and the hope of making new ones, the squeaky clean of the halls, the sheen of the freshly waxed gym floors, the smell of new books and old chalk. All these images never seem to change, generation after generation.

In Among Schoolchildren, *Tracy Kidder takes the reader into the new September classroom from the perspective of the teacher, Mrs. Zajac, a teacher both feared and loved. In some ways this is a book about the*

> *Certainly one of the great autumn rituals is the return to school.*

American educational system, and hardly a chapter goes by without the reader's being deeply immersed in the ways in which cultural problems affect the affairs of the classroom at every level. By the end of the school year, most of Mrs. Zajac's students will have rotated out of her classroom for a new school, or into her classroom from a new school. With such enormous turnover, she faces the September newness almost every week of the year.

But this is also a book about a teacher and, by extension, about all teachers. In detailing Mrs. Zajac's indomitability, her absolute commitment to the students, and her commitment to the business of education, Kidder shows that teaching is, maybe above all, a spiritual activity. For what else is it when a teacher works at establishing relationships with students? And what else is it when a child's soul is deeply affected by another?

"SEPTEMBER"

Mrs. Zajac wasn't born yesterday. She knows you didn't do your best work on this paper, Clarence. Don't you remember Mrs. Zajac saying that if you didn't do your best, she'd make you do it over? As for you, Claude, God forbid that you should ever need brain surgery. But Mrs. Zajac hopes that if you do, the doctor won't open up your head and walk off saying he's almost done, as you just said when Mrs. Zajac asked you for your penmanship, which, by the way, looks like who did it and ran. Felipe, the reason you have hiccups is, your mouth is always open and the wind rushes in. You're in fifth grade now. So, Felipe, put a lock on it. Zip it up. Then go get a drink of water. Mrs. Zajac means business, Robert. The sooner you realize she never said everybody in the room has to do the work except for Robert, the sooner you'll get along with her. And … Clarence. Mrs. Zajac knows you didn't try. You don't just hand in junk to Mrs. Zajac. She's been teaching an awful lot of years. She didn't fall off the turnip cart yesterday. She told you she was an old-lady teacher.

She was thirty-four. She wore a white skirt and yellow sweater and a thin gold necklace, which she held in her fingers, as if holding her own reins, while waiting for children to answer. Her hair was black with a hint of Irish red. It was cut short to the tops of her ears, and swept back like a pair of folded wings. She had a delicately cleft chin, and she was short—the children's chairs would have fit her. Although her voice sounded conversational, it had projection. She had never acted. She had found this voice in classrooms.

Mrs. Zajac seemed to have a frightening amount of energy. She strode across the room, her arms swinging high and her hands in small fists. Taking her stand in front of the green chalkboard, discussing the rules with her new class, she repeated sentences, and her lips held the shapes of certain words, such as "homework," after she had said them. Her hands kept very busy. They sliced the air and made irate chops to mark off boundaries. They extended straight out like a traffic cop's, halting illegal maneuvers yet to be perpetrated. When they rested momentarily on her hips, her hands looked as if they were in holsters. She told the children, "One thing Mrs. Zajac expects from each of you is that you do *your* best." She said, "Mrs. Zajac gives homework. I'm sure you've all heard. The only meanie gives homework." *Mrs. Zajac.* It was in part a role. She worked her way into it every September.

At home on late summer days like these, Chris Zajac wore shorts or blue jeans. Although there was no dress code for teachers here at Kelly School, she always went to work in skirts or dresses. She dressed as if she were applying for a job, and hoped in the back of her mind that someday, heading for job interviews, her students would remember her example. Outside school, she wept easily over small and large catastrophes and at sentimental movies, but she never cried in front of students, except once a few years ago when the news came over the intercom that the Space Shuttle had exploded and Christa McAuliffe had died—and then she saw in her students' faces that the sight of Mrs. Zajac crying had frightened them, and she made herself stop and then explained.

At home, Chris laughed at the antics of her infant daughter and egged the child on. She and her first-grade son would sneak up to the radio when her husband wasn't looking and change the station from classical to rock-and-roll music. "You're regressing, Chris," her husband would say. But especially on the first few days of school, she didn't let her students get away with much. She was not amused when, for instance, on the first day, two of the boys started dueling with their rulers. On nights before the school year started, Chris used to have bad dreams: her principal would come to observe her, and her students would choose that moment to climb up on their desks and give her the finger, or they would simply wander out the door. But a child in her classroom would never know that Mrs. Zajac had the slightest doubt that students would obey her.

The first day, after going over all the school rules, Chris spoke to them about effort. "If you put your name on a paper, you should be proud of it," she said. "You should think, This is the best I can do and I'm proud of it and I want to hand this in." Then she asked, "If it isn't your best, what's Mrs. Zajac going to do?"

Many voices, most of them female, answered softly in unison, "Make us do it over."

"Make you do it over," Chris repeated. It sounded like a chant.

"Does anyone know anything about Lisette?" she asked when no one answered to that name.

Felipe—small, with glossy black hair—threw up his hand.

"Felipe?"

"She isn't here!" said Felipe. He wasn't being fresh. On those first few days of school, whenever Mrs. Zajac put the sound of a question in her voice, and sometimes before she got the question out, Felipe's hand shot up.

In contrast, there was the very chubby girl who sat nearly motionless at her desk, covering the lower half of her face with her hands. As usual, most of their voices sounded timid the first day, and came out of hiding gradually. There were twenty children. About half were Puerto Rican. Almost two-thirds of the twenty needed the forms to obtain free lunches. There was a lot of long and curly hair. Some boys wore little rattails. The eyes the children lifted up to her as she went over the rules—a few eyes were blue and many more were brown—looked so solemn and so wide that Chris felt like dropping all pretense and laughing. Their faces ranged from dark brown to gold, to pink, to pasty white, the color that Chris associated with sunless tenements and too much TV. The boys wore polo shirts and T-shirts and new white sneakers with the ends of the laces untied and tucked behind tongues. Some girls wore lacy ribbons in their hair, and some wore pants and others skirts, a rough but not infallible indication of religion—the daughters of Jehovah's Witnesses and Pentecostals do not wear pants. There was a lot of prettiness in the room, and all of the children looked cute to Chris.

So did the student teacher, Miss Hunt, a very young woman in a dress with a bow at the throat who sat at a table in the back of the room. Miss Hunt had a sweet smile, which she turned on the children, hunching her shoulders when they looked at her. At times the first days, while watching Chris in action, Miss Hunt seemed to gulp. Sometimes she looked as frightened as the children. For Chris, looking at Miss Hunt was like looking at herself fourteen years ago.

The smell of construction paper, slightly sweet and forest-like, mingled with the fading, acrid smell of roach and rodent spray. The squawk box on the wall above the closets, beside the clock with its jerky minute hand, erupted almost constantly, adult voices paging adults by their surnames and reminding staff of deadlines for the census forms, attendance calendars, and United Way contributions. Other teachers poked their heads inside the door to say hello to Chris or to ask advice about how to fill out forms or to confer with her on schedules for math and reading. In between interruptions, amid the usual commotion of the first day, Chris taught short lessons, assigned the children seat work, and attended to paperwork at her large gray metal desk over by the window.

For moments then, the room was still. From the bilingual class next door to the south came the baritone of the teacher Victor Guevara, singing to his students in Spanish. Through the small casement windows behind Chris came sounds of the city—Holyoke, Massachusetts—trailer truck brakes releasing giant sighs now and then, occasional screeches of freight trains, and, always in the background, the mechanical hum of ventilators from the school and from Dinn Bros. Trophies and Autron, from Leduc Corp. Metal Fabricators and Laminated Papers. It was so quiet inside the room during those moments that little sounds were loud: the rustle of a book's pages being turned and the tiny clanks of metal-legged chairs being shifted slightly. Bending over forms and the children's records, Chris watched the class from the corner of her eye. The first day she kept an especially close eye on the boy called Clarence.

Clarence was a small, lithe, brown-skinned boy with large

eyes and deep dimples. Chris watched his journeys to the pencil sharpener. They were frequent. Clarence took the longest possible route around the room, walking heel-to-toe and brushing the back of one leg with the shin of the other at every step—a cheerful little dance across the blue carpet, around the perimeter of desks, and along the back wall, passing under the American flag, which didn't quite brush his head. Reaching the sharpener, Clarence would turn his pencil into a stunt plane, which did several loop-the-loops before plunging in the hole.

The first morning, Chris didn't catch one of the intercom announcements. She asked if anyone had heard the message. Clarence, who seemed to stutter at the start of sentences when he was in a hurry to speak, piped up right away, "He he say to put the extra desks in the hall." Clarence noticed things. He paid close attention to the intercom. His eyes darted to the door the moment a visitor appeared. But he paid almost no attention to her lessons and his work. It seemed as if every time that she glanced at Clarence he wasn't working.

"Take a look at Clarence," Chris whispered to Miss Hunt. She had called Miss Hunt up to her desk for a chat. "Is he doing anything?"

The other children were working. Clarence was just then glancing over his shoulder, checking on the clock. Miss Hunt hunched her shoulders and laughed without making a sound. "He has such huge eyes!" she said.

"And they're looking right through me," said Chris, who lifted her voice and called, "Clarence, the pencil's moving, right?" Then Chris smiled at Miss Hunt, and said in a half whisper, "I can see that Clarence and I will have a little chat out in the hall, one of these days."

Miss Hunt smiled, gulped, and nodded, all at once.

Chris had received the children's "cumulative" records, which were stuffed inside salmon-colored folders known as "cumes." For now she checked only addresses and phone numbers, and resisted looking into histories. It was usually better at first to let her own opinions form. But she couldn't help noticing the thickness of some cumes. "The thicker the cume, the more trouble," she told Miss Hunt. "If it looks like *War and Peace....*" Clarence's cume was about as thick as the phone book. And Chris couldn't help having heard what some colleagues had insisted on telling her about Clarence. One teacher whom Chris trusted had described him as probably the most difficult child in all of last year's fourth grade classes. Chris wished she hadn't heard that, nor the rumors about Clarence. She'd heard confident but unsubstantiated assertions that he was a beaten child. These days many people applied the word "abused" to any apparently troubled student. She had no good reason to believe the rumors, but she couldn't help thinking, "What if they're true?" She wished she hadn't heard anything about Clarence's past at this early moment. She found it hard enough after thirteen years to believe that all fifth graders' futures lay before them out of sight, and not in plain view behind.

She'd try to ignore what she had heard and deal with problems as they came. Clarence's were surfacing quickly. He came to school the second morning without having done his homework. He had not done any work at all so far, except for one math assignment, and for that he'd just written down some numbers at random. She'd try to nip this in the bud. "No work, no recess," she told Clarence late the second morning. He had quit even pretending to work about half an hour before.

Just a little later, she saw Clarence heading for the pencil sharpener again. He paused near Felipe's desk. Clarence glanced back at her. She could see that he thought she wasn't looking.

Clarence set his jaw. He made a quick, sharp kick at Felipe's leg under the desk. Then he stalked, glancing backward at Chris, to the pencil sharpener. Felipe didn't complain.

Maybe Felipe had provoked the kick. Or maybe this was Clarence's way of getting even with her for threatening to keep him in from recess. It wasn't a pleasant thought. She let the incident pass. She'd have to watch Clarence carefully, though.

The afternoon of that second day of class, Chris warned Clarence several times that she would keep him after school if he didn't get to work. Detention seemed like a masochistic exercise. Sometimes it worked. It was a tool she'd found most useful at the beginning of a year and after vacations. In her experience, most children responded well to clearly prescribed rules and consequences, and she really didn't have many other tangible weapons. The idea was to get most of the unpleasantness, the scoldings and detentions, out of the way early. And, of course, if she threatened to keep Clarence after school, she had to keep her word. Maybe he would do some work, and she could have a quiet talk with him. She didn't plan to keep him long.

The other children went home, and so did Miss Hunt. Chris sat at her desk, a warm late-summer breeze coming through the little casement window behind her. She worked on her plans for next week, and from under cover of her bowed head, she watched Clarence. The children's chairs, the plastic backs and seats of which came in primary colors, like a bag full of party balloons, were placed upside down on the tops of their desks. Clarence sat alone at his desk, surrounded by upended chairs. He had his arms folded on his chest and was glaring at her. The picture of defiance. He would show her. She felt like laughing for a moment. His stubbornness was impressive. Nearly an hour passed, and the boy did no work at all.

Chris sighed, got up, and walked over to Clarence.

He turned his face away as she approached.

Chris sat in a child's chair and, resting her chin on her hand, leaned her face close to Clarence's. He turned his farther away.

"What's the problem?"

He didn't answer. His eyelashes began to flutter.

"Do you understand the work in fifth grade?"

He didn't answer.

"I hear you're a very smart boy. Don't you want to have a good year? Don't you want to take your work home and tell your mom, 'Look what I did'?"

The fluorescent lights in the ceiling were pale and bright. One was flickering. Tears came rolling out of Clarence's eyes. They streaked his brown cheeks.

Chris gazed at him, and in a while said, "Okay, I'll make a deal with you. You go home and do your work, and come in tomorrow with all your work done, and I'll pretend these two days never happened. We'll have a new Clarence tomorrow. Okay?"

Clarence still had not looked at her or answered.

"A new Clarence," Chris said. "Promise?"

Clarence made the suggestion of a nod, a slight concession to her, she figured, now that it was clear she would let him leave.

Her face was very close to his. Her eyes almost touched his tear-stained cheeks. She gazed. She knew she wasn't going to see a new Clarence tomorrow. It would be naive to think a boy with a cume that thick was going to change overnight. But she'd heard the words in her mind anyway. She had to keep alive the little voice that says, Well, you never know. What was the alternative? To decide an eleven-year-old was going to go on failing, and there was nothing anyone could do about it, so why try? Besides, this was just the start of a campaign. She was trying to tell him, "You don't have to have another bad year. Your life in school can begin to change." If she could talk him into believing that, maybe by June there *would* be a new Clarence.

"We always keep our promises?" Chris said.

He seemed to make a little nod.

"I bet everyone will be surprised. We'll have a new Clarence," Chris said, and then she let him go.

PART FOUR

Harvest

INTRODUCTION

During the mid-1950s, the nature writer Edwin Way Teale drove along the shoreline of western Michigan, "overcome by autumn wanderlust." He marveled at the vast abundance and the promise of a rich harvest economy in this fruit region: "Roadside stands were laden. Vines were redolent with their blue burden and apple trees bent low with the weight of the autumn harvest. Mile after mile we rode among gray-barked peach trees where fallen fruit on the ground below outlined the form of the trees like shadows at noontime.... [T]his was harvest time, payoff time, the season of profit and plenty." We understand this vision: Work has been done; it's time for the payoff.

But harvest prayers from around the world look at autumn in a very different manner. A Meusan prayer from Ethiopia directs the eye up to the autumn moon:

> May you be for us a moon of joy and happiness. Let the young become strong and the grown man maintain his strength, the pregnant woman be delivered and the woman who has given birth suckle her child. Let the stranger come to the end of his journey and those who remain at home dwell safely in their house. Let the flocks that go to feed in the pastures return happily. May you be a moon of harvest and of calves. May you be a moon of restoration and of good health.

A very different prayer from a very different culture—one of the Psalms of David—looks not to the sky but to the land all around.

> Thou visitest the earth, and waterest it: thou greatly enrichest it with the river of God, which is full of water: thou preparest them corn, when thou hast so provided for it. Thou waterest the ridges thereof abundantly: thou settlest the furrows thereof: thou makest it soft with showers: thou blessest the springing thereof. Thou crownest the year with thy goodness, and thy paths drop fatness. They drop upon the pastures of the wilderness: and the little hills rejoice on every side. The pastures are clothed with flocks; the valleys also are covered over with corn; they shout for joy, they also sing.

These prayers have an orientation different from that of Teale, though they share Teale's awe at autumnal abundance. The Ethiopian prayer is a prayer of hope in the harvest; many of the sentences begin with a petition: "Let the.... " Psalm 65 is a prayer of praise and gratitude for the abundance that God has given. Profit is mentioned in neither.

Both of these spiritual states—hope and gratitude—are a part of the notion of harvest, and they look in different directions. Autumn, in its harvest, helps us to look back. There has been the planting in spring, and the care during the heat of the summer. Now, because of what we have given, we receive the good fruits of labor. But harvest is not only for the farmer. It is for the parent who has given so much of himself over the years, and who now sees his child grown into a full and healthy adult. It is for the business owner who has treated her employees with justice and generosity for many years, and who sees them flourishing and growing in their skills and happiness. It is for the teacher who watches young students, so untried at the beginning of the year, come to new knowledge, awarenesses, and sensitivities. It is for the legislator who sees the fruit of a bill aimed at relieving distress. The autumn harvest points back to our good labor and reminds us that work can actually bring about nothing less than a redemption.

But the harvest also points toward the future. Harvest is not only for the now. In the same way that the farmer stores away hay and grain for the cold months that will surely come, so too does the parent, the teacher, the employer, and the legislator look forward to the continuing good of their work. No teacher would be satisfied with knowledge dropped after the last bus leaves for summer break in June; no legislator should be satisfied with addressing only superficial needs and not root causes, and so dealing only with the immediate and not the long term. The harvest is the bounty brought in, but it is a bounty that asks a question: What will you do with this now?

The Psalmist's answer is unequivocal: The hills shout and sing for joy.

It is a joyous answer echoed by John Burroughs, in his sheer delight in the simple apple, which becomes to him an archetypal image of the harvest. It is echoed by Wyman Richardson, rowing off the shores of Cape Cod, so extraordinarily sensitive to the gifts that are set before his eyes. And it is echoed by the mystic Julian of Norwich, whose keen sense of the unity of love and the world often seems to lift her prose into poetry.

But the irony in all of this is one of sight: Henry David Thoreau suggests that the harvest we gather is the one we look for; if we are not looking, then there won't be a harvest at all. We might miss it all.

During most of Robert Lawson's children's classic *Rabbit Hill* (1944), the animals wonder whether the New Folks moving in are planting folks. The hope, of course, is that they will be, and the animals begin to dream of nightly raids. It turns out that they are indeed planting folks, and the animals watch greedily as the garden is tilled, seeded, weeded—and finally begins to yield its bounty. The evening is chosen, and the animals gather to raid—but the New Folks are there, waiting. As the animals hesitate, the Man draws a tarp away from a shape at the edge of the garden, and a statue is revealed: that of St. Francis.

Suddenly the animals understand: The garden has been planted for them! There is no need to raid. Enough has been planted for everyone. They draw in their breaths, and as the New Folks watch quietly, the animals eat what they need. Then, in an image of the New Creation, they process quietly around the garden—the deer, the fox, the field mice, the badgers, the rabbits, the pheasants, the raccoons, the chipmunks, and the squirrels as the New Folks hold their breaths.

How easy it would have been, Thoreau might have suggested, to have missed the rich harvests of that night. Greed, a sense of possession, jealousy, the claims of ownership—any of these might have made the animals miss the love given to them, and any of these might have made the New Folks miss the love given back. For the harvest of that garden was love. And it is that harvest, of course, that we so often miss, that we so often throw away as though it were abundant and common.

The prayers and hymns that conclude this section capture some of that sense of the real joy in the harvest—the gathering in not only of physical plenty but of grace-filled gifts. The grain is sweet because the God of the grain is "brimful of sweetness." The barley is inexhaustible, as are those who tend it with love. The world is God's own field, and even while giving wholesome grain, God tends us. Mwene-Nyanga [God] grants not only rain and the harvest but peace and calm and health; the stuff of the body and the stuff of the spirit are one. The harvest, perhaps most powerfully, links the physical matter of our world with the spiritual matter of our deepest lives, and insists on their unity.

FROM THE BOOK OF RUTH IN THE HEBREW BIBLE

If harvest is a time of fulfillment, then this short selection from the book of Ruth fairly bursts with harvests. The barley has been brought into the barn, its floor humming with the sounds of threshing, feasting, and dancing. Naomi, too, senses that the time is right to harvest the love that has been growing between Boaz and Ruth. Secrecy and stealth—even the last-minute obstacle of a nearer kinsman—only heighten the anticipation and remind us that even at harvest time we should take nothing for granted. Here there is still the need to be attentive, to lay plans and carry them through to completion. Yet, here is also feasting and joy. And here is the time to lie down, secure under the wings of love where we have found our refuge.

> *Here there is still the need to be attentive, to lay plans and carry them through to completion. Yet, here is also feasting and joy.*

FROM THE BOOK OF RUTH

Then Naomi said to Ruth, "My daughter, shall I not seek out a home for you, that you may prosper? And is not Boaz our kinsman? Tonight he is winnowing barley on the threshing floor. Wash and anoint yourself, put on your best clothes, and go down to the barn. But don't let Boaz see you until he has finished eating and drinking.

When he lies down to sleep, observe his place; then go and lift up the covers and lie down at his feet. He will tell you what to do."

Ruth answered, "Everything that you have said, I will do."

So Ruth went down to the barn and did everything that Naomi had told her. When Boaz had finished eating and drinking and making merry, he lay down beside a heap of grain. Then Ruth came up softly and lifted the coverings and lay down at his feet. At midnight, Boaz awoke, startled, to find a woman at his feet.

Boaz said, "Who are you?"

Ruth answered, "I am Ruth, your handmaid. Spread your wings over me, for you are my nearest kinsman."

Boaz said, "May the Lord bless you, my daughter, for your kindness is better now than at the beginning. You have not sought out younger men, whether rich or poor. So now, my daughter, do not be afraid. I will do all that you ask, for all this city of Bethlehem knows that you are a woman of virtue. However, although I am your kinsman, there is one who is closer in kinship to you. Remain here tonight, and when morning is come, if he will marry you, then let it be so. But if he will not marry you, then as surely as the Lord lives, I will marry you. Lie still until the morning."

So Ruth lay at his feet until the early morning. Before anyone else was awake, she rose up. And Boaz said to her, "Let no one know that a woman came to the barn." And he also said, "Bring your cloak and hold it up."

When Ruth held up her cloak, Boaz poured into it six measures of barley and gave it to her. Then Ruth returned to the city. When she came to her mother-in-law, Naomi said to her, "How is it with you, my daughter?"

And Ruth told Naomi all that Boaz had done for her and said, "These six measures of barley he gave me and said, 'You shall not return to your mother-in-law empty-handed.'"

Then Naomi said, "My daughter, sit still until you know how this matter will turn out. For Boaz will not rest until he has settled this affair."

John Burroughs

FROM "THE APPLE,"
FROM *WINTER SUNSHINE*

John Burroughs's paean to apples runs the gamut from nutrition—apples are "full of sugar and mucilage" that act as a "gentle spur and tonic to the whole biliary system"—to aesthetics: apples are pleasing to see, to touch, to smell, even to hear as they fall with a "mellow thump" to the ground. Apples bear the bright full harvest of autumn right through the frigid winter months. Whether forming a pert centerpiece or steaming in a fresh-baked pie, apples carry within themselves the promise of October's Indian summer. For Burroughs, sometimes called the dean of American nature writers, apples are the fruit of youth and of a young, strong America whose people are bound together by the communal ties of harvest rituals.

For Burroughs, sometimes called the dean of American nature writers, apples are the fruit of youth and of a young, strong America whose people are bound together by the communal ties of harvest rituals.

FROM "THE APPLE"

Lo! sweetened with the summer light,
The full-juiced apple, waxing over-mellow,
Drops in a silent autumn night.
—ALFRED, LORD TENNYSON, "SONG OF THE LOTOS-EATERS"

Not a little of the sunshine of our northern winters is surely wrapped up in the apple. How could we winter over without it? How is life sweetened by its mild acids! A cellar well filled with apples is more valuable than a chamber filled with flax and wool. So much sound, ruddy life to draw upon, to strike one's roots down into, as it were.

Especially to those whose soil of life is inclined to be a little clayey and heavy, is the apple a winter necessity. It is the natural antidote of most of the ills the flesh is heir to. Full of vegetable acids and aromatics, qualities which act as refrigerants and antiseptics, what an enemy it is to jaundice, indigestion, torpidity of liver, etc.! It is a gentle spur and tonic to the whole biliary system. Then I have read that it has been found by analysis to contain more phosphorus than any other vegetable. This makes it the proper food of the scholar and the sedentary man; it feeds his brain and it stimulates his liver. Neither is this all. Beside its hygienic properties, the apple is full of sugar and mucilage, which make it highly nutritious. It is said "the operators of Cornwall, England, consider ripe apples nearly as nourishing as bread, and far more so than potatoes. In the year 1801—which was a year of much scarcity—apples, instead of being converted into cider, were sold to the poor, and the laborers asserted that they could 'stand their work' on baked apples without meat; whereas a potato diet required either meat or some other substantial nutriment. The French and Germans use apples extensively; so do the inhabitants of all European nations. The laborers depend upon them as an article of food, and frequently make a dinner of sliced apples and bread."

The apple is the commonest and yet the most varied and beautiful of fruits. A dish of them is as becoming to the centre-table in winter as was the vase of flowers in the summer,—a bouquet of spitzenburgs and greenings and northern spies. A rose when it blooms, the apple is a rose when it ripens. It pleases every sense to which it can be addressed, the touch, the smell, the sight, the taste; and when it falls, in the still October days, it pleases the ear. It is a call to a banquet, it is a signal that the feast is ready. The bough would fain hold it, but it can now assert its independence; it can now live a life of its own.

Daily the stem relaxes its hold, till finally it lets go completely and down comes the painted sphere with a mellow thump to the earth, toward which it has been nodding so long. It bounds away to seek its bed, to hide under a leaf, or in a tuft of grass. It will now take time to meditate and ripen! What delicious thoughts it has there nestled with its fellows under the fence, turning acid into sugar, and sugar into wine!

How pleasing to the touch! I love to stroke its polished rondure with my hand, to carry it in my pocket on my tramp over the winter hills, or through the early spring woods. You are company, you red-checked spitz, or you salmon-fleshed greening! I toy with you; press your face to mine, toss you in the air, roll you on the ground, see you shine out where you lie amid the moss and dry leaves and sticks. You are so alive! You glow like a ruddy flower. You look so animated I almost expect to see you move! I postpone the eating of you, you are so beautiful! How compact; how exquisitely tinted! Stained by the sun and varnished against the rains. An independent vegetable existence, alive and vascular as my own flesh; capable of being wounded, bleeding, wasting away, or almost of repairing damages!

How they resist the cold! holding out almost as long as the red cheeks of the boys do. A frost that destroys the potatoes and other roots only makes the apple more crisp and vigorous; they peep out from the chance November snows unscathed. When I see the fruit-vender on the street corner stamping his feet and beating his hands to keep them warm, and his naked apples lying exposed to the blasts, I wonder if they do not ache, too, to clap their hands and enliven their circulation. But they can stand it nearly as long as the vender can.

Noble common fruit, best friend of man and most loved by him, following him, like his dog or his cow, wherever he goes! His homestead is not planted till you are planted, your roots intertwine with his; thriving best where he thrives best, loving the limestone and the frost, the plow and the pruning-knife: you are indeed suggestive of hardy, cheerful industry, and a healthy life in the open air. Temperate, chaste fruit! you mean neither luxury nor sloth, neither satiety nor indolence, neither enervating heats nor the frigid zones. Uncloying fruit,—fruit whose best sauce is the open air, whose finest flavors only he whose taste is sharpened by brisk work or walking knows; winter fruit, when the fire of life burns brightest; fruit always a little hyperborean, leaning toward the cold; bracing, sub-acid, active fruit! I think you must come from the north, you are so frank and honest, so sturdy and appetizing. You are stocky and homely like the northern races. Your quality is Saxon. Surely the fiery and impetuous south is not akin to you. Not spices or olives, or the sumptuous liquid fruits, but the grass, the snow, the grains, the coolness, is akin to you. I think if I could subsist on you, or the like of you, I should never have an intemperate or ignoble thought, never be feverish or despondent. So far as I could absorb or transmute your quality, I should be cheerful, continent, equitable, sweet-blooded, long-lived, and should shed warmth and contentment around.

The boy is indeed the true apple-eater, and is not to be questioned how he came by the fruit with which his pockets are filled. It belongs to him, and he may steal it if it cannot be had in any other way. His own juicy flesh craves the juicy flesh of the apple. Sap draws sap. His fruit-eating has little reference to the state of his appetite. Whether he be full of meat or empty of meat, he wants the apple just the same. Before meal or after meal it never comes amiss. The farm-boy munches apples all day long. He has nests of them in the haymow, mellowing, to which he makes frequent visits. Sometimes old Brindle, having access through the open door, smells them out and makes short work of them.

In some countries the custom remains of placing a rosy apple in the hand of the dead, that they may find it when they enter paradise. In northern mythology the giants eat apples to keep off old age.

The apple is indeed the fruit of youth. As we grow old we crave apples less. It is an ominous sign. When you are ashamed to be seen eating them on the street; when you can carry them in your pocket and your hand not constantly find its way to them; when your neighbor has apples and you have none, and you make no nocturnal visits to his orchard; when your lunch-basket is without them, and you can pass a winter's night by the fireside with not thought of the fruit at your elbow,—then be assured you are no longer a boy, either in heart or in years.

The genuine apple-eater comforts himself with an apple in their season, as others with a pipe or a cigar. When he has nothing else to do, or is bored, he eats an apple. While he is waiting for the train he eats an apple, sometimes several of them. When he takes a walk he arms himself with apples. His traveling-bag is full of apples. He offers an apple to his companion, and takes one himself. They are his chief solace when on the road. He sows their seed all along the route. He tosses the core from the car window and from the top of the stage-coach. He would, in time, make the land one vast orchard. He dispenses with a knife. He prefers that his teeth shall have the first taste. Then he knows that the best flavor is immediately beneath the skin, and that in a pared apple this is lost. If you will stew the apple, he says, instead of baking it, by all means leave the skin on. It improves the color and vastly heightens the flavor of the dish.

Emerson, I believe, has spoken of the apple as the social fruit of New England. Indeed, what a promoter or abettor of social intercourse among our rural population the apple has been, the company growing more merry and unrestrained as soon as the basket of apples was passed round! When the cider followed, the introduction and good understanding were complete. Then those rural gatherings that enlivened the autumn in the country, known as "apple-cuts," now, alas! nearly obsolete, where so many things were cut and dried besides apples! The larger and more loaded the orchard, the more frequently the invitations went round and the higher the social and convivial spirit ran. Ours is eminently a country of the orchard. Horace Greeley said he had seen no land in which the orchard formed such a prominent feature in the rural and agricultural districts. Nearly every farmhouse in the Eastern and Northern States has its setting or its background of apple-trees, which generally date back to the first settlement of the farm. Indeed, the orchard, more than almost any other thing, tends to soften and humanize the country, and give the place of which it is an adjunct a settled, domestic look. The apple-tree takes the rawness and wildness off any scene. On the top of a mountain, or in remote pastures, it sheds the sentiment of home. It never loses its domestic air, or lapses into a wild state. And in planting a homestead, or in choosing a building-site for the new house, what a help it is to have a few old, maternal apple-trees near by,—regular old grandmothers, who have seen trouble, who have been sad and glad through so many winters and summers, who have blossomed till the air about them is sweeter than elsewhere, and borne fruit till the grass beneath them has become thick and soft from human contact, and who have nourished robins and finches in their branches till they have a tender, brooding look! The ground, the turf, the atmosphere of an old orchard, seem several stages nearer to man than that of the adjoining field, as if the trees had given back to the soil more than they had taken from it; as if they had tempered the elements, and attracted all the genial and beneficent influences in the landscape around.

Robert Frost

A Gathering of Autumn Poems

For Robert Frost, as for John Burroughs, apple-picking represents all of autumn's harvests, but Frost draws our attention to a single picker. He recollects sore arches and wearied limbs, the sheer abundance of the harvest reducing cherished fruit to routine and even nightmare. For autumn may bring a harvest of sorrow as well as joy, each as full and rich in its own way as the other. In these poems, the apple-picking ladder remains pointed toward the heavens, its wooden legs planted in the still-warm soil while the apple's sad, sweet juice lingers as a memory on our tongues and in our hearts. And from the quiet fields, the poet picks one last blue aster for his love.

In these poems, the apple-picking ladder remains pointed toward the heavens, its wooden legs planted in the still-warm soil while the apple's sad, sweet juice lingers as a memory on our tongues and in our hearts.

After Apple-Picking

My long two-pointed ladder's sticking through a tree
Toward heaven still,
And there's a barrel that I didn't fill
Beside it, and there may be two or three
Apples I didn't pick upon some bough.
But I am done with apple-picking now.
Essence of winter sleep is on the night,
The scent of apples: I am drowsing off.
I cannot rub the strangeness from my sight
I got from looking through a pane of glass
I skimmed this morning from the drinking trough
And held against the world of hoary grass.
It melted, and I let it fall and break.
But I was well
Upon my way to sleep before it fell,
And I could tell
What form my dreaming was about to take.
Magnified apples appear and disappear,
Stem end and blossom end,
And every fleck of russet showing clear.
My instep arch not only keeps the ache,
It keeps the pressure of a ladder-round.
I feel the ladder sway as the boughs bend.
And I keep hearing from the cellar bin
The rumbling sound
Of load on load of apples coming in.
For I have had too much
Of apple-picking: I am overtired
Of the great harvest I myself desired.

There were ten thousand thousand fruit to touch,
Cherish in hand, lift down, and not let fall.
For all
That struck the earth,
No matter if not bruised or spiked with stubble,
Went surely to the cider-apple heap
As of no worth.
One can see what will trouble
This sleep of mine, whatever sleep it is.
Were he not gone,
The woodchuck could say whether it's like his
Long sleep, as I describe its coming on,
Or just some human sleep.

My November Guest

My Sorrow, when she's here with me,
Thinks these dark days of autumn rain
Are beautiful as days can be;
She loves the bare, the withered tree;
She walks the sodden pasture lane.

Her pleasure will not let me stay.
She talks and I am fain to list:
She's glad the birds are gone away,
She's glad her simple worsted gray
Is silver now with clinging mist.

The desolate, deserted trees,
The faded earth, the heavy sky,
The beauties she so truly sees,

She thinks I have no eye for these,
And vexes me for reason why.

Not yesterday I learned to know
The love of bare November days
Before the coming of the snow,
But it were vain to tell her so,
And they are better for her praise.

A Late Walk

When I go up through the mowing field,
The headless aftermath,
Smooth-laid like thatch with the heavy dew,
Half closes the garden path.

And when I come to the garden ground,
The whir of sober birds
Up from the tangle of withered weeds
Is sadder than any words.

A tree beside the wall stands bare,
But a leaf that lingered brown,
Disturbed, I doubt not, by my thought,
Comes softly rattling down.

I end not far from my going forth
By picking the faded blue
Of the last remaining aster flower
To carry again to you.

Wyman Richardson

"Around the Horn,"
from *The House on Nauset Marsh*

The House on Nauset Marsh *is one of the great classics of Cape Cod literature, a line begun with Henry David Thoreau's own posthumous* Cape Cod. *Here, the physician and nature writer Wyman Richardson recorded, at first through a series of articles in the* Atlantic, *and later in book form, his many precise and detailed observations of life on the Cape—particularly bird life. Writing from his family's farmhouse, Richardson noted the passing of the seasons, the changing patterns of wildlife, and the personalities of many of the people on Cape Cod that he had come to know.*

> *B*ut Richardson is surprising, in that he wants to paint a very different image of autumn on the shores of Cape Cod.

In this passage, Richardson, accompanied by his wife and several others, canoes through the marsh to round their own mythical Horn. The date is October 9, and most readers might expect that there is a general emptying out, a movement of life away from the activities of the summer and toward the hibernation and sleep of winter. But Richardson is surprising, in that he wants to paint a very different image of autumn on the shores of Cape Cod. Here there is nothing like emptying out; instead, there is a great fecundity of life, bird and fish and plant, that is startling in its diversity and activity. As he canoes through the marsh, his eye, trained to observe, picks out what he calls a few of the marsh's autumn secrets; readers will believe that he has picked out more than a few.

"Around the Horn"

The Nauset Marsh at Eastham is an unusual salt marsh. Most such marshes are protected to the seaward by a barrier beach through which an estuary enters. This estuary is widest at its mouth, and divides into smaller and smaller branches which lead into denser and denser bodies of solid sedge.

Not so the Nauset Marsh. It contains more water than sedge and has large bays at the upper end. Even the Main Channel, while nearly two miles from the Inlet, is a quarter of a mile wide. (The Inlet is the passage through the barrier beach.) The sedge is divided into sections. A large one is called "flat" or "marsh," and a small one "hummock." The largest such piece, Porchy Marsh, is about a mile and a half from north to south. Its nearest, or north, edge is about a mile from the Farm House, and the south end about two and a half miles. We call the southernmost tip Cape Horn, and the shallow passageway that makes a tiny island of it, the Straits of Magellan.

One of our best expeditions is "rounding the Horn" in the canoe. To do this, conditions must be just right. In the first place, there must not be so much wind that paddling becomes a task. In the second place, the tide must serve in such a manner that we can drop down the Main Channel on the ebb, meet the flood at the Horn, come up with it, and get home at a comfortable hour for dinner.

It is not too often that all these factors are combined on the same day, so that "rounding the Horn" is a rather infrequent occurrence. And besides all this, let it be said that it requires an expert knowledge of the vagaries of Nauset Marsh tides, as well as a good guess, to hit the "furthest south" at exactly the right moment. Even at best, we are likely to get stuck on the flats below our hill on the way up and have to wait for them to be flooded.

The tide comes right for us this time on the ninth of October. There is a light breeze from the northeast and the air is clean and fresh. From the Farm House piazza the water in the marsh channels is a clear blue, while through the dips in the dunes we can see the deeper blue of the Atlantic Ocean.

As we leave the mouth of the Salt Pond Creek and begin to negotiate the twists and turns of the upper channels, we see many ducks which are strung all the way along the edge of Tom Doane's Hummock. Most of them are black ducks, although we note two hen mallards, one pintail, and perhaps half a dozen baldpates. As we approach, the black ducks begin to take notice. Their necks become straight, long, and stiff, at least twice as long as a duck's neck should be. The nearer ones separate from one another and luff up into the wind, a sure sign that they are about to fly. And off they go, with that spectacular jump of theirs. They drag off others which are not so close, and these in turn drag off others, until at last the whole caboodle is in the air in a great, straggling, lacy flock. Most of them go off straight to the eastward out across the dunes to the ocean, where presumably they will spend the rest of the day asleep.

We soon come to that deep part of the channel, south of the Cedar Bank, where we put out a bucktail fly and begin trolling with our fly rod. This is simply to protect ourselves; for what with the bright sun and very low water, it does not seem like a good chance. The flats are pretty well covered with shore birds. "Winter" yellowlegs and black-bellied plover represent the larger birds, while the smaller ones consist mostly of thousands of red-backed sandpipers. Then suddenly we hear their shrill alarm note and at once every bird is in the air.

"Must be a duck hawk around," I observe.

My wife, in some alarm, snatches off her white hat. A day or two before, when she was sketching, a duck hawk had come along. She had taken up her binoculars and, just as she had them focussed on the hawk, he had made a pass at her hat. This, as seen through her glasses, had been truly terrifying.

"Leave it on," I suggest. "You may attract him."

"Here," she says, "you wear it."

"I guess I won't," I reply.

White hat or no white hat, a handsome full-plumaged male duck hawk comes directly over our heads. Soon he begins to soar and in an incredibly short time has disappeared to the northeast.

And it is just at this point that five huge shore birds come low over our heads and light on the flat in front of us. A quick glance through the glasses shows that they are all godwits, four marbled and one Hudsonian. We all have a good look at these magnificent birds, the largest of all our shore birds. We take a chance on reeling in our line, but the sound does not seem to disturb them. Then we let the canoe drift up toward them.

Three of the marbled godwits are large, and one is considerably smaller. And, as is the case with many nations as well as humans, the larger ones are all picking on the small one. Every time he digs a succulent worm from the ooze, the others go for him, and then what a racket there ensues! I have never heard anything quite like it. It is a sort of cross between Gabriel blowing his horn and the cackling of a hen after she has laid an egg: "*Too*-kity, *Yoo*-kity, Yook!"

We drift up to within thirty feet of them and they don't fly. The marbled godwits show at the base of their long, up-turned bills an orange tinge which we have never noticed before. The Hudsonian is considerably darker and there is a bit of the white patch at the base of his tail which is so obvious when he flies. We leave them to their bickerings and their worms as the ebb takes us slowly past.

We go on down past Hay Island, where some bass boil ahead of the canoe and corroborate the old adage that "A boiling bass never bites." Past the mouth of Jeremiah's Creek, where we put a night heron in a dither as to whether or not to fly. Past the outermost end of Porchy Bar, which so many neophytes have tried to cheat by cutting across too soon, only to find themselves hopelessly stuck on the sand riffles. Past Broad Creek, now, at low water, almost dry except for a few deep holes here and there. Past Deep Water Point, which is no longer a point and where there is no deep water. And finally, down to the sand bar to the south of the Horn.

We see that this sand bar is covered with herring gulls, perhaps two hundred of them, and we wonder why they are standing so still and so erect with all eyes turned in the same direction. There is not a gull in the air and no sound comes from them. And then the reason for this rapt attention becomes apparent.

At the upper end of the bar, austerely aloof, is a large brown bird, about as big as the gulls. When we get the glasses focussed on him, we realize he is a brown gyrfalcon. He seems to be eyeing the gulls with a malevolent expression. As we approach, he turns his baleful eye on us, as if to say: "Get the hell out of here."

But it is he at last who moves. He allows us to come within about fifty yards and finally takes off. As he does so, every gull turns and faces him. He flies directly over them and makes several dives at them. Each time, the target gull spreads his wings, opens his beak wide and screams. And each time, the gyrfalcon swoops up, inches from the gull's head, without touching him.

The gyrfalcon does this about three times and then, off to the east, he spies a marsh hawk. He dashes away and comes down on the marsh hawk from above. But just before he gets there, the marsh hawk flips over on his back, with upraised talons, and again the gyrfalcon swoops up and away. Time after time this performance is repeated, until finally the gyrfalcon tires of the sport and lazily flies away to the south. In fact, what with his lazy flight and his overall brown color, one could almost mistake him for a year-old herring gull.

I have been diffident about reporting gyrfalcons. These birds have been considered to be exceedingly rare, if not of accidental occurrence, in Massachusetts. If one tells of seeing a gyrfalcon, one can almost hear the unspoken thought, "Probably was a duck hawk." However this may be, I am convinced that gyrfalcons appear regularly on outer Cape Cod. Ever since 1948, when, from October to June, I kept running across the one I wrote about in

"Gyrfalcon Pays a Visit," I have seen them at least once a year, usually in October. This is the month when we see the greatest number of duck hawks, and skeptics will make the most of this point.

After this excitement, we go ashore at the end of the sand flat for a stroll and to wait for the flood tide to take hold. We succeed where the gyrfalcon failed—that is, all the gulls take off and begin making slow circles in the air. We walk barefoot over the riffled sand, looking for items of interest, but we find nothing more unusual than that savage shellfish, *Polynices heros.* He is the common big round "snail" which makes a trail in the sand, ending in a very suggestive hump. He is equipped not only with a powerful foot but with an effective rasp as well. He it is who destroys so many mollusks, and he who fashions that smooth sand collar which never meets in the middle, and which holds many thousands of polynices eggs.

When we went ashore, the tide was rising on the flats while still ebbing in the channels. This is a peculiarity of estuaries which is not too difficult to understand. One can see how the water, while still running out of the estuary system, must meet the flow from the sea. In the resulting struggle the water may, and generally does, rise while it is still flowing out. After about twenty minutes or so, in the Nauset Marsh, the current will coincide with the rise.

But it is rather more difficult to visualize the reverse process. The tide will generally start to fall even while it is still flooding. And this brings up a very curious situation. At the mouth of the estuary the tide will be ebbing and falling, and, at the head, flooding and rising. What happens at that critical point in the middle? It would seem as if the two parts of the watershed must separate and leave a dry place in between. Of course, no such thing occurs. I have been much puzzled by this matter, but I have taken comfort in finding that Hilaire Belloc reports, in *The Cruise of the Nona,* his own mystification.

At any rate, when we climb back into the canoe the tide is flooding strongly. We make our southing and turn with the tide, leaving Cape Horn to starboard. The channel takes us close to the

Tonset Shore where eelgrass, the kind that is five or six feet long, has come in thick. We skirt the edge of it and are just approaching the rocks when suddenly the rod man's reel begins to screech.

I back water sharply to stop the canoe's progress, but the fish continues to tear off line. Not only that, but he starts weaving around some lobster buoys which are always to be found in this region. I do my best, in the strong current, to weave the canoe around after him, and must confess to a feeling of relief when he suddenly kicks off.

At this moment someone spies a large white object in the Skiff Hill pastures a quarter of a mile ahead. Various suggestions as to its identity are made, such as a white parasol, an inflated laundry bag, a small tent.

"It's a mushroom," say I, by way of a joke.

At the foot of the pastures we land and climb the green slope. And a mushroom it is! Nine and one-half inches across the top it measures, with a stem an inch and three quarters thick. In the old Farm House log my father wrote of mushrooms as big as dinner plates. Well, this pasture is full of dinner plates and we pick a mess of them to bring home.

These mushrooms, we find later, are not the common field mushroom, *Campestris agaricus,* but a close relative, *Campestris arvensis* or horse mushroom. They are as good to eat if not better, than their smaller cousin. The very young ones have white gills and we are chary of them. For although we think we know the deadly *Amanita phalloides,* our rule is never to eat a white-gilled mushroom of any kind. Consequently, we are careful to pick only those more mature ones with delicate pink or brown gills.

The mushroom-picking diversion has allowed the tide to catch up with us and we all pile back into the canoe. Even so, the upper flats are still out. The Skiff Hill Channel is plenty deep, but it shoals to nothing when we get up towards our hill. We follow a run which turns and twists through the West Cove flats. For some time it is satisfyingly deep. It peters out, however, just as we are approaching the first bend of the Main Channel. When we come to a stop, there is some talk about getting out and dragging. But the hazards, both psychological and physical, of wading in bare feet through soft mud, are too great. We prefer to wait.

And we are repaid for our waiting. As we sit quietly, an army of sandpipers lights beside us. Each little bird begins frantically to scurry to and fro, constantly probing the soft surface with his bill, and evidently getting something to his liking. We watch them through our glasses, trying to tell the difference between the semipalmated and the least sandpiper. The least is darker and has greenish legs, and the semipalmated is lighter and has black legs. I am told that each species breeds true. I hope so, as we spend so much time trying to distinguish them.

They look very small beside their cousins with the down-curved bills, the redbacks. The latter, who are winter visitors, seem to specialize on a small, pink worm which they carefully dunk in the water before swallowing.

So engrossed do we become looking for darker backs and greener legs that we are surprised when the canoe suddenly begins to move. The tide is not only rising, it is flooding. We go along with it into the channel, up into the Salt Pond Creek and back to the boathouse. We park the canoe alongside and somewhat wearily trudge up the hill to the Farm House.

But fatigue gives way as we sit on the piazza and sip a refreshing drink. Soon someone will have enough energy to start producing a hearty Farm House meal. Meanwhile, strangely content, we look out over the marsh with its blue water slowly spreading over the flats.

A few of its secrets have this day been bared to us. Sometime, another day will come when conditions are just right. Then perhaps we may wrest more secrets from the Nauset Marsh, as once again we round the Horn.

Henry David Thoreau

"Autumnal Tints"

At first blush, Henry David Thoreau's "Autumnal Tints," published just months after his death in May 1862, seems to be merely a collection of notes that Thoreau has taken while walking through an autumnal wood. Even if simply read this way, the notes represent lovely expressions of the colors of leaves, of their changes, and of their fall into the woodlots, yards, rivers, and roadsides of Concord, Massachusetts. But Thoreau is doing in this essay what he had earlier done in Walden: *asking, challenging, imploring the reader to see with a new set of eyes. While the inhabitants of the Old World have only sere woods, he writes, the inhabitants of the New World have a glorious woods—if they can see it. When the farmer looks with an eye trained only for economy, he can see only the dull though useful timothy grass, but he will miss the beauty of the purple grasses that thrive beside his fields. This essay is Thoreau's attempt to wake us up so that we will see the true harvest of the woods: Beauty.*

This essay is Thoreau's attempt to wake us up so that we will see the true harvest of the woods: Beauty.

And it is not accidental that Thoreau refers to that beauty as one of ripeness. The red maples he calls "burning bushes," signs that the trees are coming to real fruition, and their colors are harbingers not of death and decay but of fullness and richness—a parable of the life to which we are called.

Autumn, in this sense, is truly a time of harvest, but as the leaves them-selves suggest, it is a harvest of beauty enjoyed only by those with the eye to see, with the spirit to perceive, and with the heart to yearn toward fruition.

"Autumnal Tints"

Europeans coming to America are surprised by the brilliancy of our autumnal foliage. There is no account of such a phenomenon in English poetry, because the trees acquire but few bright colors there. The most that Thomson says on this subject in his "Autumn" is contained in the lines,—

> *But see the fading many-colored woods,*
> *Shade deepening over shade, the country round*
> *Imbrown; a crowded umbrage, dusk and dun,*
> *Of every hue, from wan declining green to sooty*
> *dark:—*

and in the line in which he speaks of

> *Autumn beaming o'er the yellow woods.*

The autumnal change of our woods has not made a deep impression on our own literature yet. October has hardly tinged our poetry.

A great many, who have spent their lives in cities, and have never chanced to come into the country at this season, have never seen this, the flower, or rather the ripe fruit, of the year. I remem-ber riding with one such citizen, who, though a fortnight too late for the most brilliant tints, was taken by surprise, and would not believe that there had been any brighter. He had never heard of this phenomenon before. Not only many in our towns have never witnessed it, but it is scarcely remembered by the majority from year to year.

Most appear to confound changed leaves with withered ones,

as if they were to confound ripe apples with rotten ones. I think that the change to some higher color in a leaf is an evidence that it has arrived at a late and perfect maturity, answering to the maturity of fruits. It is generally the lowest and oldest leaves which change first. But as the perfect-winged and usually bright-colored insect is short-lived, so the leaves ripen but to fall.

Generally, every fruit, on ripening, and just before it falls, when it commences a more independent and individual existence, requiring less nourishment from any source, and that not so much from the earth through its stem as from the sun and air, acquires a bright tint. So do leaves. The physiologist says it is "due to an increased absorption of oxygen." That is the scientific account of the matter,—only a reassertion of the fact. But I am more interested in the rosy cheek than I am to know what particular diet the maiden fed on. The very forest and herbage, the pellicle of the earth, must acquire a bright color, an evidence of its ripeness,—as if the globe itself were a fruit on its stem, with ever a cheek toward the sun.

Flowers are but colored leaves, fruits but ripe ones. The edible part of most fruits is, as the physiologist says, "the parenchyma or fleshy tissue of the leaf" of which they are formed.

Our appetites have commonly confined our views of ripeness and its phenomena, color, mellowness, and perfectness, to the fruits which we eat, and we are wont to forget that an immense harvest which we do not eat, hardly use at all, is annually ripened by Nature. At our annual Cattle Shows and Horticultural Exhibitions, we make, as we think, a great show of fair fruits, destined, however, to a rather ignoble end, fruits not valued for their beauty chiefly. But round about and within our towns there is annually another show of fruits, on an infinitely grander scale, fruits which address our taste for beauty alone.

October is the month for painted leaves. Their rich glow now flashes round the world. As fruits and leaves and the day itself acquire a bright tint just before they fall, so the year nears its setting. October is its sunset sky; November the later twilight.

I formerly thought that it would be worth the while to get a specimen leaf from each changing tree, shrub, and herbaceous plant, when it had acquired its brightest characteristic color, in its transition from the green to the brown state, outline it, and copy its color exactly, with paint, in a book, which should be entitled *"October, or Autumnal Tints"*;—beginning with the earliest reddening,—Woodbine and the lake of radical leaves, and coming down through the Maples, Hickories, and Sumachs, and many beautifully freckled leaves less generally known, to the latest Oaks and Aspens. What a memento such a book would be! You would need only to turn over its leaves to take a ramble through the autumn woods whenever you pleased. Or if I could preserve the leaves themselves, unfaded, it would be better still. I have made but little progress toward such a book, but I have endeavored, instead, to describe all these bright tints in the order in which they present themselves. The following are some extracts from my notes.

The Purple Grasses

By the twentieth of August, everywhere in woods and swamps we are reminded of the fall, both by the richly spotted Sarsaparilla-leaves and Brakes, and the withering and blackened Skunk-Cabbage and Hellebore, and, by the river-side, the already blackening Pontederia.

The Purple Grass (*Eragrostis pectinacea*) is now in the height of its beauty. I remember still when I first noticed this grass particularly. Standing on a hillside near our river, I saw, thirty or forty rods off, a stripe of purple half a dozen rods long, under the edge of a wood, where the ground sloped toward a meadow. It was as high-colored and interesting, though not quite so bright, as the patches of Rhexia, being a darker purple, like a berry's stain laid on close and thick. On going to and examining it, I found it to be a kind of grass in bloom, hardly a foot high, with but few green blades, and a fine spreading panicle of purple flowers, a shallow, purplish mist trembling around me. Close at hand it appeared but a

dull purple, and made little impression on the eye; it was even difficult to detect; and if you plucked a single plant, you were surprised
to find how thin it was, and how little color it had. But viewed at
a distance in a favorable light, it was of a fine lively purple, flow-
er-like, enriching the earth. Such puny causes combine to produce
these decided effects. I was the more surprised and charmed because
grass is commonly of a sober and humble color.

With its beautiful purple blush it reminds me, and supplies
the place, of the Rhexia, which is now leaving off, and it is one of
the most interesting phenomena of August. The finest patches of it
grow on waste strips or selvages of land at the base of dry hills, just
above the edge of the meadows, where the greedy mower does not
deign to swing his scythe; for this is a thin and poor grass, beneath
his notice. Or, it may be, because it is so beautiful he does not
know that it exists; for the same eye does not see this and timothy.
He carefully gets the meadow hay and the more nutritious grasses
which grow next to that, but he leaves this fine purple mist for the
walker's harvest,—fodder for his fancy stock. Higher up the hill,
perchance, grow also Blackberries, John's-Wort, and neglected,
withered, and wiry June-Grass. How fortunate that it grows in such
places, and not in the midst of the rank grasses which are annually
cut! Nature thus keeps use and beauty distinct. I know many such
localities, where it does not fail to present itself annually, and paint
the earth with its blush. It grows on the gentle slopes, either in a
continuous patch or in scattered and rounded tufts a foot in diame-
ter, and it lasts till it is killed by the first smart frosts....

We love to see any redness in the vegetation of the temperate
zone. It is the color of colors. This plant [poke berry] speaks to our
blood. It asks a bright sun on it to make it show to best advantage,
and it must be seen at this season of the year. On warm hill-sides
its stems are ripe by the twenty-third of August. At that date I
walked through a beautiful grove of them, six or seven feet high,
on the side of one of our cliffs, where they ripen early. Quite to the
ground they were a deep, brilliant purple, with a bloom contrasting
with the still clear green leaves. It appears a rare triumph of Nature

to have produced and perfected such a plant, as if this were enough for a summer. What a perfect maturity it arrives at! It is the emblem of a successful life concluded by a death not premature, which is an ornament to Nature. What if we were to mature as perfectly, root and branch, glowing in the midst of our decay, like the Poke! I confess that it excites me to behold them. I cut one for a cane, for I would fain handle and lean on it. I love to press the berries between my fingers, and see their juice staining my hand. To walk amid these upright, branching casks of purple wine, which retain and diffuse a sunset glow, tasting each one with your eye, instead of counting the pipes on a London dock, what a privilege! For Nature's vintage is not confined to the vine. Our poets have sung of wine, the product of a foreign plant which commonly they never saw, as if our own plants had no juice in them more than the singers. Indeed, this has been called by some the American Grape, and, though a native of America, its juices are used in some foreign countries to improve the color of the wine; so that the poetaster may be celebrating the virtues of the Poke without knowing it. Here are berries enough to paint afresh the western sky, and play the bacchanal with, if you will. And what flutes its ensanguined stems would make, to be used in such a dance! It is truly a royal plant. I could spend the evening of the year musing amid the Poke-stems. And perchance amid these groves might arise at last a new school of philosophy or poetry. It lasts all through September....

A man shall perhaps rush by and trample down plants as high as his head, and cannot be said to know that they exist, though he may have cut many tons of them, littered his stables with them, and fed them to his cattle for years. Yet, if he ever favorably attends to them, he may be overcome by their beauty. Each humblest plant, or weed, as we call it, stands there to express some thought or mood of ours; and yet how long it stands in vain! I had walked over those Great Fields so many Augusts, and never yet distinctly recognized these purple companions that I had there. I had brushed against them and trodden on them, forsooth; and now, at last, they, as it were, rose up and blessed me. Beauty and true wealth are always thus cheap and despised. Heaven might be defined as the place which men avoid. Who can doubt that these grasses, which the farmer says are of no account to him, find some compensation in your appreciation of them? I may say that I never saw them before,—though, when I came to look them face to face, there did come down to me a purple gleam from previous years; and now, wherever I go, I see hardly anything else. It is the reign and presidency of the Andropogons.

The Red Maple

By the twenty-fifth of September, the Red Maples generally are beginning to be ripe. Some large ones have been conspicuously changing for a week, and some single trees are now very brilliant. I notice a small one, half a mile off across a meadow, against the green wood-side there, a far brighter red than the blossoms of any tree in summer, and more conspicuous. I have observed this tree for several autumns invariably changing earlier than its fellows, just as one tree ripens its fruit earlier than another. It might serve to mark the season, perhaps. I should be sorry if it were cut down. I know of two or three such trees in different parts of our town, which might, perhaps, be propagated from, as early ripeners or September trees, and their seed be advertised in the market, as well as that of radishes, if we cared as much about them.

At present these burning bushes stand chiefly along the edge of the meadows, or I distinguish them afar on the hillsides here and there. Sometimes you will see many small ones in a swamp turned quite crimson when all other trees around are still perfectly green, and the former appear so much the brighter for it. They take you by surprise, as you are going by on one side, across the fields, thus early in the season, as if it were some gay encampment of the red men or other foresters, of whose arrival you had not heard.

Some single trees, wholly bright scarlet, seen against others of their kind still freshly green, or against evergreens, are more memorable than whole groves will be by and by. How beautiful, when a whole tree is like one great scarlet fruit full of ripe juices, every leaf, from lowest limb to topmost spire, all aglow, especially if you look toward the sun! What more remarkable object can there be in the landscape? Visible for miles, too fair to be believed. If such a phenomenon occurred but once, it would be handed down by tradition to posterity, and get into the mythology at last.

The whole tree thus ripening in advance of its fellows attains a singular preëminence, and sometimes maintains it for a week or two. I am thrilled at the sight of it, bearing aloft its scarlet standard for the regiment of green-clad foresters around, and I go half a mile out of my way to examine it. A single tree becomes thus the crowning beauty of some meadowy vale, and the expression of the whole surrounding forest is at once more spirited for it.

A small Red Maple has grown, perchance, far away at the head of some retired valley, a mile from any road, unobserved. It has faithfully discharged the duties of a Maple there, all winter and summer, neglected none of its economies, but added to its stature in the virtue which belongs to a Maple, by a steady growth for so many months, never having gone gadding abroad, and is nearer heaven than it was in the spring. It has faithfully husbanded its sap, and afforded a shelter to the wandering bird, has long since ripened its seeds and committed them to the winds, and has the satisfaction of knowing, perhaps, that a thousand little well-behaved Maples are already settled in life somewhere. It deserves well of Mapledom. Its leaves have been asking it from time to time, in a whisper, "When shall we redden?" And now, in this month of September, this month of traveling, when men are hastening to the sea-side, or the mountains, or the lakes, this modest Maple, still without budging an inch, travels in its reputation,—runs up its scarlet flag on that hill-side, which shows that it has finished its summer's work before all other trees, and withdraws from the contest. At the eleventh hour of the year, the tree which no scrutiny could have detected here when it was most industrious is thus, by the tint of its maturity, by its very blushes, revealed at last to the careless and distant traveler, and leads his thoughts away from the dusty road into those brave solitudes which it inhabits. It flashes out conspicuous with all the virtue and beauty of a Maple,—*Acer rubrum.* We may now read its title, or *rubric,* clear. Its *virtues,* not its sins, are as scarlet....

As I go across a meadow directly toward a low rising ground this bright afternoon, I see, some fifty rods off toward the sun, the top of a Maple swamp just appearing over the sheeny russet edge of the hill, a stripe apparently twenty rods long by ten feet deep, of the most intensely brilliant scarlet, orange, and yellow, equal to any flowers or fruits, or any tints ever painted. As I advance, lowering the edge of the hill which makes the firm foreground or lower frame of the picture, the depth of the brilliant grove revealed steadily increases, suggesting that the whole of the inclosed valley is filled with such color. One wonders that the tithing-men and fathers of the town are not out to see what the trees mean by their high colors and exuberance of spirits, fearing that some mischief is brewing. I do not see what the Puritans did at this season, when the Maples blaze out in scarlet. They certainly could not have worshiped in groves then. Perhaps that is what they built meeting-houses and fenced them round with horse-sheds for.

The Elm

Now too, the first of October, or later, the Elms are at the height of their autumnal beauty, great brownish-yellow masses, warm from their September oven, hanging over the highway. Their leaves are perfectly ripe. I wonder if there is any answering ripeness in the lives of the men who live beneath them. As I look down our street, which is lined with them, they remind me both by their form and color of yellowing sheaves of grain, as if the harvest had indeed come to the village itself, and we might expect to find some maturity and *flavor* in the thoughts of the villagers at last. Under those bright rustling yellow piles just ready to fall on the heads of the walkers, how can any crudity or greenness of thought or act prevail? When I stand where half a dozen large Elms droop over a house, it is as if I stood within a ripe pumpkin-rind, and I feel as mellow as if I were the pulp, though I may be somewhat stringy and seedy withal. What is the late greenness of the English Elm, like a cucumber out of season, which does not know when to have done, compared with the early and golden maturity of the American tree? The street is the scene of a great harvest-home. It would be worth the while to set out these trees, if only for their autumnal value. Think of these great yellow canopies or parasols held over our heads and houses by the mile together, making the village all one and compact,—an *ulmarium,* which is at the same time a nursery of men! And then how gently and unobserved they drop their burden and let in the sun when it is wanted, their leaves not heard when they fall on our roofs and in our streets; and thus the village parasol is shut up and put away! I see the market-man driving into the village, and disappearing under its canopy of Elm-tops, with *his* crop, as into a great granary or barn-yard. I am tempted to go thither as to a husking of thoughts, now dry and ripe, and ready to be separated from their integuments; but, alas! I foresee that it will be chiefly husks and little thought, blasted pig-corn, fit only for cob-meal,—for, as you sow, so shall you reap.

Fallen Leaves

By the sixth of October the leaves generally begin to fall, in successive showers, after frost or rain; but the principal leaf-harvest, the acme of the *Fall,* is commonly about the sixteenth. Some morning at that date there is perhaps a harder frost than we have seen, and ice formed under the pump, and now, when the morning wind rises, the leaves come down in denser showers than ever. They suddenly form thick beds or carpets on the ground, in this gentle air, or even without wind, just the size and form of the tree above. Some trees, as small Hickories, appear to have dropped their leaves instantaneously, as a soldier grounds arms at a signal; and those of the Hickory, being bright yellow still, though withered, reflect a blaze of light from the ground where they lie. Down they have come on all sides, at the first earnest touch of autumn's wand, making a sound like rain.

Or else it is after moist and rainy weather that we notice how great a fall of leaves there has been in the night, though it may not yet be the touch that loosens the Rock-Maple leaf. The streets are thickly strewn with the trophies, and fallen Elm-leaves make a dark brown pavement under our feet. After some remarkably warm Indian-summer day or days, I perceive that it is the unusual heat which, more than anything, causes the leaves to fall, there having been, perhaps, no frost nor rain for some time. The intense heat suddenly ripens and wilts them, just as it softens and ripens peaches and other fruits, and causes them to drop.

The leaves of late Red Maples, still bright, strew the earth, often crimson-spotted on a yellow ground, like some wild apples,— though they preserve these bright colors on the ground but a day or two, especially if it rains. On causeways I go by trees here and there all bare and smoke-like, having lost their brilliant clothing; but there it lies, nearly as bright as ever, on the ground on one side, and making nearly as regular a figure as lately on the tree. I would rather say that I first observe the trees thus flat on the ground like a permanent colored shadow, and they suggest to look for the boughs that bore them. A queen might be proud to walk where these gallant trees have spread their bright cloaks in the mud. I see wagons roll over them as a shadow or a reflection, and the drivers heed them just as little as they did their shadows before.

Birds' nests, in the Huckleberry and other shrubs, and in trees, are already being filled with the withered leaves. So many have fallen in the woods that a squirrel cannot run after a falling nut without being heard. Boys are raking them in the streets, if only for the pleasure of dealing with such clean, crisp substances. Some sweep the paths scrupulously neat, and then stand to see the next breath strew them with new trophies. The swamp-floor is thickly covered, and the *Lycopodium lucidulum* looks suddenly greener amid them. In dense woods they half-cover pools that are three or four rods long. The other day I could hardly find a well-known spring, and even suspected that it had dried up, for it was completely concealed by freshly fallen leaves; and when I swept them aside and revealed it, it was like striking the earth, with Aaron's rod, for a new spring. Wet grounds about the edges of swamps look dry with them. At one swamp, where I was surveying, thinking to step on a leafy shore from a rail, I got into the water more than a foot deep....

How they are mixed up, of all species, Oak and Maple and Chestnut and Birch! But Nature is not cluttered with them; she is a perfect husbandman; she stores them all. Consider what a vast crop is thus annually shed on the earth! This, more than any mere grain or seed, is the great harvest of the year. The trees are now repaying the earth with interest what they have taken from it. They are discounting. They are about to add a leaf's thickness to the depth of the soil. This is the beautiful way in which Nature gets her muck, while I chaffer with this man and that, who talks to me about sulphur and the cost of carting. We are all the richer for their decay. I am more interested in this crop than in the English grass alone or in the corn. It prepares the virgin mould for future corn-fields and forests, on which the earth fattens. It keeps our homestead in good heart.

For beautiful variety no crop can be compared with this. Here is not merely the plain yellow of the grains, but nearly all the colors that we know, the brightest blue not excepted: the early blushing Maple, the Poison-Sumach blazing its sins as scarlet, the mulberry Ash, the rich chrome yellow of the Poplars, the brilliant red Huckleberry, with which the hills' backs are painted, like those of sheep. The frost touches them, and, with the slightest breath of returning day or jarring of earth's axle, see in what showers they come floating down! The ground is all party-colored with them. But they still live in the soil, whose fertility and bulk they increase, and in the forests that spring from it. They stoop to rise, to mount higher in coming years, by subtle chemistry, climbing by the sap in the trees; and the sapling's first fruits thus shed, transmuted at last, may adorn its crown, when, in after-years, it has become the monarch of the forest.

It is pleasant to walk over the beds of these fresh, crisp, and rustling leaves. How beautifully they go to their graves! how gently lay themselves down and turn to mould!—painted of a thousand hues, and fit to make the beds of us living. So they troop to their last resting-place, light and frisky. They put on no weeds, but merrily they go scampering over the earth, selecting the spot, choosing a lot, ordering no iron fence, whispering all through the woods about it,—some choosing the spot where the bodies of men are mouldering beneath, and meeting them half-way. How many flutterings before they rest quietly in their graves! They that soared so loftily, how contentedly they return to dust again, and are laid low, resigned to lie and decay at the foot of the tree, and afford nourishment to new generations of their kind, as well as to flutter on high! They teach us how to die. One wonders if the time will ever come when men, with their boasted faith in immortality, will lie down as gracefully and as ripe,—with such an Indian-summer serenity will shed their bodies, as they do their hair and nails.

When the leaves fall, the whole earth is a cemetery pleasant to walk in. I love to wander and muse over them in their graves. Here are no lying nor vain epitaphs. What though you own no lot at Mount Auburn? Your lot is surely cast somewhere in this vast cemetery, which has been consecrated from of old. You need attend no auction to secure a place. There is room enough here. The Loosestrife shall bloom and the Huckleberry-bird sing over your bones. The woodman and hunter shall be your sextons, and the children shall tread upon the borders as much as they will. Let us walk in the cemetery of the leaves,—this is your true Greenwood Cemetery.

The Sugar-Maple

But think not that the splendor of the year is over; for as one leaf does not make a summer, neither does one falling leaf make an autumn. The smallest Sugar-Maples in our streets make a great show as early as the fifth of October, more than any other trees there. As I look up the Main Street, they appear like painted screens standing before the houses; yet many are green. But now, or generally by the seventeenth of October, when almost all Red Maples and some White Maples are bare, the large Sugar-Maples also are in their glory, glowing with yellow and red, and show unexpectedly bright and delicate tints. They are remarkable for the contrast they often afford of deep blushing red on one half and green on the other. They become at length dense masses of rich yellow with a deep scarlet blush, or more than blush, on the exposed surfaces. They are the brightest trees now in the street.

The large ones on our Common are particularly beautiful. A delicate but warmer than golden yellow is now the prevailing color, with scarlet cheeks. Yet, standing on the east side of the Common just before sundown, when the western light is transmitted through them, I see that their yellow even, compared with the pale lemon yellow of an Elm close by, amounts to a scarlet, without noticing the bright scarlet portions. Generally, they are great regular oval masses of yellow and scarlet. All the sunny warmth of the season, the Indian summer, seems to be absorbed in their leaves. The lowest and inmost leaves next the bole are, as usual, of the most delicate yellow and green, like the complexion of young men brought up in the house. There is an auction on the Common to-day, but its red flag is hard to be discerned amid this blaze of color.

Little did the fathers of the town anticipate this brilliant success, when they caused to be imported from farther in the country some straight poles with their tops cut off, which they called Sugar-Maples; and, as I remember, after they were set out, a neighboring merchant's clerk, by way of jest, planted beans about them. Those which were then jestingly called bean-poles are to-day far the most beautiful objects noticeable in our streets. They are worth all and more than they have cost,—though one of the selectmen, while setting them out, took the cold which occasioned his death,—if only because they have filled the open eyes of children with their rich color unstintedly so many Octobers. We will not ask them to yield us sugar in the spring, while they afford us so fair a prospect in the autumn. Wealth in-doors may be the inheritance of few, but it is equally distributed on the Common. All children alike can revel in this golden Harvest....

No wonder that we must have our annual Cattle-Show, and Fall Training, and perhaps Cornwallis, our September Courts, and the like. Nature herself holds her annual fair in October, not only in the streets, but in every hollow and on every hill-side. When lately we looked into that Red-Maple swamp all a-blaze, where the trees were clothed in their vestures of most dazzling tints, did it not suggest a thousand gypsies beneath,—a race capable of wild delight,—or even the fabled fauns, satyrs, and wood-nymphs come back to earth? Or was it only a congregation of wearied wood-choppers, or of proprietors come to inspect their lots, that we thought of? Or, earlier still, when we paddled on the river through that fine-grained September air, did there not appear to be something new going on under the sparkling surface of the stream, a shaking of props, at least, so that we made haste in order to be up in time? Did not the rows of yellowing Willows and Button-Bushes on each side seem like rows of booths, under which, perhaps, some fluviatile egg-pop equally yellow was effervescing? Did not all these suggest that man's spirits should rise as high as Nature's,—should hang out their flag, and the routine of his life be interrupted by an analogous expression of joy and hilarity?…

A village needs these innocent stimulants of bright and cheering prospects to keep off melancholy and superstition. Show me two villages, one embowered in trees and blazing with all the glories of October, the other a merely trivial and treeless waste, or with only a single tree or two for suicides, and I shall be sure that in the latter will be found the most starved and bigoted religionists and the most desperate drinkers. Every wash-tub and milk-can and gravestone will be exposed. The inhabitants will disappear abruptly behind their barns and houses, like desert Arabs amid their rocks, and I shall look to see spears in their hands. They will be ready to accept the most barren and forlorn doctrine,—as that the world is speedily coming to an end, or has already got to it, or that they themselves are turned wrong side outward. They will perchance crack their dry joints at one another and call it a spiritual communication.

The Scarlet Oak

By the twenty-sixth of October the large Scarlet Oaks are in their prime, when other Oaks are usually withered. They have been kindling their fires for a week past, and now generally burst into a blaze. This alone of *our* indigenous deciduous trees (excepting the Dogwood, of which I do not know half a dozen, and they are but large bushes) is now in its glory. The two Aspens and the Sugar-Maple come nearest to it in date, but they have lost the greater part of their leaves. Of evergreens, only the Pitch-Pine is still commonly bright.

But it requires a particular alertness, if not devotion to these phenomena, to appreciate the wide-spread, but late and unexpected glory of the Scarlet Oaks. I do not speak here of the small trees and shrubs, which are commonly observed, and which are now withered, but of the large trees. Most go in and shut their doors, thinking that bleak and colorless November has already come, when some of the most brilliant and memorable colors are not yet lit.

This very perfect and vigorous one, about forty feet high, standing in an open pasture, which was quite glossy green on the twelfth, is now, the twenty-sixth, completely changed to bright dark-scarlet,—every leaf, between you and the sun, as if it had been dipped into a scarlet dye. The whole tree is much like a heart in form, as well as color. Was not this worth waiting for? Little did you think, ten days ago, that that cold green tree would assume such color as this. Its leaves are still firmly attached, while those of other trees are falling around it. It seems to say,—"I am the last to blush, but I blush deeper than any of ye. I bring up the rear in my red coat. We Scarlet ones, alone of Oaks, have not given up the fight."

The sap is now, and even far into November, frequently flowing fast in these trees, as in Maples in the spring; and apparently their bright tints, now that most other Oaks are withered, are connected with this phenomenon. They are full of life. It has a pleasantly astringent, acorn-like taste, this strong Oak-wine, as I find on tapping them with my knife.

Looking across this woodland valley, a quarter of a mile wide, how rich those Scarlet Oaks embosomed in Pines, their bright red branches intimately intermingled with them! They have their full effect there. The Pine-boughs are the green calyx to their red petals. Or, as we go along a road in the woods, the sun striking endwise through it, and lighting up the red tents of the Oaks, which on each side are mingled with the liquid green of the Pines, makes a very gorgeous scene. Indeed, without the evergreens for contrast, the autumnal tints would lose much of their effect.

The Scarlet Oak asks a clear sky and the brightness of late October days. These bring out its colors. If the sun goes into a cloud they become comparatively indistinct. As I sit on a cliff in the southwest part of our town, the sun is now getting low, and the woods in Lincoln, south and east of me, are lit up by its more level rays; and in the Scarlet Oaks, scattered so equally over the forest, there is brought out a more brilliant redness than I had believed was in them. Every tree of this species which is visible in those directions, even to the horizon, now stands out distinctly red. Some great ones lift their red backs high above the woods, in the next town, like huge roses with a myriad of fine petals; and some more slender ones, in a small grove of White Pines on Pine Hill in the east, on the very verge of the horizon, alternating with the Pines on the edge of the grove, and shouldering them with their red coats, look like soldiers in red amid hunters in green. This time it is Lincoln green, too. Till the sun got low, I did not believe that there were so many redcoats in the forest army. Theirs is an intense, burning red, which would lose some of its strength, methinks, with every step you might take toward them; for the shade that lurks amid their foliage does not report itself at this distance, and they are unanimously red. The focus of their reflected color is in the atmosphere far on this side. Every such tree becomes a nucleus of red, as it were, where, with the declining sun, that color grows and glows. It is partly borrowed fire, gathering strength from the sun on its way to your eye. It has only some comparatively dull red leaves for a rallying-point, or kindling-stuff, to start it, and it becomes an intense scarlet or red mist, or fire, which finds fuel for itself in the very atmosphere. So vivacious is redness. The very rails reflect a rosy light at this hour and season. You see a redder tree than exists.

If you wish to count the Scarlet Oaks, do it now. In a clear day stand thus on a hill-top in the woods, when the sun is an hour high, and every one within range of your vision, excepting in the west, will be revealed. You might live to the age of Methuselah and never find a tithe of them, otherwise. Yet sometimes even in a dark day I have thought them as bright as I ever saw them. Looking westward, their colors are lost in a blaze of light; but in other directions the whole forest is a flower-garden, in which these late roses burn, alternating with green, while the so-called "gardeners," walking here and there, perchance, beneath, with spade and water-pot, see only a few little asters amid withered leaves....

Let your walks now be a little more adventurous; ascend the hills. If, about the last of October, you ascend any hill in the outskirts of our town, and probably of yours, and look over the forest, you may see—well, what I have endeavored to describe. All this you surely *will* see, and much more, if you are prepared to see it,—if you *look* for it. Otherwise, regular and universal as this phenomenon is, whether you stand on the hill-top or in the hollow, you will think for threescore years and ten that all the wood is, at this season, sere and brown. Objects are concealed from our view, not so much because they are out of the course of our visual ray as because we do not bring our minds and eyes to bear on them; for there is no power to see in the eye itself, any more than in any other jelly. We do not realize how far and widely, or how near and narrowly, we are to look. The greater part of the phenomena of Nature are for this reason concealed from us all our lives. The gardener sees only the gardener's garden. Here, too, as in political economy, the supply answers to the demand. Nature does not cast pearls before swine. There is just as much beauty visible to us in the landscape as we are prepared to appreciate,—not a grain more. The actual objects which one man will see from a particular hilltop are just as different from those which another will see as the beholders are different. The Scarlet Oak must, in a sense, be in your eye when you go forth. We cannot see anything until we are possessed with the idea of it, take it into our heads,—and then we can hardly see anything else. In my botanical rambles, I find, that, first, the idea, or image, of a plant occupies my thoughts, though it may seem very foreign to this locality,—no nearer than Hudson's Bay,—and for some weeks or months I go thinking of it, and expecting it, unconsciously, and at length I surely see it. This is the history of my finding a score or more of rare plants which I could name. A man sees only what concerns him. A botanist absorbed in the study of grasses does not distinguish the grandest Pasture Oaks. He, as it were, tramples down Oaks unwittingly in his walk, or at most sees only their shadows. I have found that it required a different intention of the eye, in the same locality, to see different plants, even when they were closely allied, as *Juncaceae* and *Gramineae:* when I was looking for the former, I did not see the latter in the midst of them. How much more, then, it requires different intentions of the eye and of the mind to attend to different departments of knowledge! How differently the poet and the naturalist look at objects!

Take a New England selectman, and set him on the highest of our hills, and tell him to look,—sharpening his sight to the utmost, and putting on the glasses that suit him best, (aye, using a spy-glass if he likes,)—and make a full report. What, probably, will he *spy?*—what will he *select* to look at? Of course, he will see a Brocken spectre of himself. He will see several meeting-houses, at least, and, perhaps, that somebody ought to be assessed higher than he is, since he has so handsome a wood-lot. Now take Julius Caesar, or Immanuel Swedenborg, or a Fegee- [Figi-]Islander, and set him up there. Or suppose all together, and let them compare notes afterward. Will it appear that they have enjoyed the same prospect? What they will see will be as different as Rome was from Heaven or Hell, or the last from the Fegee Islands. For aught we know, as strange a man as any of these is always at our elbow.

Why, it takes a sharp-shooter to bring down even such trivial game as snipes and woodcocks; he must take very particular aim, and know what he is aiming at. He would stand a very small chance, if he fired at random into the sky, being told that snipes were flying there. And so is it with him that shoots at beauty; though he wait till the sky falls, he will not bag any, if he does not already know its seasons and haunts, and the color of its wing,—if he has not dreamed of it, so that he can *anticipate* it; then, indeed, he flushes it at every step, shoots double and on the wing, with both barrels, even in corn-fields. The sportsman trains himself, dresses, and watches unweariedly, and loads and primes for his particular game. He prays for it, and offers sacrifices, and so he gets it. After due and long preparation, schooling his eye and hand, dreaming awake and asleep, with gun and paddle and boat, he goes out after meadow-hens, which most of his townsmen never saw nor dreamed of, and paddles for miles against a head wind, and wades in water up to his knees, being out all day without his dinner, and *therefore* he gets them. He had them half-way into his bag when he started, and has only to shove them down. The true sportsman can shoot you almost any of his game from his windows: what else has he windows or eyes for? It comes and perches at last on the barrel of his gun; but the rest of the world never see it *with the feathers on.* The geese fly exactly under his zenith, and honk when they get there, and he will keep himself supplied by firing up his chimney; twenty musquash [muskrats] have the refusal of each one of his traps before it is empty. If he lives, and his game spirit increases, heaven and earth shall fail him sooner than game; and when he dies, he will go to more extensive and, perchance, happier hunting-grounds. The fisherman, too, dreams of fish, sees a bobbing cork in his dreams, till he can almost catch them in his sink-spout. I knew a girl who, being sent to pick huckleberries, picked wild gooseberries by the quart, where no one else knew that there were any, because she was accustomed to pick them upcountry where she came from. The astronomer knows where to go star–gathering, and sees one clearly in his mind before any have seen it with a glass. The hen scratches and finds her food right under where she stands; but such is not the way with the hawk.

These bright leaves which I have mentioned are not the exception, but the rule; for I believe that all leaves, even grasses and mosses, acquire brighter colors just before their fall. When you come to observe faithfully the changes of each humblest plant, you find that each has, sooner or later, its peculiar autumnal tint; and if you undertake to make a complete list of the bright tints, it will be nearly as long as a catalogue of the plants in your vicinity.

Donald Culross Peattie

FROM *AN ALMANAC FOR MODERNS*

Donald Culross Peattie draws together the naturalist's interest in the minute details of the physical world with the writer's delight in finding—and creating—rich connections. The harvest moon can be described in astronomical terms, but it is also "wise, ripe, and portly," an old god to bear company with Longfellow's goddess strewing bounty over the land. And, indeed, bounty is just what Peattie sees again and again in the season of autumn—the pear trees bowed down with fruit, the heaped hayricks, the ripening nuts.

> The patron saint in Peattie's modern almanac is Johnny Appleseed, whose patient toil helped create this yearly bounty.

The patron saint in Peattie's modern almanac is Johnny Appleseed, whose patient toil helped create this yearly bounty. But perhaps we are most drawn to the cheeky choirboys, the mice and squirrels, hauling away their loot before autumn takes her bow and yields Nature's stage to winter.

FROM *AN ALMANAC FOR MODERNS*

September Twenty-Fourth

I try each year to disbelieve what my senses tell me, and to look at the harvest moon in a cold and astronomical light. I know that it is a small cold sphere of rock, airless, jagged and without activity. But the harvest moon is not an astronomical fact. It is a knowing thing, lifting its ruddy face above the rim of the world. Even to the thoroughly civilized mind, where caution for the future is supposed to rule all impulse, the orange moon of autumn invites the senses to some saturnalia.... The harvest moon has no innocence, like the slim quarter moon of a spring twilight, nor has it the silver penny brilliance of the moon that looks down upon the resorts of summertime. Wise, ripe, and portly, like an old Bacchus, it waxes night after night.

September Twenty-Fifth

Now is that opulent moment in the year, the harvest, a time of cream in old crocks in cool, newt-haunted springhouses, of pears at the hour of perfection on old trees bent like women that, as the Bible says, bow down with child. In this field the grain stands, a harsh forest of golden straw nodding under the weight of the bearded spikes, and in that, it has been swept and all its fruitfulness carried off to fill the barns.

One will not see here, save in the steep tilted Blue Ridge farms, the man reaping by sickle in his solitary field, while his daughters bind the sheaves, nor the bouquet of wheat and pine boughs hung above the grange gable that is crammed to the doors. But we have our own sights and sounds at harvest time. There is the roar and the amber dust of the threshing machines, the laughter of the children riding home on the hayricks, the warfare of the crows and grackles in the painted woods, and the seething of juice in the apple presses. Then night falls and the workers sleep. The fields are stripped, and only the crickets chant in the midnight chill of the naked meadow.

October Sixth

Nobody knows the birth date of John Chapman, known as Johnny Appleseed, so that I shall put him where, I am sure, he would have preferred his biography to be inserted, in apple time. Sandburg and Stephen Benet and Vachel Lindsay have all sung his praises, and from his obscurity John (not Jonathan, as he is sometimes inaccurately called) has emerged as a national hero. Perhaps the only American who resembles an early Christian saint, he too went his barefoot way in sackcloth, subsisting upon roots, thundering out denunciations of pioneer vanity—store calico and tea drinking—and planting apple seeds wherever he set foot.

Legend concerning him has grown to almost homeric proportions. Many cities and states claim that their apples are descended from his sowing. The sober facts seem to be that he arrived on the Ohio about 1801, being then some twenty-six years in age, a completely daft young Elijah with a dash of Daniel Boone and General William Booth who went about in Ohio and Indiana starting orchards from seed. He regarded cutting and grafting as immoral and contrary to the will of God. In flouting horticultural experience he seems to have been motivated by a compassion for apple trees, a devout belief that they should not be deprived of regular sexual fertilization. There is no record that any woman ever looked with favor upon poor ragged Johnny. At sixty-five he died of exhaustion, after a hundred mile trip afoot to one of his orchards. Mad he undoubtedly was, but Saint Paul would have approved of him, and so would Whitman, and Francis of Assisi.

October Twenty-Fifth

Autumn is the time of fattening. Now the beech nuts ripen their oily kernels; the walnut swells its rich meat through black wooden labyrinths; the wild rice stands high the marshes, and the woods are filled with their jolly harvest of berries, blue buckthorn and scarlet bittersweet, black catbrier, holly and mistletoe and honeysuckle. The great green cannonballs of the osage orange drop from the prickly hedges with a thud; under the little hawthorns a perfect windfall of scarlet pomes lies drifted, and in the sun the bitter little wild crabs reach their one instant of winy, tangy, astringent perfection.

This is the moment of abundance for all our brother animals. The harvest mouse is now a wealthy little miser; squirrels can afford the bad investments they make. Opossums paw over the persimmons and pawpaws, picking only the tastiest, and like a cloud the cowbirds and grackles and bobolinks wing southward over the wild rice fields, so fat and lazy that the fowler makes an easy harvest of them. Everywhere, on frail bird bones, under the hides of chipmunk and skunk and all four-footed things, fat, the animal's own larder and reserve, is stored away against the bitter Months, against lean hunger and long sleep.

November First

What I love best in autumn is the way that Nature takes her curtain, as the stage folk say. The banners of the marshes furl, droop and fall. The leaves descend in golden glory. The ripe seeds drop and the fruit is cast aside. And so with slow chords in imperceptible fine modulations the great music draws to its close, and when the silence comes you can scarce distinguish it from the last far-off strains of the woodwinds and the horns.

Julian of Norwich

FROM *THE SHOWINGS OF DIVINE LOVE*

Julian of Norwich was a fourteenth-century mystic, writer, and teacher. She lived in an anchorage, a small room attached to a parish church in the English seacoast town of Norwich, where she devoted herself to prayer and to helping all those who came to seek her counsel. Here, as she reflects on one tiny fruit of the harvest, a hazelnut, she sees its fragility as harboring a miraculous promise: God will spread a mantle of love over us more tenderly—and faithfully—than the most devoted human parent.

Harvest then, for Julian and for us, is a time to come home. Yet Julian recognizes that our homes, our fathers and mothers, our siblings, our spouses often disappoint us, and so at harvest time our hearts are also gently pulled toward a better home, toward a father-mother who will never let us down, in whom we find our beginning that never has an end.

> ℋere, as she reflects on one tiny fruit of the harvest, a hazelnut, she sees its fragility as harboring a miraculous promise: God *will* spread a mantle of love over us more tenderly—and faithfully—than the most devoted human parent.

FROM *THE SHOWINGS OF DIVINE LOVE*

At this same time our Lord showed me a spiritual sight of His homely loving. I saw that He is to us everything that is good and comfortable for us. He is our clothing that for love wraps us, clasps us, and all encloses us for tender love, that He may never leave us. He is to us everything that is good.

Also in this He showed me a little thing, the quantity of an hazelnut, in the palm of my hand, and it was as round as a ball. I looked thereupon with eye of my understanding, and thought, "What may this be?"

And it was answered generally thus, "It is all that is made."

I marveled how it might last, for I thought it might suddenly have fallen to nothing for littleness.

And I was answered in my understanding, "It lasts now and ever shall last because God loves it."

And so everything has its being by the love of God. In this little hazelnut I saw three properties. The first is that God made it; the second is that God loves it; the third is that God keeps it. But what is to me truly the Maker, the Keeper, and the Lover, I cannot tell. For until I am joined to Him substantially, I may never have full rest nor true bliss, that is to say, until I be so fastened to Him, that there is nothing at all between my God and me.

It is necessary that we know the littleness of creatures and to hold as nothing everything that is made so that we may love and have God that is unmade. For this is the cause why we are not all in ease of heart and soul, because we seek here rest in those things that are so little, wherein is no rest, and know not our God that is All-mighty, All-wise, All-good. For He is the Very Rest. God wills to be known, and it pleases Him that we rest in Him; for all that is beneath Him does not satisfy us. And this is the cause why no soul is at rest until it is made nothing as to all things that are made. When it is willingly made nothing for love, to have Him that is all, then is it able to receive spiritual rest.

Also our Lord God showed that it is most pleasant to Him that a helpless soul come to Him simply and plainly and homely. For this is the natural yearning of the soul when it is touched by the Holy Ghost, "God, of Thy goodness, give me Thyself; for Thou art enough to me, and I may ask nothing that is less, that may be full worship to Thee. And if I ask anything that is less, I will still feel the lack. But only in Thee I have all."

And these words are full lovely to the soul, and they full nearly touch the will of God and His goodness. For His goodness comprehends all His creatures and all His blessed works and surpasses them without end. For He is the endlessness, and He hath made us only for Himself, and restored us by His blessed passion, and keeps us in His blessed love, and all this of His goodness.

And thus in our making, God All-mighty, is our nature's father, and God All-wisdom is our nature's mother, with the love and the goodness of the Holy Ghost, which is all one God, one Lord. And in the knitting and the joining, He is our very, true spouse, and we are His loved wife, His fair maiden: with which wife He is never displeased. For He says, "I love you and you love me, and our love shall never be parted in two."

This fair lovely word *Mother*, it is so sweet and so natural that it may not truly be said of any but of *Him* and to her that is very mother of Him and of all. To the property of motherhood belongs natural love, wisdom, and knowing, and it is good. For though our body's birth be but little, low, and simple when compared to our spiritual birth, yet it is He who does it in the creatures by whom it is done. The kindly, loving mother that knows and understands the need of her child, she keeps that child full tenderly, as the nature and condition of motherhood will. And as the child grows older, she changes her working, but not her love. And when the child is yet older, she allows punishment to beat down vices and to make the child receive virtues and graces. This working, with all that is fair and good, our Lord does in them by whom it is done. Thus He is our mother in nature by the working of grace in the lower part for love of the higher part. And He wills that we know this, for He will have all our love fastened to Him.

And in this I saw that all our duty that we owe, by God's bidding, to fatherhood and motherhood, we do so because God's fatherhood and motherhood is fulfilled in true loving of God, which blessed love Christ works in us.

God said to me full merrily, "I am the Ground of your beseeching."

For truly I saw and understood in our Lord's meaning that He showed it because He wills to have it known more than it is, so that He may give us grace to love Him and cleave to Him. For He beholds His heavenly treasure with so great love on earth that He wills to give us more light and solace in heavenly joy, in drawing our hearts to Him because of the sorrow and darkness which we are in.

And from that time that it was showed I desired oftentimes to learn what was our Lord's meaning. And fifteen years later, I was answered in my spiritual understanding:

> *Wouldst thou learn your Lord's meaning in this*
> *thing?*
> *Learn it well.*
> *Love was His meaning.*
> *Who showed it thee?*
> *Love.*
> *What showed He thee?*
> *Love.*
> *Wherefore showed it He?*

For Love.

Hold yourself in love and you shall learn and know
    more of the same. But without love you will
    never know anything.

Thus I learned that love was our Lord's meaning. And I saw for a certainty that before God made us, He loved us, and this love never lessened nor shall it ever. And in this love He hath done all His works, and in this love He hath made all things profitable for us, and in this love our life is everlasting. In our making we had a beginning, but the love wherein He made us was in Him from without beginning, in which love we have our beginning. And all this shall we see in God, without end.

A GATHERING OF
PRAYERS AND HYMNS

The impulse to pray is more than mere intuition—or desperation. It is a response to an irresistible call, to the penetrating knowledge that we are not alone and we are not our own. Whether chanted, recited, or sung, prayers—each of which is specific to its own tradition—probe the deepest parts of the human heart and reach out to the God who hears.

The Vedic prayers included here are about fruitfulness and fecundity, powerfully evocative in India, a land that has seen so much drought and famine. Perhaps that context makes the expressions of the sweet nature of the world so moving and the images of God as provider and reaper so powerful. A similar image of God as provider anchors the "Verse of the Throne"

*W*hether chanted, recited, or sung, prayers— each of which is specific to its own tradition—probe the deepest parts of the human heart and reach out to the God who hears.

from the Qur'an, a verse that is often recited in Muslim prayers. Particularly powerful are the assurances that God never slumbers and that the preservation of heaven and earth "is no burden to him."

In American hymnody of the nineteenth century, autumn often serves as a parable. In the same manner in which the farmer gathers the harvest, so too does the Lord gather people together, bringing them finally—rejoicing—to God's own harvest home. The African prayers of harvest are also rooted in a strong sense of home and immediate experience. Yet, in the starkness of the pleas—against illness, against hunger, for plenitude, for healthy children—lurks the reminder that the prayers may not be answered: that however plentiful the harvest, it can never be taken for granted.

Vedic Harvest Prayers

Brimful of sweetness is the grain,
brimful of sweetness are my words;
when everything is a thousand times sweet,
how can I not prosper?

I know one who is brimful of sweetness,
the one who has given abundant corn,
the God whose name is Reaper-God;
him we invoke with our song.

He swells in the home of even the lowly
who are debarred from sacrifice.
The God whose name is Reaper-God,
him we invoke with our song.

Let the five directions and races of men
bring to our doors prosperity,
as after the rains (in a swollen flood)
a river carries down driftwood.

As a spring gushes forth in a hundred, a thousand,
streams, and yet stays inexhaustible,
so in a thousand streams may our corn
flow inexhaustibly!

Reap, you workers, one hundred hands,
garner, you workers, one thousand hands!
gather in the bounteous corn that is cut
or still waits on the stalk.

Three measures I apportion to the Spirits,
four measures to the mistress of the house,
while you I touch with the amplest measure
(of all that the field has yielded).

Reaper and Garnerer are your two
distributors, O Lord of creation.
May they convey hither an ample store
of riches never decreasing!

Spring up, become fair, be distended, O barley,
with your own increase!
Burst all vessels designed to contain you!
May lightning not smite you
in that place where we make our appeal to you.

In response, divine barley, to our invocation,
rise up there tall as the sky, inexhaustible
as the boundless sea!

> *May those who tend you prove inexhaustible,*
> *inexhaustible their barns,*
> *inexhaustible those who offer you in sacrifice*
> *and those who consume you.*

The Verse of the Throne

God! There is no God but he; the living, the self-subsisting: neither slumber nor sleep seizeth him; to him belongeth whatsoever is in heaven, and on earth. Who is he that can intercede with him, but through his good pleasure? He knoweth that which is past, and that which is to come unto them, and they shall not comprehend anything of his knowledge, but so far as he pleaseth. His throne is extended over heaven and earth, and the preservation of both is no burden unto him. He is the high, the mighty.

Evangelistic Hymns

Come, Ye Thankful People, Come

> *Come, ye thankful people, come, raise the song of*
> *   harvest home;*
> *All is safely gathered in, ere the winter storms begin;*
> *God, our Maker, doth provide for our want to be*
> *   supplied;*
> *Come to God's own temple, come, raise the song of*
> *   harvest home.*
>
> *All the world is God's own field, fruit unto his*
> *   praise to yield;*
> *Wheat and tares together sown, unto joy or sorrow*
> *   grown;*

First the blade, and then the ear, then the full corn
    shall appear;
Lord of harvest, grant that we wholesome grain and
    pure may be.

For the Lord, our God shall come, and shall take his
    harvest home;
From his field shall in that day all offenses purge
    away,
Give his angels charge at last in the fire the tares to
    cast,
But the fruitful ears to store in his garner evermore.

Even so, Lord, quickly come to thy final harvest
    home;
Gather thou thy people in, free from sorrow, free
    from sin;
There forever purified, in thy presence to abide;
Come, with all thine angels, come, raise the glorious
    harvest home.

Sing to the Lord of Harvest

Sing to the Lord of harvest, sing songs of love and
    praise;
With joyful hearts and voices your alleluias raise.
By him the rolling seasons in fruitful order move;
Sing to the Lord of harvest a joyful song of love.

God makes the clouds drop fatness, the deserts bloom
and spring;
The hills leap up in gladness, the valleys laugh and
sing.
He fills from his great fullness all things with large
increase;
He crowns the year with goodness, with plenty, and
with peace.

Heap on his sacred altar the gifts his goodness gave,
The golden sheaves of harvest, the souls Christ died
to save.
Your hearts lay down before him when at his feet
you fall,
And with your lives adore him who gave his life for
all.

African Harvest Prayers

Leader: Mwene-Nyanga [God], you who have
brought us rain and have given us a good
harvest, let people eat grain of this harvest
calmly and peacefully.

People: Peace, praise ye, Ngai [God], peace be
with us.

Leader: Do not bring us any surprise or depression.

People: Peace, praise ye, Ngai, peace be with us.

Leader: *Guard us against illness of people and our herds and flocks, so that we may enjoy this season's harvest in tranquility.*

People: *Peace, praise ye, Ngai, peace be with us.*

This is yours, Kazooba [the Sun],
This is yours, Ruhanga [the Creator],
This is yours, Rugaba [the Giver].

May our grain bear so much fruit that it be forgotten on the ground and that it lets fall along the path so much that next year when we go forth to seed, the fields and the pathways will be covered with green grain.

God! give us health
God! give us raided cattle
God! give us the offspring
Of men and cattle.

See my lords
I have presented to you
I have given you this food.
Eat and be satisfied so that I may have health.

PART FIVE

Thanksgiving

INTRODUCTION

On Thanksgiving Day, November 21, 1793, Samuel Lane, of Stratham, New Hampshire, woke early. It was to be a busy day, but before it all started, Lane began to think about the meaning of the holiday and about his life as a farmer, tanner, cobbler, and surveyor. He turned to his diary and began listing those things for which he was thankful, listing particulars, and so giving an account of his good life.

> *The Life & health of myself and family, and also of so many of my Children, grand Children, and great grand-children; also of my other Relations and friends & Neighbors, for Health peace and plenty amongst us.*
>
> *for my Bible and Many other good and Useful Books, Civil & Religious Priviledges,*
>
> *for the ordinances of the gospel; and for my Minister.*
>
> *for my Land, House and Barn and other Buildings, & that they are preserv'd from fire & other accidents.*
>
> *for my wearing Clothes to keep me warm, my Bed & Beding to rest upon.*
>
> *for my Cattle, Sheep & Swine & other Creatures, for my support.*
>
> *for my Corn, Wheat, Rye Grass and Hay; Wool, flax, Syder, Apples, Pumpkins, Potatoes, Cabages, turnips, Carrots, Beets, peaches and other fruits.*

for my Clock and Watch to measure my passing time by Day and
by Night, Wood, Water, Butter, Cheese, Milk, Pork, Beefe, &
fish, &c

for Tea, Sugar, Rum, Wine, Gin, Molasses, peper, Spice & Money
for to bye other Necessaries and to pay my Debts & Taxes &c.

for my Lether, Lamp oyl & Candles, Husbandry Utensils, & other
tools of every sort &c &c &c.

Bless the Lord O my Soul and all that is within me Bless his holy
Name. Bless the Lord O my Soul and forget not all his benefits,
who Satisfieth thy mouth with good things.

When Lane thinks about what he should be thankful for, he thinks
not of large elements but of particulars. He does not think about
global trends but of the local, what is given to him within his own
reach. And he does not consider the abstract but the concrete, even
ending his prayer with a reference to the concrete: God is the one
who satisfies his mouth with good things. On this day, it would be
good food to satisfy him, eaten in company with friends and family.

The season of autumn, which begins with so many perturba-
tions, with so much uncertainty, with a sense of endings, concludes
with this great festival of gratitude. Like the Pilgrims who stood on
that first Thanksgiving, we recognize that our lives are full of uncer-
tainties and that we cannot control our fates: autumn has shown us
the inevitability of our passing. And yet, our understanding of that
passing does not diminish the sense that we should be grateful for
what we are given now. It is right and proper to celebrate; we do
not ignore the fact of our passing, but we celebrate the fact of our
life.

This is what several of the pieces in this section focus upon.
Sarah Josepha Hale evokes the past in her joyful recounting of the
abundance built into American Thanksgiving traditions. David
Kline celebrates the sense of what Annie Dillard, in *Pilgrim at Tin-
ker Creek,* has called the fecundity of the world—the sense of the
creator's overwhelming and extravagant abundance. And Hahm
Dong-seon revels in the kind of particularities of life that Samuel

Lane enjoyed, poetically using them to evoke a sense of autumn as a time of poignant and powerful memory.

Nonetheless, in celebrating life, autumn still does remind us of passing. And here, there is thanksgiving of a different sort. Both Robert Louis Stevenson and P. D. James locate their autumn pieces, at least in part, in a graveyard—but they are not the grave-yards of Halloween. They are graveyards full of rich harvests of memories. Here there is thanksgiving for the gatherings of lives well lived and gratitude for the witness of those lives. When James describes walking through the autumnal light that slants upon the stones, she invests that time and place with a sense of thanksgiving. When Stevenson looks at a grave with flowers strewn across it, he understands the role of gratitude in our lives.

The Pilgrims saw their Thanksgiving holiday as a celebration not only of personal survival—though they certainly were thank-ful for that. Instead they also saw it as a celebration of gratitude to God for providing for their needs and not allowing their dream to perish. Though there were only half as many of them as there had been a year before, Plimoth town was well established. There was smoke rising from a handful of houses, a fort begun, and good trea-ties concluded. But they could also look up from the harbor and see Burial Hill, where their first governor and so many of their loved ones bore witness to the depth of their commitment to the ideal.

So they celebrated. Their choice of autumn for their celebra-tion seems in one sense obvious: the harvest was in, and food was abundant. But in fact, the choice was a radical affirmation and gains in significance when we set it against the previous year, when this group had lived through a horrific winter. This November, having learned the lessons of the past American winter, they had every reason and every incentive to hoard. But like Dillard's extravagant Creator, they spent the wad. Trusting God, they celebrated fully and extravagantly and—for Pilgrims—wildly.

Thanksgiving is an affirmation of gratitude for the past and an expression of confidence in the future. It is autumn looking for-ward toward winter, and not being frightened by the coming cold.

It is change and ending, the loss of summer light and play, and the inner assurance that they will come again. Autumn is the expression of hope in the certainty and promise of renewal. It is the gladness in our hearts that once again the harvest has come, and we have not been disappointed.

Autumn is the bracing knowledge that there is joy in the morning.

FROM THE BOOK OF RUTH IN THE HEBREW BIBLE

In the complicated transaction that completes the book of Ruth, two things are clear: Boaz loves Ruth, and he is willing to spend extravagantly to buy back her inheritance. As the kinsman removes the shoe that witnesses to Boaz's purchase, we can imagine Boaz willingly, jubilantly, grasping it as he celebrates her redemption. And what blesses Ruth also blesses Naomi.

No longer can she call herself "Mara" or say, "I went away full, but the Lord brought me back empty," for now she is full to overflowing: daughter, son, grandson, and a restored inheritance.

What response to such richness, but joy and laughter that ripples out to all the people of Bethlehem? For though autumn may begin in loneliness and sorrow, it must end with communal thanksgiving, with invitations to widows and orphans, with songs that begin "Blessed be the Lord." And in the middle sits Ruth: serene, confident, a woman of virtue, the mother of kings.

> For though autumn may begin in loneliness and sorrow, it must end with communal thanksgiving, with invitations to widows and orphans, with songs that begin "Blessed be the Lord."

THE BOOK OF RUTH

Then Boaz went to the gate of the city and sat down. When the kinsman came by, Boaz said, "Come and sit here," and the man sat down. Boaz also called ten elders and said, "Come and sit here," and they sat down.

Boaz said to his kinsman, "Naomi is returned from the country of Moab and wishes to sell a parcel of land that belonged to Elimelech, our brother. Here in the presence of the people of Bethlehem and the elders, tell me. Do you wish to redeem it? If so, purchase it now. But if not, tell me so that I may redeem it."

The kinsman said, "I will redeem the land."

The Boaz said, "The day you purchase the land from Naomi you must also take Ruth the Moabite, the wife of the dead Mahlon, to be your wife. You must raise up children to carry on his inheritance."

The kinsman said, "Then I cannot redeem the land, for it will mar my own inheritance. Redeem the land yourself, for I cannot."

And the kinsman took off his shoe and gave it to Boaz, for such was the custom in Israel. The shoe bore witness to all the people.

So Boaz said to the elders and all the people of Bethlehem, "You are witnesses this day that I have bought from Naomi all that was Elimelech's and Chilion's and Mahlon's. And I have also taken Ruth the Moabite, the wife of Mahlon, to be my wife. I will raise up children for the dead that his name may not be put away from his people or from the gate of his place. You are the witnesses this day."

And all the people at the gate and all the elders said, "We are witnesses. May the Lord make Ruth to be like Rachel and Leah, who built the house of Israel. May you also be valiant in Ephrata and famous in Bethlehem. May your house be like that of Perez, whom Tamar bore to Judah, springing from the seed that the Lord shall give to Ruth."

So Boaz took Ruth and she became his wife. The Lord granted her a son.

The women of Bethlehem said to Naomi, "Blessed be the

Lord who has not left you bereft but who has given you a name in Israel, life, and one to cherish you in your old age. For Ruth, your daughter-in-law who loved you, has borne you a child, and she is better to you than seven sons."

Naomi took the child and laid him in her lap and nursed him. And her neighbors said, "A child is born to Naomi," and named him Obed. And Obed became the father of Jesse and Jesse the father of David the king.

These are the generations of Perez: Perez begat Hezron; Hezron begat Ram; Ram begat Amminadab; Amminadab begat Nahshon; Nahshon begat Salmon; Salmon begat Boaz; Boaz begat Obed; Obed begat Jesse; Jesse begat David.

William Bradford and Edward Winslow

FROM *JOURNALL OF THE ENGLISH PLANTATION AT PLIMOTH*

Writing in his History of Plymouth Plantation, *William Bradford recalled the first Thanksgiving in Plymouth in words that suggest a kind of incredulity: "All ye somer [of 1621] ther was no wante. And now begane to come in store of foule, as winter aproached, of which this place did abound ... And besids water foule, ther was great store of wild Turkies, of which they tooke many, besids venison, &c. Besids they had aboute a peck a meale a weeke to a person, or now since harvest, Indean corne to y^t proportion." Bradford's incredulity at this bounty is set within the context of this day of joyous Thanksgiving. But that day followed a most awful year. Half the company had died through exposure and sickness. Almost all the women were gone. Prospects had been made even bleaker by a harsh land that did not yield easily to settlement, a cold sea that did not easily yield fish to those who had been trained to be farmers, and the prospect of battles with the powerful Narragansett and the Massachusetts.*

> *B*ut, for the Pilgrims, the feast was an act of gratitude. It was a feast to acknowledge and celebrate the presence of real grace and goodness in the center of hardship and privation.

Facing yet another long and harsh winter whose early frosts had already come upon them, the joyous feasting seems difficult to comprehend—or even to condone. But, for the Pilgrims, the feast was an act of gratitude. It was a feast to acknowledge and celebrate the presence of real grace and goodness in the center of hardship and privation. It was an affirmation of faith in a world that seemed to pose only challenge. In this sense, Thanksgiving represents fruition, but it also represents our proper and heady celebration of promises given and kept.

FROM *JOURNALL OF THE ENGLISH PLANTATION AT PLIMOTH*

Loving, and old Friend; although I received no Letter from you by this Ship, yet for as much as I know you expect the performance of my promise, which was, to write unto you truly and faithfully of all things, I have therefore at this time sent unto you accordingly. Referring you for further satisfaction to our more large Relations, you shall understand, that in this little time that a few of us have been here, we have built seven dwelling houses, and four for the use of the Plantation, and have made preparation for divers others. We set the last Spring some twenty Acres of Indian Corn, and sowed some six Acres of Barley and Peas, and according to the manner of the Indians, we manured our ground with Herrings or rather Shads, which we have in great abundance, and take with great ease at our dories. Our Corn did prove well, & God be praised, we had a good increase of Indian Corn, and our Barley was indifferent but good, and our Peas not worth the gathering, for, we feared, they were too late sown; they came up well, and blossomed, but the Sun parched them in the blossom. Our harvest being gotten in, our Governor [William Bradford] sent four men on fowling, that so we might after a more special manner rejoice together, after we had gathered the fruit of our labors; they four in one day killed as much fowl, as with a little help beside, served the Company almost a week. At which time amongst other Recreations, we [also] exercised our Arms. Many of the Indians [came] amongst us, and amongst the rest their greatest King Massasoit, with some ninety men, whom for three days we entertained and feasted. And they went out and killed five Deer, which they brought to the Plantation and bestowed on our Governor, and upon the Captain [Miles Standish], and others. And although it be not always so plentiful, as it was at this time with us, yet by the goodness of God, we are so far from want, that we often wish you partakers of our plenty. We have found the Indians very faithful in their Covenant of Peace with us; very loving and ready to pleasure us: we often go to them, and they come to us; some of us have been fifty miles by Land in the Country with them; the occasions and Relations whereof you shall understand by our general and more full Declaration of such things as are worth the noting....

Sarah Josepha Hale

FROM *NORTHWOOD:*
A TALE OF NEW ENGLAND
AND *TRAITS OF AMERICAN LIFE*

Sarah Josepha Hale was one of the leading voices in the early nineteenth century advocating for the creation of a national Thanksgiving holiday, and many felt that it was principally her influence that led Abraham Lincoln to proclaim the holiday a national event for the first time in 1863. But, in fact, the holiday had been celebrated around the country—though most particularly in New England—for a very long time. By the first quarter of the eighteenth century, it had already acquired familiar traits and observances and, as shown here, familiar understandings.

As she reminds us in the second selection, feasting is necessary and proper—an outward demonstration of our own inner joy.

In the scene from North-wood, young Sidney Rome-lee has just returned to his New Hampshire ancestral home, seeing his parents and family for the first time in thirteen years. He brings with him a friend named Frankford from South Carolina who is an Englishman, and Hale writes of the feast of Thanksgiving from Frankford's rather amazed perspective. While young Frankford wonders whether such feasting might not be an unwarranted indulgence, neither Squire Romelee nor Hale herself will brook such nonsense. As she reminds us in the second selection, feasting is necessary and proper— an outward demonstration of our own inner joy. And such joy can only come from a heart that has schooled itself to look on the world with delight.

FROM NORTHWOOD: A TALE OF NEW ENGLAND

The table, covered with a damask cloth, vieing in whiteness, and nearly equalling in texture, the finest imported, though spun, woven and bleached by Mrs. Romelee's own hand, was not intended for the whole household, every child having a seat on this occasion, and the more the better, it being considered an honor for a man to sit down to his Thanksgiving supper surrounded by a large family. The provision is always sufficient for a multitude, every farmer in the country being, at this season of the year, plentifully supplied, and every one proud of displaying his abundance and prosperity.

The roasted turkey took precedence on this occasion, being placed at the head of the table; and well did it become its lordly station, sending forth the rich odour of its savoury stuffing, and finely covered with the frost of the basting. At the foot of the board a surloin of beef, flanked on either side by a leg of pork and joint of mutton, seemed placed as a bastion to defend innumerable bowls of gravy and plates of vegetables disposed in that quarter. A goose and pair of ducklings occupied side stations on the table, the middle being graced, as it always is on such occasions, by that rich burgomaster of the provisions, called a chicken pie. This pie, which is wholly formed of the choicest parts of fowls, enriched and seasoned with a profusion of butter and pepper, and covered with an excellent puff paste, is, like the celebrated pumpkin pie, an indispensable part of a good and true Yankee Thanksgiving; the size of the pie usually denoting the gratitude of the party who prepares the feast. The one now displayed could never have had many peers. Frankford had seen nothing like it, and recollected nothing in description bearing a comparison.... Plates of pickles, preserves, and butter, and all the necessaries for increasing the seasoning of the viands to the demand of each palate, filled the interstices on the table, leaving hardly sufficient room for the plates of the company, a wine glass and two tumblers for each, with a slice of wheat bread lying on one of the inverted tumblers. A side table was literally loaded with the preparations for the second course, placed there to obviate the necessity of leaving the apartment during the repast. Mr. Romelee keeping no domestic, the family were to wait on themselves, or on each other. There was a huge plum pudding, custards, and pies of every name and description ever known in Yankee land; yet the pumpkin pie occupied the most distinguished niche. There were also several kinds of rich cake, and a variety of sweetmeats and fruits. On the sideboard was ranged a goodly number of decanters and bottles; the former filled with currant wine and the latter with excellent cider and ginger beer, a beverage Mrs. Romelee prided herself on preparing in perfection. There were no foreign wines or ardent spirits, Squire Romelee being a *consistent* moralist; and while he deprecated the evils an indulgence in their use was bringing on his countrymen, and urged them to correct the pernicious habit, he *practised* what he *preached*. Would that all declaimers against intemperance followed his example.

Such, as I have attempted to describe, was the appearance of the apartment and the supper, when Mr. Frankford, ushered by his host and followed by Sidney and the whole family, entered and took their stations around the table. The blessing, which "the saint, the father and the husband" now fervently besought, was not merely a form of words, mechanically mumbled over to comply with an established custom, or perform an irksome duty—It was the breathings of a good and grateful heart acknowledging the mercies received, and sincerely thanking the Giver of every good gift for the plenteous portion he had bestowed. And while enumerating the varied blessings with which the year had been crowned, Squire Romelee alluded to the return of the long absent child, and expressed his joy in thus, once more, being permitted to gather all his dear family around his table, his voice quivered;—but the tear which fell slowly down his cheek was unnoted by all save

Frankford; the others were endeavoring to repress or conceal their own emotion.

The eating of the supper then commenced in earnest. There was little of ceremony, and less of parade; yet the gratified hospitality, the obliging civility and unaffected happiness of this excellent family left, on the heart of the foreigner, a lasting impression of felicity while the recollection of many a splendid *fete* in gorgeous halls had passed away. The conversation during the repast, though chiefly employed in comparing the respective qualities of the several dishes, and explaining the manner of their preparation, was more interesting than a discussion of the same subjects would have been at a nobleman's table. Because those who supported or listened to the discourse were more immediately concerned in the decision of the various questions proposed, and more gratified by the eulogiums which the quality of the provisions and the perfection of the cookery received from the two guests, Mrs. Romelee attended particularly to them;—helping them to the choicest bits, and replenishing their plates so often and so bountifully that the appetite of the Englishman, craving as it had been, was completely satiated. Yet he could not forget how hungry he had been, and while refusing the "pudding which Lucy had made," and the "custard Sophia had prepared," he looked around on the still loaded table, with a kind of sorrowful disappointment that he must leave so many good things untasted.... The Squire proceeded, without noticing it, to descant on temperance and industry, and on the necessity of inculcating the practice of those virtues on the rising generation, till Mr. Frankford archly interrupted him.

"You must then," said he, "abolish your Thanksgivings entirely, for who can practice temperance when set down to such a table as this? If you were a hermit, and our meal had been roots and water, I might have listened, much edified, to your discourse; but now, sir, I confess my excellent supper has totally disqualified me from receiving any benefit from a homily on temperance; nor can you, while placing me in the midst of temptation, wonder if I fall into the snare."

"Well, well," replied the Squire, laughing, "I may at least recommend industry, for all this variety you have seen before you on the table, excepting the spices and salt, has been furnished from my own farm and procured by our own labor and care."

"If that be the case," returned Frankford, looking around on the various and complicated dishes with a half incredulous stare, "you are privileged to enjoy them. The fruits of his own labor every man may surely partake. You think the indulgence in domestic luxuries perfectly innocent?"

"No; but I think them less dangerous and less apt to be indulged to excess. And the exertion to procure them cherishes a spirit of patriotism, independence, and devotion. We should love our native land were it a sterile rock; but we love it better when to our cultivation it yields an ample increase; and the farmer instead of sighing for foreign dainties, looks up to heaven, and depends on his own labors; and when they are crowned with a blessing, he thanks God, as tens of thousands throughout our state are doing this day. Let us join our voices with theirs."

FROM *TRAITS OF AMERICAN LIFE*

Our good ancestors were wise, even in their mirth. We have a standing proof of this in the season they chose for the celebration of our annual festival, the Thanksgiving. The funeral-faced month of November is thus made to wear a garland of joy, and instead of associating the days of fog, like our English relations, with sadness and suicide, we hail them as the era of gladness and good living.

There is a deep moral influence in the periodical seasons of rejoicing, in which a whole community participate. They bring out, and bring together, as it were, the best sympathies of our nature. The rich contemplate the enjoyments of the poor with complacency, and the poor regard the entertainments of the rich without envy, because *all* are privileged to be happy in their own way. Yet enjoyment does not always imply happiness. There is a disposition of mind which cannot, by any single word in our language, be expressed. Philanthropy will best signify it: yet its influence is so different, as displayed in different situations, that it is called, alternately, contentment, charity, resignation, fortitude and love. These are all but modifications of the desire to diffuse happiness—a spirit that leads us to rejoice, to cheer the unfortunate, and always to look on the sunny side of our path, gathering flowers where the repining (usually the selfish) would see only thorns and gravel.

It takes but little to make one happy when the heart is right: but a repining disposition never yet enjoyed a Thanksgiving.

Hahm Dong-seon

Three Poems

Hahm Dong-seon, professor emeritus at Chung Ang University in Seoul, writes his poetry out of a sense of exile: Though his hometown was located in the South when the war began, that town was apportioned to the North after the partition of Korea. Perhaps this is one reason why he dwells so lovingly— and longingly—on the particulars of the world he sees around him. Though he picks out physical moments in a setting, they do seem more like moments than like a physical reality, as if they might pass away, evaporate, on the instant.

Yet, there is gratitude here, a thankful grasping of the fleeting moment. His poems of autumn evoke powerful sets of images that begin in the eye, then move quickly to the heart, where, Professor Hahm writes, "a parched leaf is always sculling past."

> *H*is poems of autumn evoke powerful sets of images that begin in the eye, then move quickly to the heart.

A Rough Sketch of Autumn

Shadows of the bluish-black pine forest
Harbor the trestle, the field of eulalia
And graze along the first footholds of the mountain.
A dragonfly threading the curved creek bank
Seems stunned by the shadows
And lights on a cosmos
That blooms in a tilt as though counting on the wind
*   to come back soon.*
At the gates of the village
The long sound of autumn comes in a quaver,
The throat notes of someone singing pansori.
Over a grandmother's stooped shoulders,
The sun in autumn, whether it wants to or not,
Disappears as soon as it nears the horizon.
In my heart
A parched leaf is always sculling past.

Autumn Sanjo

The cosmos are out along the field-paths.
The noon light that falls on the petals in October
Clears its throat when the clouds pass over.
Flying in from who knows where a worn out honeybee
That could likely not buzz another ten li
Sinks inside the petals as if it had journeyed all that
*   way just to collapse there.*
Its breath is like moonlight on a knife-blade.
Wind weathers the leaves of the grapevine;
The season is restless, ready to follow
The crowd of wind-scattered petals

That fall like the tears of a woman who met her
     desire late one autumn
And confessed that love.

Landscape

After the rain
Fell hard on the autumn roofs,
From the most far-flung house to the nearest village
You can hear the ripe persimmons
Heavy with the sun's red setting
Muttering now amongst themselves
That they are on the verge of falling.
As soon as the sun went under
As if hiccupped by the horizon,
The wind pulled in behind a train arriving from the
     suburbs
And let the night swell across
The field that turns
An annual crop, more or less, for fifty homes.
Before long electric bulbs are hot with light
And the first night of frost goes warm
Like the spot on the floor above the heat piped in
     from the kitchen fire,
A crescent moon pokes out its face
Like the curved back of a long-toothed comb.

David Kline

"OCTOBER,"
FROM *GREAT POSSESSIONS:*
AN AMISH FARMER'S JOURNAL

David Kline's evocative description of autumn in Ohio comes out of his deep sense of gratitude and celebration for the bounties of the harvest. Kline, who is a member of an Old Order Amish community, farms 120 acres. In his writing and in his farming he unifies the activities of mind and body, even as he unifies work and land in ways that much of contemporary North American society has rejected—consciously or unconsciously.

In his writing and in his farming he unifies the activities of mind and body, even as he unifies work and land in ways that much of contemporary North American society has rejected—consciously or unconsciously.

In his introduction to the book, Wendell Berry suggests that Kline, having brought a sense of Amish reverence to his work, "announces on every page that the world is good, an article of faith that is here brought to rest upon experience." Thus, images of migrating mallards, blue skies, air tinged with the scent of skunk, frosts, and the corn harvest come together to create a sense of a season that is very much tied to the land, and which, Kline suggests, should lead us to give thanks to the Provider of all things.

"OCTOBER"

There is something about October that no other month can match. The brilliant colors of the hardwoods, the crisp morning air spiked with a faint tinge of skunk, the clear skies laced with a few cumulus clouds drifting lazily across it—all these spell October.

Along with October comes a certain sadness because the spring we so eagerly awaited has passed, and so has the summer; now we realize that winter is waiting in the wings. However, this melancholy is soon overwhelmed by the spell of the season as we gather walnuts, hickory nuts, and chestnuts, and hustle to get the corn cribbed.

Though we regret the passing of summer, the time does arrive when we look forward to a killing frost so that we can cease our battles with the lamb's-quarters, pigweeds, and purslane, and hang up our hoes for the year. Most gardeners probably reach this point sometime during the fall. In a few months the new seed catalogs will be arriving in the mail, and our struggles with the weeds will be forgotten. Resolutions will be made to start the melons earlier, and maybe set out the Siberian tomatoes a week sooner so that we'll have ripe tomatoes by the fourth of July.

For the small-scale dairy farmer, October is almost perfect. The cool nights have eliminated the bothersome flies, and the cows, content on legume pastures, have a desire to produce large quantities of milk.

Along about the middle of the month we hear a sound we've been waiting for—the quacking and gabbling of migrating ducks and geese. Every autumn since 1975 hundreds and often thousands of migrating waterfowl visit our pond, Levi D. Miller's, and some other ponds in the area, and linger, feeding on waste grain in the picked cornfields until snow and cold weather in late November drive them farther south. Though primarily mallards, there are also a considerable number of black ducks, American wigeons, and pintails, and a lesser number of blue- and green-winged teal, shovelers, wood ducks, lesser scaups, and coots.

We have often wondered why these thousands of wild ducks, especially the wary black ducks, come to these farm ponds, as you could say, in the middle of nowhere.

There may be several reasons. One, the forty-five-hundred-acre Killbuck Wildlife Area, the largest inland area of swamp and marshland in Ohio, is only ten miles west of our farm. This "wasteland" was privately owned until around twelve years ago when the state began buying it. As the land was purchased, it was opened for public hunting, and then, because of the heavy hunting pressure, the ducks were forced to seek sanctuary elsewhere.

A second reason is that in the early seventies we had some semi-wild mallards on our pond and, after several years of good hatches, we were overstocked. So a friend and I live-trapped thirty-five and released them in the Killbuck marshes. A farmer from that area, who was with us when we turned ducks loose, told me later that many of the ducks were shot soon afterward by poachers. Could some of these mallards have survived and then, in the following fall, shown their wild kin the way to our farm for food and protection?

The first ducks begin coming in to the pond the day the duck season opens. For some reason they do not stay on the pond at night, except occasionally during a full moon, but prefer to return to the marshes. They leave the pond about a half hour before dark and return in the morning just after daybreak. Thus their departure and arrival from the marshes are after and before legal shooting hours. And to think that some people call them dumb ducks.

We very seldom feed the ducks because we want them to retain their wild ways, and besides, we like to see them fly. As someone said, "one duck flying is worth ten on the water." It is especially exciting to watch the graceful birds come in when there's a brisk west wind. Since ducks almost always land into the wind, they set their wings and come in over the house. To hear the air rush through their pinion feathers is truly thrilling.

The ducks usually reach peak numbers during the third week in November. After the first significant snow and cold snap, they depart. Where do they go? According to John Latecki, a state game protector, most of the band returns from ducks banded in the Killbuck Wildlife Area have been from Arkansas. So apparently many of the ducks spend the winter months along the lower Mississippi River and in the surrounding wetlands. I'm reminded of the words written by William Cullen Bryant in his poem "To a Waterfowl":

> *Thou'rt gone; the abyss of heaven*
> *Hath swallowed up thy form; yet on my heart*
> *Deeply hath sunk the lesson thou hast given,*
> *And shall not soon depart.*

> *He who from zone to zone*
> *Guides through the boundless sky thy certain flight*
> *In the long way that I must tread alone*
> *Will lead my steps aright.*

Toward the end of October, with the corn harvest in, we have time to walk in the woods, replenish the woodpile, and reflect on the summer's toils and sweat. There's time, too, for giving thanks to the Provider of all things for another bounteous year.

Garret Keizer

"I Am the Clock-Winder," from *A Dresser of Sycamore Trees*

When he moved to New England, Garret Keizer little realized that to the professions of teacher and pastor he would add that of clock-winder. But so he did, and as summer's apprenticeship lengthened into autumn, his twice-weekly trips up into the church spire grew from routine to ritual. For clocks mark the hours of work: the railroad man's clanging hammer; the farmer's pitched bales of hay; the mother's watchful care. But clocks also mark out the ritual of our days, the ascent up and down the clock tower, the slip between memory and the present, the friendships that endure through the years. And for such rituals we give our thanks.

Keizer discovers on the first cold day in autumn that mechanical clocks align themselves with the weather: The colder it is, the faster they run. As he struggles to make his clock keep time, he senses the futility of perfectionism. "There I was," he writes, "waiting for my poor, fallible clock to act like a machine." As Alix Kates Shulman adjusted herself to the long

thought of nature's extravagant abundance, so does Keizer tune his clock—
and himself—to autumn's rhythmic imprecision.

For such rhythms bespeak our better natures—our halting, messy,
faithful making and keeping of promises. "What time is it?" he asks, but
the clock cannot answer. Only the clock-winder, walking among the people of
Island Pond, can learn to know the times and the seasons of thanksgiving.

"I Am the Clock-Winder"

And God will wipe away every tear from their eyes.
                                              —Revelation 7:17

I am the town clock-winder for Island Pond, Vermont. I have
been so almost as long as I have been the lay vicar of its Episcopal
Church. Twice a week, on Thursday and Sunday, I climb through
the vertical tunnel inside the Carpenter Gothic spire of my church
up to the little wooden house that holds the clockworks. With a
key like an antique car crank, I wind two drums of steel cable, one
for the time on the four clock faces and one for the great bell that
rings the hours. I also make adjustments, minor repairs, and lubricate the bearings with a special oil made for the few mechanical
clocks still keeping time in our towns.

Along with my ministry this minor job has given me a focus
for thinking about work, faith, and time, and about the particular places in which individuals come to reckon with those things.
From a vantage point much higher than a pulpit, I have looked out
from behind the clock faces at the railroad tracks far below, and
wondered about my own coming and going, and about the town's
history and future.

Island Pond was made and almost unmade by the railroad.
It stood as the chief junction between Montreal and Portland,
Maine—I like to say, between Canada and the sea. The railroad
yard in town was once thick with tracks, as if a giant had pulled a
broad rake over the valley and each tooth had left rails and ties in
its wake. There were fifty locomotives stabled here, sometimes so

many cars that whole trains of them had to be moved down the line for storage. A legion of local men worked for the Grand Trunk in those days: brakemen, bridge builders, section men, ticket takers, freight conductors, engineers, machinists, stokers, boiler welders, inspectors—all shifts, all year, every hour the trains came and went packed with wheat, lumber, bauxite, machines, and passengers. And on a hill over this railroad town, above the train yard in work time and strike time, over the black locomotives huddled thick like pollywogs in the spring, above the steam of engines, the mist off the pond, and the breaths of men working in the subzero cold, was the clock. A former railroad man tells me he could hear and see it clearly from the yard, always running, always right.

The town prospered with the railroad, which means, of course, that it contained some prosperous citizens, and the rest had work. There were no fewer than five hotels in operation at any one time. Choice cuts of lumber came on the train to build the church that would hold the clock. Then, having built it, the workers along with their bosses filled the pews. The pipe organ also came, piece by piece over the rails—followed by the clock, up from the E. Howard Company in Boston. The organ pipes played like melodious train whistles, thanks to the boys who pumped the bellows and left their initials in the little curtained closet behind the instrument. And at the first moment of the liturgy, the clock rang, wound twice each week by one of those same boys, dreaming in his tower of the day he'd exchange his meager clock-winder's wage for that of a full-fledged railroad man.

Island Pond began to decline at roughly the same time as railroading did, more specifically when diesel replaced steam, and when the Canadian National bought out the Grand Trunk. The descent was gradual; a generation grew old as the railroad went down, many retiring in what for them was the very nick of time. As the tracks began to be pulled up, families came up with them, like wheat with tares, and Island Pond joined the list of those places where an industry has enjoyed a good time, and is happy to help tidy up a little on the way out, and will be pleased to see its hosts if they ever happen to be in South Carolina or Singapore.

After the railroad, Island Pond's dubious fame rests with a controversial religious sect that moved here more than a decade ago, and with the fact that Rudy Vallee was born here. His house still stands. Old-timers tell me that the man with the megaphone never took any pains to announce the place of his origin. But now his music is as quaint as a steam locomotive; his name is almost as obscure as the town's. The bell that tolled for Island Pond tolled for thee, Rudy.

Then the bell was still. For years, ever since the railroad declined, and long before "the church people" arrived, the clock in Christ Church tower was broken. The motionless hands on each of its four faces pointed to different numbers, and no sound came from its belfry but the cooing of pigeons. One day, for a reason they might not know themselves, the people in the church under the clock, who number fifteen on a good Sunday, maybe thirty-five on an Easter, elected to repair its faces, the steeple above, and the machine behind. They found a clock repairer and a clock-winder. The town graciously supplied them with funds to pay both. Somewhat fitfully, like a steam locomotive starting from a long standstill, the clock began to run.

I first met Bob Ross, the clock repairer, at the top of the tower in the clock house that lies squarely under the cone of the copper-shingled steeple. It was only my second or third climb up, and I still clung very deliberately to each of the iron rungs, which appear to have come from the side of a boxcar.

The first part of the ascent is on a short ladder outside the church sacristy. One goes straight up about a dozen feet to a wooden trap door; on that day in July it was already pushed up and open. Once through the hole, the climber is standing on the roof of the sacristy, looking up at least twenty feet to the ceiling, or belfry floor. This first high-ceilinged room, dimly lit by one bulb, is cobwebby and barnlike, its floor littered with old rope, straw, clock weights, a piece of log. At diagonal corners, one by the first ladder, are upright wooden tracks in which the clock weights rise and descend on cables. The entire steeple is built with the same sturdiness and doubtless some of the same materials and know-how once found in wooden railroad trestles. Single timbers, one piece each, run straight up the corners. What trees they must have been hewn from!

The second ladder, this one at a slant, takes me as high as the belfry. The few remaining rungs are bolted to the steeple side and lead to the last floor, on which the clock house sits. The belfry is a squat room, lit during the day by slatted windows in the steeple and at night by nothing but the moon. The bell is about one third the size of the Liberty Bell, uncracked, and hangs in a carriage of gray wooden studding. Raised letters around the waist of the bell read: "Cast by Henry N. Hooper & Co. Boston 1862," indicating that the bell is about fifteen years older than the church. It is rung by a sledgehammer set on a spring by its side and connected to the clock house above by a metal rod, and to the sacristy below by a new bell rope. In the past, there was no way to ring the bell from downstairs. One of the parishioners told me that on Easters some years ago he would put coveralls over his Sunday clothes and climb to the belfry with a croquet mallet to ring in the holiday. "I don't think I could go up there now," he added with a look of sincere worry that someone might ask him, at eighty-four, to perform the feat again.

I found Bob Ross under the light bulb in the clock house, wiping a clock part with a rag. He and his assistant, a fellow industrial arts teacher from New Hampshire, had spent a good part of that morning cleaning the clock, the clock house, and the area around it, some of which had been cleaned earlier by the crew that repaired the steeple. But there was still some more cleaning to do, even when I arrived, and, as I was to learn, cleanliness is essential to the smooth running of a mechanical clock. Outside the clock house were several grocery bags full of pigeon skeletons, egg shells, and droppings; apparently the former condition of the steeple had afforded good housing to several generations of pigeons. Inside, the partially disassembled clock, its heavy pendulum asleep on the floor, was being wiped and rewiped, and, where appropriate, lubricated with light machine oil. Boards in the clock faces had been removed, providing extra light, a breeze, a glimpse at the back sides of several clock hands—so much larger when closer—and four commanding views of the town.

I introduced myself to Bob Ross as the man who would be winding and looking after the clock; he greeted me, warmly and immediately began to tell me everything he knew about that clock, working as he went. Listening to him I had the impression of standing before a benevolent but zealous archivist with a greasy rag. His language was as exact as the toothiest gear of the clock—no thingamajigs, but no impatience either when I asked for repeated or simpler explanations.

Under his tutelage the clock became intelligible. It was the same as a grandfather's clock or cuckoo clock, he said; the three of us had stepped into the works of a giant's timepiece. In between two cast-iron arches bolted to the floor are the gears of two separate but cooperative mechanisms, one for the clock and one for the bell. Each is driven by the pull of weights lowered when the pendulum swings and the bell rings, respectively. The pendulum, kept ticking by this pull, regulates a succession of gears that move the clock hands; it "feeds into" (Ross said this better) the clock by means of an escapement, an object like a curved pair of open calipers that swings with the pendulum, its points rocking in and out between the teeth of a rotating wheel. When the pendulum is lengthened— that is, lowered—the clock runs more slowly since the pendulum moves in a greater arc. A vertical shaft rising out of the timing mechanism turns the gears of four horizontal rods, which form a cross over the clock and extend through four holes in the clock house to each of the faces. Ross had tied red rags on these rods to prevent our bumping our heads on them—I felt dizzy enough following his tour at the same time as I tried to stay out of the way.

Mostly I was interested in the maintenance of the clock, though I have since found myself grateful for Ross's "theoretical" information, without which I would have been unable to improvise the few repairs I have had to make. Ross showed me how to set the clock by pulling a pin to disengage the faces from the mechanism and moving a dial marked for sixty minutes. He also instructed me to lubricate bearings, pulley sheaves, and the universal joints behind each face. I have since learned from a helpful man at the E. Howard Company that the exposed works of the clock itself, which suffer no friction, should receive no lubricant whatsoever. They should be kept as clean as possible. But Bob anticipated even this; he concluded his directions by saying that if I studied the clock, I would soon know things about it that he could never have told me.

By early evening the clock was reassembled. We wanted an hour or so in which to check its accuracy, and eat our supper. After washing up we headed down the street to a restaurant. On the way, we met Bob's sister Andrea, who was responsible for bringing him to the clock, and who was just then coming home from work. She said that if a simple meal of chicken, potatoes, and salad was to our liking, the three of us were welcome for supper. She and her husband would stop at the store for some things; we knew the way over.

Andrea and Larry Roth live with their three daughters in a new log cabin at the foot of a mountain in East Brighton, just outside of Island Pond. One crosses a railroad track at his "own risk" and enters a dense woods on a bumpy driveway that climbs to the cabin. It is an impressive dwelling, with five or six different pitches to the roof, completely surrounded by forest. They have seen a bear, a moose, and a bald eagle, literally in their backyard; their daughter, Aggie, fishes for trout in the brook behind the garage, and rabbits tear back and forth across the clearing chased by the family hound. The Roths will be as good a choice as any if ever an American family goes into outer space as emissaries or pioneers. They are all hearty, hospitable, and handsome. They built their cabin from the ground up, Ross working alongside his brother-in-law on those tricky roofs. They make their own soap, grow their own vegetables, slaughter and dress their own chickens. Larry, a local boy who journeyed to Los Angeles via the navy and stayed for the car craze, who has a hot-rodder's lean and intrepidly optimistic look, took the risk of opening an auto parts business in Island Pond, which has proven a smart venture in a town twenty miles from the nearest spare parts, a town that runs on cars—hopped-up cars, wood haulers, collections of junk cars one tries at inspection time like a ring of skeleton keys. At supper we asked about the auto parts trade, and the Roths talked about the clock trade, and then we got down to business and talked about Indians.

The ones in the woodland were as fierce as any, Larry says, and I agree, having read the public library out of Indian books as a kid, and Ross, behold, an American history buff who casts and fires replica Civil War cannons, begins the round of stories—how one chief mustered ten thousand braves from as far away as Michigan and Kentucky, and not a white person in the East had wind of their movements until the first tomahawk struck; how the Sauk and Fox and Ojibwa played lacrosse outside the stockade of an army fort, passed the rawhide ball through the gates, and ran screaming past the blue-clad spectators only to run out again with everyone's scalp—we stopped with a "shhh." It was eight, and Ross wanted to listen for the clock ringing far away. All quiet, we looked out the cabin windows into the shadowy woods in the direction of town. I really don't remember whether we heard the bell or not; it was faint at any rate, perhaps too faint to count.

We returned to the clock after nightfall and made a few minor adjustments. It appeared to be keeping good time; the metal slide that regulates the number of chimes, to which Ross had welded three new teeth to replace broken ones, was in its correct post–eight o'clock position. After a few final squirts of lubricant, a few parting wipes of the rag, Ross and his friend wrote their names and the date on the inside walls of the clock house, urging me to do the same. I felt I had not earned a place there, but Ross said I had, probably meaning that in time I would have. We picked up the tools, lowered them down the ladders with a rope, closed the trap door, shut out the lights, locked the church. I was left to learn the secret idiosyncrasies that were lost years ago when the clock and its most intimate tenders had stopped ticking.

When you acquire the use of a new word, you suddenly begin to see it everywhere. I began to see clocks, clocks, clocks. Like a hungry traveler, antique postcard collector, gravestone rubber, or boozer, I'd drive into an unfamiliar town with hunting eyes and one question behind them: "They got a public clock in this place or what?" I had seldom worn a watch before; now I often carried two, one with the exact time as told by radio station or phone operator or, in the case of divergent readings, as figured from an average of the two; the other set by the clock in Island Pond the last time I had driven to check it, which was usually no later than yesterday, sometimes no later than that morning—and I live more than twenty miles out of town. Against these two I was likely to check any other timepiece I saw.

I began noticing the number of clocks on town halls and churches that do not run or run wrong. Island Pond had not been so unusual in this respect after all. I also realized that the public keeping of time has passed from the church and possibly the municipal building to the branch bank. In most towns of any size, that is the place to look for a digital display of the right time. The location of the public clock has something to say, I think, about the way a culture gives meaning to time. It was logical for a church to tell people the time when one of the things they needed to know time for was when to pray, and when church feasts and holy days colored the calendar. Equally logical is it that the bank should tell the hours to a populace for whom time is not liturgical but financial, who inhabit a fiscal year broken into quarters and the maturation periods of certificates of deposit.

Island Pond also has a bank clock, albeit a modest one with hands, inside the bank window, but I do not check that clock against the steeple, though one can check both standing in the same place. The latter clock has been running erratically, I suspect not merely slow or fast, but slow *and* fast, and correctly some short times in between. I prefer to have a more comprehensive report comparing real time and Island Pond time over a twelve-hour period, so I stop first at one of the service stations in town, not only because the elders leaning back on chairs inside the office will have such a report, but because I want an excuse to lean back in one of those chairs myself. I love a garage, a store, a barber shop with a circle of regulars—each one a third part customer, a fifth part helper, and the remaining part permanent fixture. I find this one of the things most wanting in my work as a teacher: we are a sadly croniless profession. Oh, for some wizened old geezer with a reserved seat under the bulletin board and his own dog-eared copy of *The Great Gatsby* lying next to a spare cane on the radiator cover to totter in of an afternoon and say, "How they doin' with their compositions? I just been down the hall. You ought to see old Harding givin' 'em hell on the Punic Wars. Think it'll rain?"

The men on chairs give me a list of scattered data with commentary. "It was five minutes fast at six 'clock this morning." "What's an ol' fella like you doing up at six o'clock? You was probably still half asleep. It was running fine when I seen it—that was at ten o'clock. Just taken my wife for her beauty appointment. I stood right outside and listened to the bell—was ten on the nose." "You should've gone in with her, Frank." "I just been over for a paper, and I think it's a minute or two *slow*. What time you got now?" Everyone looks down at his watch; no one has the same time. "Well how's the bell?" I ask. "Is it ringing the right number of times?" "Yup. Least it did at three."

I get my tank filled and go over to the church. The clock is three minutes slow, not a considerable discrepancy in itself, but I set it correctly and made an adjustment the day before, when it was two minutes fast from the day previous. I have apparently overcorrected. My goal is to have it lose or gain no time in four days; accuracy beyond that is immaterial since I wind it every four days anyway and the clock can be reset then. For some reason I am unable to calibrate what fraction of a turn on the adjusting wheel will quicken the clock by a minute in twenty-four hours. I have kept logs, made charts—all useless. The adjusting wheel is unmarked except for a dot of paint on the circumference and a curved, two-pointed arrow marked "S" and "F" for "slow" and "fast," which Bob Ross scratched into the metal. I am to turn the wheel in the "F" direction to make the clock run faster—or am I? I begin to wonder if I may have misunderstood his instructions, if the "F" direction is for when the clock is *running fast,* not for making it run faster.

Framed on the clock-house wall are the antique "Instructions for a Tower Clock," which I had not bothered to read before, thinking I had all the information I needed by word of mouth, thinking also that my source had himself read the plaque. According to *that,* one turns the wheel left to make the clock run faster—the opposite of what Ross said, or at least of what I remember him saying.

So, I change the meanings of "S" and "F" and adjust accordingly for a week. If anything, the clock runs worse. But I have forgotten those "theoretical" principles that Ross took such pains to teach me; in my independent study I have grown careless of what I learned in the required courses. The pertinent question is not "What did Ross really say about turning the wheel?" but "Which direction on the adjusting wheel makes the pendulum shorter?" That a shorter pendulum makes a faster clock is beyond dispute.

With a little measuring, I find out that Ross was right if he said what I remember him saying; turning the wheel in the "F" direction shortens the pendulum and thus makes the clock run faster. The original instructions hanging on the wall were undoubtedly right, too, when the clock had all of its original parts and threadings. Nevertheless, having finally established how to raise and lower the pendulum, and thus how to make the clock run faster or slower, I am still unable to make it run as accurately as I wish, as accurately as the old people in town remember it. For that part, I can tell myself that the memory of the aged always makes the past more perfect than it was, and that in the days before the quartz crystal and television, people were less likely to notice or be disturbed by a slightly quick or sluggish clock. But I cannot even make the clock consistently quick or sluggish; it seems to run at will, a propensity made all the more maddening by brief periods when the clock keeps literally perfect time. I feel like those physicists who abandoned the clock model of creation, who watched as Newtonian law gave way to relativity and relativity to uncertainty, their quarks like my clock's quirks—nothing but vapors and winds to stand on.

And how much more troubling is the clock's misbehavior in an age of microseconds, when precision is as sought after as youth. A man can scarcely enjoy listening to recorded music because his space-age sound system picks up the tiniest motes and scratches like a radio telescope catching nebulae light-years away; he chases hysterically after his wife accusing her of the infidelity of his record—perhaps she has been lending it to his best friend on the sly, a dissolute man with a cheap turntable. I struggle with my erratic clock as computers are fed the archprogram: "Be ye perfect, even as your father at the drawing board is not perfect."

I discovered the secret of my clock's imperfection in the autumn, which comes to Vermont like a painted Indian brave with cold flint arrows that never miss. During the first frigid spell, the clock began accumulating twenty to thirty extra minutes in a three-day period. The clock is affected by the weather. Cold temperatures make it run faster, presumably because the moving parts contract somewhat and work with less resistance. By turning the adjusting wheel and by varying the number of weights on the cables—another determiner, discovered at the suggestion of Larry Roth—I can make my clock keep very good time providing that the temperature is roughly constant. But I can as easily make a perfectly precise adjustment as I can predict the weather—the Vermont weather no less. With the whole world waiting for its machines to start acting human, there I was, waiting for my poor, fallible clock to act like a machine.

The Clock-Winder

It is dark as a cave,
Or a vault in the nave
When the iron door

Is closed, and the floor
Of the church relaid
With trowel and spade.

But the parish-clerk
Cares not for the dark
As he winds in the tower
At a regular hour
The rheumatic clock
Whose dilatory knock
You can hear when praying
At the day's decaying,
Or at any lone while
From a pew in the aisle.

Up, up from the ground,
Around and around
In the turret stair
He clambers, to where
The wheelwork is,
With its tick, click, whizz,
Reposefully measuring
Each day to its end
That mortal men spend
In sorrowing and pleasuring.
Nightly thus does he climb
To the trackway of Time.

Him I followed one night
To this place without light,
And, ere I spoke, heard

Him say, word by word,
At the end of his winding,
The darkness unminding:

"So I wipe out one more,
My Dear, of the sore
Sad days that still be,
Like a drying Dead Sea,
Between you and me!"

Who she was no man knew:
He had long borne him blind
To all womankind;
And was ever one who
Kept his past out of view.

When Thomas Hardy published this poem in 1917, my clock was also punctuating the prayers of a decaying day, though inaudibly; one does not hear its "dilatory knock" until halfway up the steeple. Unlike Hardy's winder, I have a wife, a past cheerfully open to view, the desire to live long, and plenty of fragile reasons to believe that I shall. Perhaps because of this contrast, I am not without some care of the darkness, which Hardy's bereaved parish clerk had climbed through and beyond.

I drive over to Island Pond on a Thursday night after a well-cooked meal and a teacher's day of youthful enthusiasms and impertinence, a myriad of death-defying distractions; after winding the clock, I return to a place where even the refrigerator has a cozy light within, and four hands pull the covers up when darkness has at last settled throughout the house. So in the tower, even in the darkened Gothic church below, I am in an unfamiliar place, with a somewhat unfamiliar me, and sometimes I am afraid.

I twist the old-fashioned turn switch at the foot of the ladder, and a light visible through a crack in the trap door tells whatever may be up there that I am coming. The black hatch thuds away from the hole; my head emerges facing the corner of the first room. I turn around almost immediately, and complete my entrance looking behind. The light of the one bulb here is quite diffuse in the high room, but I have enough to see all the rungs of the next ladder, which makes a dull knocking against the steeple side as I climb it. Nevertheless, the ladder is steady, its iron rungs firm underfoot and to the grasp—but so chilling on winter nights that I wear gloves. The belfry is pitch-dark, except when a little moonlight slips in. It is here, and above, that I often hear a pattering around the outsides of the steeple—and perhaps up in the rafters under the apex—what, I do not know. I have looked with a flashlight for bats and seen none. I have grown somewhat used to the pattering now, but I confess that the first few times I heard it were unnerving. Once, as I climbed with a sideways glance at the dark hulk of the bell, dreadfully silent in the moonlit midst of that pattering, my heart jumped at the sound of a loud slam, followed by an awful hiss. Several seconds passed before I came to the logical explanation: two freight cars coupling outside on the tracks below the church.

One thinks of the damnedest things clambering up a steeple on a howling winter night. A picture comes to mind: bright in my head, an icon in the Orthodox monastery of St. Catherine in the Sinai desert—terror with a footnote—shows gray-bearded ascetics climbing a ladder to heaven, a ladder that, as I remember or contrive, looks exactly like this one, while demons cast lassos and grappling hooks to yank the unwary down to perdition. And thinking of pictures, I go on to remember learning in an anthropology class about some tribe or tribes that cannot discern the images of a photograph; the point of the example was that the ability to read three dimensions in two is acquired, not innate, something we learn in our parents' laps with storybooks held open before us. So it occurs to me: what if we *un*learn the reading of other images, if we are as blind as pictureless aborigines to the demons leering from the closet because we were repeatedly told as children that there was nothing in there but clothes and shoes? If I lost some of my childhood vision, if some inner eye was closed by an adult's conditioning, I'd prefer not to have it opened now as I climb to the clock.

On the uppermost level, with the bright light shining through the clock house's lone and dirty window, I complete my ascent from superstition to a sublimer awe. Inside are the ticking and the light, no longer vague as at the ladder's lower rungs, but distinct and canny as my breath and heartbeat. Here in the night, floating almost among the clouds, yet anchored by long, arboreal bones to the earth, unseen, unthought of, discreet and patiently relentless, the clock marks time, turns its moon-colored arms each minute of the sixty in the twenty-fourth part of the earth's rotation in a darker, infinitely vaster steeple. I am the mystic now, at the top of his tower, flinging open the door to behold the vision of the clockworks and the light—as inviting as a snack bar on a dark wooded road in summer—homely, as more than one of the adepts have described it.

The pendulum is the most mysterious of all, the tool of hypnotists, and dowsers, too, I learned. One morning I ate breakfast with a couple of dowsers, and tried to augur their gentle, Quakerish faces. They showed my companions and me their pocket-sized pendulums, like little tops swung from strings. It is a common misconception that dowsers use only forked sticks and dowse only for water. Dowsing is an ancient art, and the most advanced dowsers practice device-less dowsing. Jesus was one of these, according to the couple; he dowsed for "the great draught of fishes" and knew right where to tell Peter to cast his net. There are stories of dowsers being sent the floor plan of a house hundreds of miles away, and by swinging a pendulum over it, they can "find" a lost object that has eluded the house's own occupants for months. The woman said she used her pendulum to make almost every decision; she even took it with her to the supermarket. Dowsing works, I was told, by utilizing the entire nervous system of the dowser's body as an antenna to pick up the invisible energies and emanations of the cosmos. The human body has hundreds of miles of these nerves, as compared with (though no one at breakfast said so) a mere two or three pounds of brains. I smile at my pendulum and see the dowsers swinging their smaller ones over packages of sandwich meat, dowsing to decide the best brand of baloney. How quickly I have climbed from savage to seer to skeptical rationalist—all in a few tick-tocks. I think I like myself better shuddering on the lower rungs of the belfry.

What if the dowsers have something, if those two faces were not only kinder but wiser than mine? Then what of this mighty pendulum at my side—what arcane knowledge might I apprehend by shedding my sneer and hooking my central nervous system to its swing with a downturned palm on the adjusting wheel? It is true, a dowser's pendulum must be free to move with his hand, but perhaps along with deviceless dowsing there is a "way of the fixed pendulum" known only to a few initiates, masters of both dowsing and clocks. With access to that, I could become an oracle in Island Pond, a bigger business than the railroad, with five hotels of pilgrims waiting their turn to try the perilous climb to my sanctuary. And there, stiff and half blind, like a man-pigeon, an oracular bat, I would give the people knowledge, dowse the very depths of the earth, answer every question put to me—every one, that is, but "What time is it?"

To answer that question, I would need to climb down from my tall steeple, walk out of the church, and stand on the street.

Just outside the center of Island Pond is a little yellow house close to the side of a dirt lane. I go there sometimes after I've wound the clock. Behind the house are railroad tracks, and beyond these, overlooking the pond, is a steep bluff topped by tall cedars. "When I first came here," the old woman in the house tells me, "I hated to look at those trees going back and forth in the wind. They looked like crazy old women waving their arms." She says she got used to them and came to love them along with the passing train that rattles the kitchen but lets her know that "all is well." So she has her "clock" out here where the ringing of the one I wind is very faint.

There used to be an old garage next to the house, when the cedars were still crazy, and on its weathered boards, which had once fenced the tracks, she read the messages and marks the hoboes had left each other about handouts and dry places to sleep. She never understood how the authorities could lock a man up for being poor and taking his food and lodging as he found them. A former governor made her angry with his condescending talk about the disadvantaged—"as if it's really their fault." She has been poor.

Her house is the best it has ever looked, very neat inside and out, with clean paper, paint, and panels—no one can picture its former condition who did not see it, she tells me. I know several houses like this one, each with a railroad man's widow within, bought of necessity in a hard time and restored as slowly as nature restores an abused landscape, now as polished and significant and lovingly worn as a wedding ring. And I've seen several other Bibles of the kind she shows me with pride, gifts of the railroad workers' brotherhood, bound in white leather in a fragrant cedar box with the dead man's name and a colored picture on the inside of the lid showing Jesus feeding his sheep.

A year has passed, summer to summer, since the clock was repaired. Miriam takes me outside to show me her flowers and vegetable garden. She has chrysanthemums, gladiolus, lilacs, fuchsia, pansies, bee balm—and down below, on the level of the tracks, peas, corn, carrots, beans, beets, squash, lettuce, broccoli, cucumbers, tomatoes, all from seed she or a grandson planted in the ground, and which needed her as much but no more than my clock needs me. We have had to tend to both, but their changes happened without our watching, like changes in the weather, like the changes that made Miriam old. Standing in her yard, she is a strange and beautiful vision; she can barely stoop to touch the plants, she cannot chase after the birds, and because of this she seems to stand more intimate with every bird and plant than anyone younger can. They seem to reach for her, to enfold her. Naked children romping in the grass may be an image of paradise, and the man and woman lying beneath the tree, but no less is Miriam in her garden an image of paradise.

I have other stops to make going to and from the clock, other stories to hear. I see Rebecca, with her immaculate house by the river, once a dump—"That's all you could call it"—and her white Bible in its cedar box. I went to see her just after she had qualified for the Bible. She was animated by a sight in her backyard: Years ago she and Owen had torn up a patch of Indian poppies to plant their vegetable garden. No poppies had grown there since, none were there on the day the ambulance came, but that first morning of widowhood, when she looked out the kitchen … it must have come up in a night. And there it was, absurdly large and orange, bobbing in the rain like a sprung jack-in-the-box.

He had come into her life long ago, when her father hired three men on a street corner in Island Pond to help him cut hay. Owen was the only one who showed up that afternoon. He was already a railroad man. He had gone to the station asking for a job when he was only seventeen. "How old are you?" the man there had asked—then told him to come back when he was twenty-one. He showed up three days later to have the same man ask the same question. "Twenty-one," he answered, and was hired on the spot.

Rebecca's brothers were determined to show this railroad man what "real work" was. They fired him volleys of heavy bales, never letting up. He worked without a complaint. That evening, when the train stopped at the farm to pick up the cans of fresh milk, Owen showed his tormentors a trick he knew of mounting and dismounting a slowly moving train. At the right moment, a moment he knew quite well, he jumped off and waved at Rebecca's brothers as they rode helpless down the tracks. They trudged back from Island Pond and made peace with their future brother-in-law.

How is the clock running? Rebecca asks me. Do I mind the climb? Years ago she and Owen took a summer job at a forest station; they lived in the observation tower. One day when her husband was gone, she heard her two boys holler from the woods below, "Bears! Mommy, there are bears!" Down the rungs she flew, a miracle that she reached the ground with an unbroken neck, only to see a standoff between two little boys and two groundhogs.

I should let someone know whenever I intend to wind the clock, she says. It is not good that I should be alone—up in that steeple. Have I climbed it yet this morning? Have I seen Mart and Bea?

I am going there next. Mart is the man who hit the bell with a croquet mallet on those Easters long ago, and he also held a fire hose to the roof of Christ Church the whole night that the great Stewart House hotel next door burned down. He loves that church, and he loved the railroad, and he loves his beautiful Bea, his wife of sixty-five years. She nods and smiles as he plays his tape recordings of locomotive engines and whistles; they defer back and forth to each other with the telling of every story—the very curtains and cushions redolent with their mutual courtesy like a church that has burned incense for so many centuries that standing there one thinks that even if the whole place were demolished, the odor would remain. Mart worked welding and inspecting the insides of locomotive boilers, hot even after they had cooled. Bea says he would come home with spark holes all across his shirt front, and many a night he sat up in bed worrying that something was not right in the train yard; he'd dress and go down, always to find it right as he had left it, but then he could sleep.

These people are all reasons why the clock must run, and run as well as I can make it, not because it ran when they were young and their lives require that consolation, not for nostalgia or as a souvenir, but for the sake of faithfulness, which in its every nuance has been the stuff of their living.

Sometimes, it is true, I think about the good and ill uses of my clock. It tells the unemployed when they would have finished work, the disabled when their favorite game shows are on, the philandering when the third parties are due back, the child abusers how long a time their victims yet have in the closet. The bell awakens a pleasant memory, and awakens as well a person who desperately craves sleep. But I need to ponder this no more than rain and sun need to be pondered—they fall with the time on the just and the unjust, the happy and the many, the young, for whom sun and rain and time are endless, and the old, for whom the first two are ever immoderate, and the last is ever more swift.

The clock will die a second death, I am sure. Its parts cannot last indefinitely, no one manufactures mechanical tower clocks any longer, and the whole idea of a clock, how it should look and where it should be, has changed along with our theories of time itself.

Not long ago we reconciled science and what remained of religion in the "clock model of creation," which saw God as the maker and onetime winder of the cosmos. We have since outgrown that model—or at least most of us have. I confess that I find myself rather fond of it lately. But in my version, the winder is not an eighteenth-century Intelligence snoozing in a stuffed chair someplace inside the chambers of a divine Royal Society as the cosmos efficiently ticks on the mantelpiece. He puts on greasy coveralls and climbs a tower through the void, past the bones of prehistoric animals, fallen angels, and the turds of ancient bats, as the Big Bang echoes in his ears like railroad cars coupling. Rung by rung he rises through the terrible darkness. At the top of his ascent, he winds up the sun and other stars with a cranklike key, adjusts for the weathers of unknowable dimensions, and lubricates each equinox and comet. Then, stooping to a tiny gear amid the wheelwork, he wipes away the surface dirt of railroads and religious strife and, with a fresh rag, every human tear. And I am one of his ministers; I tend one of his metaphors. I am the clock-winder of Island Pond.

Robert Louis Stevenson

FROM "AN AUTUMN EFFECT"

The autumn day that Robert Louis Stevenson chooses for his walking tour of the Chiltern Hills in Buckinghamshire, England, might seem inauspicious. It is "dull, heavy, and lifeless." But for the attentive Stevenson, such a day quietly unscrolls a busy tableau of visual and vocal delights— gray-painted woods, caroling larks, "mingled green and yellow of the elm foliage," even the braying of a sassy and unrepentant small white donkey.

Stevenson takes pleasure, too, in the bustle of human activity: the "great coming and going of schoolchildren," the stout ploughmen, the shepherds leading their flocks, the startled elderly maiden. And amidst these cheerful and humorous scenes of daily life, Stevenson learns to be thankful for stillness, for lives well spent, for the love that lasts beyond the grave.

> *A*nd amidst these cheerful and humorous scenes of daily life, Stevenson learns to be thankful for stillness, for lives well spent, for the love that lasts beyond the grave.

FROM "AN AUTUMN EFFECT"

The day was a bad day for walking at best, and now began to draw towards afternoon, dull, heavy, and lifeless. A pall of grey cloud covered the sky, and its colour reacted on the colour of the land-scape. Near at hand, indeed, the hedgerow trees were still fairly green, shot through with bright autumnal yellows, bright as sunshine. But a little way off, the solid bricks of woodland that lay squarely on slope and hill-top were not green, but russet and grey, and ever less russet and more grey as they drew off into the distance. As they drew off into the distance, also, the woods seemed to mass themselves together, and lie thin and straight, like clouds, upon the limit of one's view. Not that this massing was complete, or gave the idea of any extent of forest, for every here and there the trees would break up and go down into a valley in open order, or stand in long Indian file along the horizon, tree after tree relieved, foolishly enough, against the sky. I say foolishly enough, although I have seen the effect employed cleverly in art, and such long line of single trees thrown out against the customary sunset of a Japanese picture with a certain fantastic effect that was not to be despised; but this was over water and level land, where it did not jar, as here, with the soft contour of hills and valleys. The whole scene had an indefinable look of being painted, the colour was so abstract and correct, and there was something so sketchy and merely impressional about these distant single trees on the horizon that one was forced to think of it all as of a clever French landscape. For it is rather in nature that we see resemblance to art, than in art to nature; and we say a hundred times, "How like a picture!" for once that we say, "How like the truth!" The forms in which we learn to think of landscape are forms that we have got from painted canvas. Any man can see and understand a picture; it is reserved for the few to separate anything out of the confusion of nature, and see that distinctly and with intelligence.

The sun came out before I had been long on my way; and as I had got by that time to the top of the ascent, and was now treading a labyrinth of confined by-roads, my whole view brightened considerably in colour, for it was the distance only that was grey and cold, and the distance I could see no longer. Overhead there was a wonderful carolling of larks which seemed to follow me as I went. Indeed, during all the time I was in that country the larks did not desert me. The air was alive with them from High Wycombe to Tring; and as, day after day, their "shrill delight" fell upon me out of the vacant sky, they began to take such a prominence over other conditions, and form so integral a part of my conception of the country, that I could have baptized it "The Country of Larks." This, of course, might just as well have been in early spring; but everything else was deeply imbued with the sentiment of the later year. There was no stir of insects in the grass. The sunshine was more golden, and gave less heat than summer sunshine; and the shadows under the hedge were somewhat blue and misty. It was only in autumn that you could have seen the mingled green and yellow of the elm foliage, and the fallen leaves that lay about the road, and covered the surface of wayside pools so thickly that the sun was reflected only here and there from little joints and pinholes in that brown coat of proof; or that your ear would have been troubled, as you went forward, by the occasional report of fowling-pieces from all directions and all degrees of distance.

I left the road and struck across country. It was rather a revelation to pass from between the hedgerows and find quite a bustle on the other side, a great coming and going of school-children upon by-paths, and, in every second field, lusty horses and stout country-folk a-ploughing. The way I followed took me through many fields thus occupied, and through many strips of plantation, and then over a little space of smooth turf, very pleasant to the feet, set with tall fir-trees and clamorous with rooks making ready for the winter, and so back again into the quiet road. I was now not far from the end of my day's journey. A few hundred yards farther, and, passing through a gap in the hedge, I began to go down hill through a pretty extensive tract of young beeches. I was soon in shadow myself, but the afternoon sun still coloured the upmost boughs of the wood, and made a fire over my head in the autumnal foliage. A little faint vapour lay among the slim tree-stems in the bottom of the hollow; and from farther up

I heard from time to time an outburst of gross laughter, as though clowns were making merry in the bush. There was something about the atmosphere that brought all sights and sounds home to one with a singular purity, so that I felt as if my senses had been washed with water. After I had crossed the little zone of mist, the path began to remount the hill; and just as I, mounting along with it, had got back again, from the head downwards, into the thin golden sunshine, I saw in front of me a donkey tied to a tree. Now, I have a certain liking for donkeys, principally, I believe, because of the delightful things that Sterne has written of them. But this was not after the pattern of the ass at Lyons. He was of a white colour, that seemed to fit him rather for rare festal occasions than for constant drudgery. Besides, he was very small, and of the daintiest portions you can imagine in a donkey. And so, sure enough, you had only to look at him to see he had never worked. There was something too roguish and wanton in his face, a look too like that of a schoolboy or a street Arab, to have survived much cudgelling. It was plain that these feet had kicked off sportive children oftener than they had plodded with a freight through miry lanes.

He was altogether a fine-weather, holiday sort of donkey; and though he was just then somewhat solemnised and rueful, he still gave proof of the levity of his disposition by impudently wagging his ears at me as I drew near. I say he was somewhat solemnized just then; for, with the admirable instinct of all men and animals under restraint, he had so wound and wound the halter about the tree that he could go neither back nor forwards, nor so much as put down his head to browse. There he stood, poor rogue, part puzzled, part angry, part, I believe, amused. He had not given up hope, and dully revolved the problem in his head, giving ever and again another jerk at the few inches of free rope that still remained unwound. A humorous sort of sympathy for the creature took hold upon me. I went up, and, not without some trouble on my part, and much distrust and resistance on the part of Neddy, got him forced backwards until the whole length of the halter was set loose, and he was once more as free a donkey as I dared to make him. I was pleased (as people are) with this friendly action to a fellow-creature in tribulation, and glanced back over my shoulder to see how he was profiting by his freedom. The brute was looking after me; and no sooner did he catch my eye than he put up his long white face into the air, pulled an impudent mouth at me, and began to bray derisively. If ever any one person made a grimace at another, that donkey made a grimace at me. The hardened ingratitude of his behaviour, and the impertinence that inspired his whole face as he curled up his lip, and showed his teeth, and began to bray, so tickled me, and was so much in keeping with what I had imagined to myself about his character, that I could not find it in my heart to be angry, and burst into a peal of hearty laughter. This seemed to strike the ass as a repartee, so he brayed at me again by way of rejoinder; and we went on for a while, braying and laughing, until I began to grow aweary of it, and, shouting a derisive farewell, turned to pursue my way. In so doing—it was like going suddenly into cold water—I found myself face to face with a prim little old maid. She was all in a flutter, the poor old dear! She had concluded beyond question that this must be a lunatic who stood laughing aloud at a white donkey in the placid beech-woods. I was sure, by her face, that she had already recommended her spirit most religiously to Heaven, and prepared herself for the worst. And so, to reassure her, I uncovered and besought her, after a very staid fashion, to put me on my way to Great Missenden. Her voice trembled a little, to be sure, but I think her mind was set at rest; and she told me, very explicitly, to follow the path until I came to the end of the wood, and then I should see the village below me in the bottom of the valley. And, with mutual courtesies, the little old maid and I went on our respective ways.

Wendover (which was my next stage) lies in the same valley with Great Missenden, but at the foot of it, where the hills trend off on either hand like a coast-line, and a great hemisphere of plain lies, like a sea, before one, I went up a chalky road, until I had a good outlook over the place. The vale, as it opened out into the plain, was shallow, and a little bare, perhaps, but full of graceful convolutions. From the level to which I have now attained the fields were exposed before me like a map, and I could see all that bustle of autumn field-work which had been hid from me yesterday behind the hedgerows, or shown to me only for a moment as I followed the footpath. Wendover lay well down in the midst, with mountains of foliage about it. The great plain stretched away to the northward, variegated near at hand with the quaint pattern of the fields, but growing ever more and more indistinct, until it became a mere hurly-burly of trees and bright crescents of river, and snatches of slanting road, and finally melted into the ambiguous cloud-land over the horizon. The sky was an opal-grey, touched here and there with blue, and with certain faint russets that looked as if they were reflections of the colour of the autumnal woods below. I could hear the ploughmen shouting to their horses, the uninterrupted carol of larks innumerable overhead, and, from a field where the shepherd was marshalling his flock, a sweet tumultuous tinkle of sheep-bells. All these noises came to me very thin and distinct in the clear air. There was a wonderful sentiment of distance and atmosphere about the day and the place.

I mounted the hill yet farther by a rough staircase of chalky footholds cut in the turf. The hills about Wendover and, as far as I could see, all the hills in Buckinghamshire, wear a sort of hood of beech plantation; but in this particular case the hood had been suffered to extend itself into something more like a cloak, and hung down about the shoulders of the hill in wide folds, instead of lying flatly along the summit. The trees grew so close, and their boughs were so matted together, that the whole wood looked as dense as a bush of heather. The prevailing colour was a dull, smouldering red, touched here and there with vivid yellow. But the autumn had scarce advanced beyond the outworks; it was still almost summer in the heart of the wood; and as soon as I had scrambled through the hedge, I found myself in a dim green forest atmosphere under eaves of virgin foliage. In places where the wood had itself for a background and the trees were massed together thickly, the colour became intensified and almost gem-like: a perfect fire green, that seemed none the less green for a few specks of autumn gold. None of the trees were of any considerable age or stature; but they grew well together, I have said; and as the road turned and wound among them, they fell into pleasant groupings and broke the light up pleasantly. Sometimes there would be a colonnade of slim, straight tree-stems with the light running down them as down the shafts of pillars, that looked as if it ought to lead to something, and led only to a corner of sombre and intricate jungle. Sometimes a spray of delicate foliage would be thrown out flat, the light lying flatly along the top of it, so that against a dark background it seemed almost luminous. There was a great bush over the thicket (for, indeed, it was more of a thicket than a wood); and the vague rumours that went among the tree-tops, and the occasional rustling of big birds or hares among the undergrowth, had in them a note of almost treacherous stealthiness, that put the imagination on its guard and made me walk warily on the russet carpeting of last year's leaves. The spirit of the place seemed to be all attention; the wood listened as I went, and held its breath to number my footfalls. One could not help feeling that there ought to be some reason for this stillness; whether, as the bright old legend goes, Pan lay somewhere near in siesta, or whether, perhaps, the heaven was meditating rain, and the first drops would soon come pattering through the leaves. It was not unpleasant, in such an humour, to catch sight, ever and anon, of large spaces of the open plain. This happened only where the path lay much upon the slope, and there was a flaw in the solid leafy thatch of the wood at some distance below the level at which I chanced myself to be walking; then, indeed, little scraps of foreshortened distance, miniature fields, and Lilliputian houses and hedgerow trees would appear for a moment in the aperture, and grow larger and smaller, and change and melt one into another, as I continued to go forward, and so shift my point of view.

Next morning I went along to visit the church. It is a long-backed red-and-white building, very much restored, and stands in a pleasant graveyard among those great trees of which I have spoken already. The sky was drowned in a mist. Now and again pulses of cold wind went about the enclosure, and set the branches busy overhead, and the dead leaves scurrying into the angles of the church buttresses. Now and again, also, I could hear the dull sudden fall of a chestnut among the grass—the dog would bark before the rectory door—or there would come a clinking of pails from the stable-yard behind. But in spite of these occasional interruptions—in spite, also, of the continuous autumn twittering that filled the trees—the chief impression somehow was one as of utter silence, insomuch that the little greenish bell that peeped out of a window in the tower disquieted me with a sense of some possible and more inharmonious disturbance. The grass was wet, as if with a hoar frost that had just been melted. I do not know that ever I saw a morning more autumnal. As I went to and fro among the graves, I saw some flowers set reverently before a recently erected tomb, and drawing near, was almost startled to find they lay on the grave of a man seventy-two years old when he died. We are accustomed to strew flowers only over the young, where love has been cut short untimely, and great possibilities have been restrained by death. We strew them there in token, that these possibilities, in some deeper sense, shall yet be realised, and the touch of our dead loves remain with us and guide us to the end. And yet there was more significance, perhaps, and perhaps a greater consolation, in this little nosegay on the grave of one who had died old. We are apt to make so much of the tragedy of death, and think so little of the enduring tragedy of some men's lives, that we see more to lament for in a life cut off in the midst of usefulness and love, than in one that miserably survives all love and usefulness, and goes about the world the phantom of itself, without hope, or joy, or any consolation. These flowers seemed not so much the token of love that survived death, as of something yet more beautiful—of love that had lived a man's life out to an end with him, and been faithful and companionable, and not weary of loving, throughout all these years.

P. D. James

FROM *TIME TO BE IN EARNEST: A FRAGMENT OF AUTOBIOGRAPHY*

Autumn is the occasion for P. D. James to reflect upon her own religious upbringing in what she has called "a fragment of autobiography." Though James is best known for her seventeen exquisitely crafted murder mysteries, in Time to Be in Earnest *she turns to a journal form to record the events of her seventy-seventh year—the year, says Samuel Johnson, in which one must learn to "be in earnest." The book becomes her attempt to harvest the experiences of her life, to bring them to a coherent fullness.*

> *In the autumn of her life, she is led back to earlier autumns where certainties seemed possible.*

For the harvest that she brings together here is a harvesting of images from long tradition. In the autumn of her life, she is led back to earlier autumns where certainties seemed possible. In those days, she suggests, there were the common hymns, the common grieving on Armistice Day, the common church order, the Book of Common Prayer, *the certainty of a common religious tradition, the certainty of a common national tradition. But now, autumn suggests to her a more uncertain and fading world where those commonalities have been abandoned, and James is unsure that there is anything to replace them.*

277

> *What remains is the harvest of disparate images. These must substitute for the elusive certainties.*

"Sunday, 5th October"

I was born and bred in the distinctive odour of Anglicanism, which childhood memory identifies as the smell of old prayer books, flowers, brass, stone and polished wood, the whole overlaid by the occasional sweet pungency of incense. I early grew accustomed to its services. Because Father, a middle-grade civil servant, was relatively poor, my parents employed no resident servant to help look after us children, even in those days when wages were low. This meant that, until we moved to Cambridge, when my father gave up going to church, the whole family attended Sunday Evensong together.

I must have been about five years old when we moved from Oxford to Ludlow and I can remember long autumnal Sunday evenings (my memory is always of going to church in the fading light and coming out into darkness): my brother fast asleep against my mother, my sister dozing, and myself reading the Book of Common Prayer to relieve the boredom of sermons which were not only long but invariably well above my understanding. I was fascinated by the prayer book—less by the liturgy than by the accompanying text. I can remember at a very early age being impressed by the rubric in the Communion Service that when in times of plague no one could be found to take Communion with the sick then the priest only might do so, and I would sit there in the darkened church with a vivid imagining of crosses on doors, wailing voices and the heroic figure of the cloaked priest moving silently and swiftly through the deserted streets, bearing the sacred vessels.

But my experience of church-going was even earlier. Both my parents had a deep affection for church music, my mother from nostalgia and sentiment, my father because he loved organ music, and they would frequently attend Sung Evensong in the College chapels as well as the services in the Cathedral. I would be wheeled in my pram and left outside the chapel doors (this was an age when mothers had no fear of their children being snatched), or even carried, sleeping, into the chapel. Thus listening to the music and hearing the liturgy of the church were two of my very early and formative experiences and Cranmer's magnificent cadences seeped into my first consciousness.

When we lived in the house called The Woodlands on the fringes of Ludlow our nearest church was over the bridge at Ludford. I have only two memories of Ludford church: the tortoise stove which flared dramatically when the wind changed, reminding me of the tongues of fire at Whitsun, and a remarkable prayer book which had been left in the pew in which we normally sat. It had heavy brass clasps which I would discreetly click open and shut during the service, and one of my earliest temptations was the wish somehow to conceal the prayer book and take it home with me. Surely it wouldn't be stealing. I should be returning with it every Sunday evening. It was the first object I remember wanting to possess with real passion.

I have a memory, too, of Ludford Sunday school. All the children were given a card with blank spaces and each week we were handed a coloured sticker of a biblical scene to fix to the appropriate space. I had no choice about attending Sunday school but, even if I had, it would have been important to complete my card without any humiliating blanks. After a common prayer and hymn we would disperse to sit in little groups according to age. Our group had a teacher who must have been extremely inexperienced; perhaps she was filling in for someone more orthodox. Certainly she spent little time in telling us Bible stories, but did recount the more lurid examples from *Foxe's Book of Martyrs,* which both thrilled and half-terrified us. I don't think these gory details of rackings and burnings kept me awake at night, nor did they affirm me as a natural Protestant.

My mother in particular was naturally ecumenical and had friends who were Roman Catholics and others who were Methodists or belonged to the more esoteric Protestant sects. It was never at any time suggested to me that one form of Christianity was necessarily superior to any other. My mother, indeed, was much in demand as a member of the Talkers Circuit and was frequently asked to address meetings of the Women's Bright Hour. I can remember being taken with her and sitting, legs dangling, among the female audience while my mother gave comforting and lively little homilies on "Meals in the Bible," "Journeys in the Bible," or any other similar theme on which she could hang her gentle moralizing. Mother enjoyed amateur theatricals but had no opportunity to participate except at concerts in aid of the church. I remember a performance of *Babes in the Wood* which she wrote or produced (probably both) and in which Edward was a babe, and Monica and I gnomes. Then there was the Sunday school dance troupe. Dressed in such costumes as she could improvise, we would perform deeply inauthentic folk dances, prancing uncertainly across the stage while Mother mouthed encouragement and occasional desperate instructions from the piano.

When we moved from The Woodlands to a tall terraced house in Linney View overlooking the water meadows and close to Ludlow Castle, we began attending St. Lawrence's parish church, where my father sang in the choir. Here, too, our usual service was Evensong. There seemed, as I remember, to have been a social distinction between Matins, sometimes followed by Holy Communion, and the evening service. Those who had servants to cook their Sunday lunch went in the morning; those who, like my mother, had to do all their own housework and cooking, usually found it more convenient to go in the evening. But occasionally on special days we would be taken to a Sung Holy Communion and I can remember the great glory of these occasions and my sense that something mysterious and extremely important was happening at the altar, and that, left in the pew with my brother and sister while my parents went up to receive the wafer and wine, I was temporarily deprived of something which one day would be mine also and which I would enter into as I might an inheritance. It was, too, an important Sunday for us when it was my father's turn to carry the processional cross, the pride of the occasion being somewhat dimmed for me by the terrifying fear that one day he might drop it.

My mother's faith was uncritical, unintellectual, simple and sentimental. It provided solace, nostalgia, reassurance and such social life as she enjoyed. She liked us to say our evening prayers at her knee, a practice which obviously gave her satisfaction but which I found acutely embarrassing. I accepted that there must be public prayers in church but felt that private prayer should be a matter between me and God. But religion in our home was never made into a source of guilt. We were made to feel guilty enough, but these were sins against an occasionally terrifying earthly father, not against God. God and fear seemed to me two opposing, irreconcilable ideas. And because my mother in particular took a lively part in church affairs, I never from my earliest age assumed that church-goers were necessarily morally superior to other people, since experience showed me that they were not. There were the seemingly inevitable disputes at Easter-time and Harvest Festival about who should and should not decorate the altar and pulpit, and my mother voiced her dissatisfaction at always being given one of the darkest windows. There were the usual arguments between the organist and the vicar about the hymns and the music, and the annual church fête and sale of work provoked mutterings about members of the congregation notable for their bossiness. But the church was always there, immutable, unchanging, comforting and secure, and the year given a recognizable shape by its festivals and seasons.

It was King's College Chapel which, during these years of early adolescence, provided for me my most meaningful religious experience. Evensong was sung at half-past three on Sundays and in the evening on weekdays, and I would often drop in when cycling home from school. I can recall the solemnity, the grandeur and the beauty of the building, the high, soaring magnificence of the roof, the candle-lit gloom, the decorous procession of the boys of the choir, the order and the beauty of the traditional service. This, I believed then and still do believe, was what worship should be. I think I probably realized even then that I was in danger of confusing worship of God with a strong emotional and aesthetic response to architecture, music and literature, but it seemed to me that religion could be an aesthetic experience and that God should be worshipped in the beauty of holiness.

From an early age I have taken little pleasure in sermons; it is the more reprehensible that I have occasionally succumbed to the temptation to accept invitations to deliver them.... But if as a child I disliked the sermon, I loved the hymns, and this affection has remained with me. The soaring triumph of the processional Easter hymns, the celebration of All Saints' Day, with the hymn "For All the Saints," which was my mother's favourite, and the plangent melancholy of the evening hymns, particularly "The Day Thou Gavest, Lord, Has Ended," sung while the church windows darkened and the mind moved forward to the walk through the churchyard between the gleaming tombstones in the evening dusk. Some of my early religious memories are of the hymns and my mother's rich and overloud contralto and my own piping treble. Some of them still have the power to move me to tears.

The Church of England in my childhood was the national church in a very special sense, the visible symbol of the country's moral and religious aspirations, a country which, despite great differences of class, wealth and privilege, was unified by generally accepted values and by a common tradition, history and culture, just as the Church was unified by Cranmer's magnificent liturgy. There were, of course, varieties of practice and little superficial resemblance between the multi-candled ceremonial, the incense and Stations of the Cross found in the extreme High Church and the simplicities of an evangelical church which could have been mistaken for a nonconformist chapel. But it was possible to attend different churches—on holiday, for example—and feel immediately at home, finding in the pew not a service sheet with a series number, but the familiar and unifying Book of Common Prayer.

The importance of the Church of England as the national church was perhaps most clearly shown on Armistice Day, when whole communities gathered in their parish church, united in sorrowful remembrance. To be born in 1920, two years after the end of the slaughter of a generation, was to be aware from one's earliest years of a universal grieving which was part of the air one breathed.

My early religious experience, like all the experiences of childhood, has both formed and influenced my subsequent years. I have inherited a love of and devotion to the Church of England which is still strong, although I sometimes find it difficult today to recognize the church into which I was baptized. Much of its former dignity, scholarly tolerance, beauty and order, have been not so much lost as wantonly thrown away, together with its incomparable liturgy. The King James Bible and the Book of Common Prayer have both been central to my life and to my craft as a novelist. In particular, the words of the Prayer Book are so much part of my consciousness that I do not need to remember them, search for them or concentrate on them, but can release my mind to enter into that communion with the unseen, unknowable God which I call prayer. I still see myself as a searcher after truth rather than as one confident she has found answers to the great and eternal questions of human existence, not least the problem of the suffering of the innocent, and at seventy-seven I do not think I shall find all the answers now.

ACKNOWLEDGMENTS

The editors of any book that takes the form of an anthology gather, as the book rolls along, many debts; to look at the manuscript now is to be reminded of the community of those who have been a part of its development and who have affected its final shape. Our editor, Jon Sweeney, of SkyLight Paths Publishing, is once again the chief instigator of this book—and sometimes, during the writing, we said nice things about him. Denice O'Heron, of Calvin College's Department of English, is responsible for moving words from legal pads and scrambled photocopies to crisp legible formats. Linda Naranjo-Huebl led us to the poems of the Harlem Renaissance and was one of many folks who pointed out texts for us to consider. (It is a good thing to work in an English department when pulling together a collection of poems and essays.) Kathy Struck, of Calvin College's Hekman Library, located and secured many of the old texts represented here. Conrad Bult and Kathy De Mey, also of Hekman Library, tracked down elusive authors. And Chrissie Schicktanz, our able research assistant, looked at books and scoured out scores of images, a task that eventually led us to Mary Azarian.

Our particular thanks to Mary Azarian, whose illustrations organize these pages. When we look at these images, we see not only the work of a brilliant artist but also the work of a generous and gracious soul.

As ever, our chief gratitude goes to those who have for so many years shown, in their support of our writing, their love: Douglas Felch and Anne Elizabeth Schmidt. In so many ways, this book is really your gift to us, and we give it back now to you, with love.

Woodcuts by Mary Azarian, Copyright © 2004 by Mary Azarian. Reprinted by permission of the artist.

Original woodcuts may be viewed online and purchased at www.maryazarian.com or ordered from

Mary Azaraian
Farmhouse Press
258 Gray Road
Plainfield, VT 05667

PERMISSIONS

Hahm Dong-seon: "A Rough Sketch of Autumn," "Autumn Sanjo," and "Landscape" from *Three Poets of Modern Korea: Yi Sang, Hahm Dong-seon, and Choi Young-mi,* translated by Yu Jung-yul and James Kimbrell. Copyright © 2002 by Yu Jung-yul and James Kimbrell. Reprinted by permission of Sarabande Books and the translators.

David James Duncan: "Tilt," from *My Story as Told by Water,* by David James Duncan. Copyright © 2001 by David James Duncan. Reprinted by permission of Sierra Club Books.

Robert Frost: "After Apple Picking" by Robert Frost. Copyright © 1903. "My November Guest" and "A Late Walk" by Robert Frost. Copyright © 1915. Public Domain.

A. Bartlett Giamatti: "The Green Fields of the Mind" by A. Bartlett Giamatti, from *A Great and Glorious Game: Baseball Writings of A. Bartlett Giamatti,* edited by Kenneth S. Robson. Copyright © 1998. Reprinted by permission of Algonquin Books.

Kent Gramm: "November 2" and "November 26" from *November: Lincoln's Elegy at Gettysburg* by Kent Gramm. Copyright © 2001 by Kent Gramm. Reprinted by permission of the author.

Kimiko Hahn: "Boerum Hill Tanka." Copyright © 2002. Reprinted by permission of the author.

P. D. James: From *Time to Be in Earnest* by P. D. James. Copyright © 1999 by P. D. James. Used by permission of Alfred A. Knopf, a division of Random House, Inc.

Julian of Norwich: Chapter 15 and excerpts from chapters 58, 60, and 86, from *The Revelations of Divine Love.* Modernized and reprinted from the Christian Classics Ethereal Library (www.ccel.org/ccel/julian/revelations.all.html). Public Domain.

John Keats: "To Autumn." 1819. Public Domain.

Garret Keizer: "I Am the Clock-Winder," from *A Dresser of Sycamore Trees* by Garret Keizer. Copyright © 1991 by Garret Keizer. Reprinted by permission of Garret Keizer.

Tracy Kidder: Excerpt from "September," from *Among Schoolchil-*

NOTES

Preface

The two poems by Longfellow—both titled "Autumn"—appear in *Poems by Henry Wadsworth Longfellow* (Boston: Ticknor and Fields, 1856): I: 24–25 and I: 281–82. The autumn images from Henry David Thoreau appear in "Economy," in *Walden* (1854). In Walter Harding's *Walden: An Annotated Edition* (Boston: Houghton Mifflin, 1995), this reference appears at p. 15. Debra Rienstra's "Autumn" is original to this volume.

Part One

T. C. Avery's "First Hesitations" is original to this volume.

This translation of the Book of Ruth is by the editors. The *Shema* is found in Deuteronomy 6:4–5.

Esther Popel's "October Prayer" was first published in *Opportunity* 11 (October 1933): 295. It has recently been edited in Lorraine Elena Roses and Ruth Elizabeth Randolph's *Harlem's Glory: Black Women Writing, 1900–1950* (Cambridge, MA: Harvard University Press, 1996): 438. Jean Toomer's "Cane: November Cotton Flower" was first published in 1923 and later anthologized in Countee Cullen, ed., *Caroling Dusk: An Anthology of Verse by Negro Poets* (New York: Harper and Brothers, 1927): 99. Isabel Neill's "October" is from *Opportunity* 6 (October 1928): 303. Marjorie Marshall's "Autumn" was first published in *The Crisis* 35

(November 1928): 372. The poems by Neill and Marshall have recently been edited in Maureen Honey, ed., *Shadowed Dreams: Women's Poetry of the Harlem Renaissance* (New Brunswick, NJ: Rutgers University Press, 1989): 186, 187, 188.

The sketch of E. B. White's wife is from the introduction to Katharine S. White, *Onward and Upward in the Garden* (New York: Farrar, Straus and Giroux, 1979): xvii–xix.

"Barn Raising" is from Anne Lamott, *Traveling Mercies* (New York: Pantheon Books, 1999): 147–54.

Abram Van Engen's "The Day's Peak" is original to this collection.

"A Dissolving View" was first published in *The Home Book of the Picturesque: Or American Scenery, Art, and Literature* (New York: Putnam, 1852): 79–94. The book has been reprinted in facsimile (Gainesville, FL: Scholars' Facsimiles and Reprints, 1967: 79–94), and the full essay has recently been included in Rochelle Johnson and Daniel Patterson, eds., *Susan Fenimore Cooper: Essays on Nature and Landscape* (Athens: The University of Georgia Press, 2002): 3–16.

"Tilt" is from David James Duncan, *My Story as Told by Water* (San Francisco: Sierra Club Books, 2001): 57–60.

Selections from "Autumn" are from Allen M. Young, *Small Creatures and Ordinary Places* (Madison: University of Wisconsin Press, 2000): 117–31.

Part Two

The quotation by Edwin Way Teale is from *Autumn Across America* (New York: Dodd, Mead & Co., 1956): 3. "Now fade rose and lily-flower" is the first line of Harley Lyric #23, from the fourteenth-century Middle English lyrics of MS. Harley 2253. The original Middle English is published in G. L. Brook, ed., *The Harley Lyrics: The Middle English Lyrics of MS. Harley 2253* (Manchester: Manchester University Press, 1948): 60–62. The present translation is by the editors. "The bustle in a house" (#1078) by Emily Dickinson was written in 1866 and first published in 1890. It may now be found in *The Poems of Emily Dickinson,* edited by Thomas H. Johnson (Cambridge, MA: Belknap Press of Harvard University Press, 1963): 763. William Shakespeare's sonnet #73 was first published in Thomas Thorpe's 1609 edition of *Shake-speares sonnets.* This version is modernized by the editors. Gerard Manley Hopkins's "Spring and Fall" was written in 1880 and first published in 1918. The quote from Allen

Young is found in *Small Creatures and Ordinary Places* (Madison: University of Wisconsin Press, 2000): 120. The description of Indian summer as a resurrection is attributed to Thomas De Quincey by Edwin Way Teale in *Autumn Across America* (New York: Dodd, Mead & Co., 1956): 188.

This translation of the book of Ruth is by the editors.

Siegfried Sassoon's "Break of Day" appeared in *Counter-Attack and Other Poems* (New York: E. P. Dutton, 1918): 37–39. His "October" appeared in his *The Old Huntsman and Other Poems* (New York: E. P. Dutton, 1917): 71. Edward Thomas's "There's Nothing Like the Sun" was written in November 1915, and first published in "Edward Eastaway" [Edward Thomas], *Poems* (London: Selwyn & Blount, 1917; New York: Henry Holt, 1917): 56–57. Margaret Postgate Cole's "The Falling Leaves" was first published in her *Poems* (London: Herald, 1918): 34. Henry Major Tomlinson's "An Autumn Morning" was first published in 1918 and collected in *Waiting for Daylight* (New York: Alfred A. Knopf, 1922): 65–73.

Selections from "The Island" are from Alix Kates Shulman, *Drinking the Rain* (New York: Penguin Books, 1996): 75–83. The book was first published in 1995 by Farrar, Straus and Giroux.

A. Bartlett Giamatti's "The Green Fields of the Mind" was first published in 1977 in the *Yale Alumni Magazine*. It is here reprinted from Kenneth S. Robson, ed., *A Great and Glorious Game: Baseball Writings of A. Bartlett Giamatti* (Chapel Hill, NC: Algonquin Books of Chapel Hill, 1998): 7–13.

These selections are from Kent Gramm, *November: Lincoln's Elegy at Gettysburg* (Bloomington and Indianapolis: Indiana University Press, 2001): 19–20, 22, 28–29, 249–50.

"Dry Autumn" is from Alice Meynell, *Ceres' Runaway and Other Essays* (London: Constable & Co., 1910; reprinted Freeport, NY: Books for Libraries Press, 1967): 103–8.

"No Question," "How to Take a Walk," and "Passing the Orange" are from Leo Dangel, *Old Man Brunner Country* (Granite Falls, MN: Spoon River Poetry Press, 1987): 13, 6, and 3. These poems have been most recently collected in Leo Dangel, *Home from the Field* (Granite Falls, MN: Spoon River Poetry Press, 1997): 29–30, 20–21, and 17.

Meena Alexander, "Aftermath," and Kimiko Hahn, "Boerum Hill Tanka," were first published in *110 Stories: New York Writes After September 11,* edited by Ulrich Baer (New York: New York University Press, 2002): 21, 138. "Aftermath" will appear in *Raw Silk* by Meena Alexander (Evanston, IL: Northwestern University Press, 2004).

Part Three

"Bringing in the Sheaves" was written by Knowles Shaw in 1874; he also wrote a tune for the poem, but six years later, George A. Minor wrote the melody that is today universally linked to Shaw's words. The quotation from H. W. Shepheard-Walwyn is from *The Harmonies of Nature* (New York: Dodd, Mead and Co., 1927): 126–27. The quotation from Barbara Hurd is taken from "Remains," a chapter in Barbara Hurd, *Stirring the Mud: On Swamps, Bogs, and Human Imagination* (Boston: Mariner, 2003; Beacon, 2001): 134. The tansy quotation is from Donald Culross Peattie, *An Almanac for Moderns* (New York: G. D. Putnam's Sons, 1935): 215. "A noiseless patient spider" was written by Walt Whitman in 1863 and first published by him in the final version of *Leaves of Grass* (Philadelphia, 1891–92); the poem may also be found in Whitman's *Complete Poetry and Collected Prose,* edited by Justin Kaplan (New York: The Library of America, 1982): 564–65. The traditional Vietnamese Hò, or work song, may be found in Pham Duy, *Musics of Vietnam* (Carbondale and Edwardsville: Southern Illinois University Press, 1975): 29. The English translation has been modified by the editors.

This translation of the book of Ruth is by the editors.

"The Arrival of Fall" is from Lauren Springer, *The Undaunted Garden* (Golden, CO: Fulcrum Publishing, 1994): 166–70; 178–80.

These journal entries are from May Sarton, *The House by the Sea* (New York: Norton, 1977): 143–67.

"October" is from Verlyn Klinkenborg, *The Rural Life* (Boston: Little, Brown, 2003): 169–80.

Keats's "To Autumn" was composed in September 1819, and first published the next year. The standard edition of Keats's poetry is Jack Stillinger, ed., *The Poems of John Keats* (Cambridge, MA: Belknap Press of Harvard University Press, 1978): 476–77. The description of the poem as a "distillation" is most elegantly made in W. Jackson Bate, *John Keats* (Cambridge, MA: Belknap Press of Harvard University Press, 1963): 581.

"The Music One Looks Back On" is from Stephen Dobyns's *Body Traffic* (New York: Viking Penguin, 1990): 77–78.

The excerpts from Jacob Young's autobiography are taken from Rev. Jacob Young, *Autobiography of a Pioneer: or, the Nativity, Experience, Travels, and Ministerial Labors of Rev. Jacob Young, with Incidents, Observations, and Reflections* (Cincinnati: L. Swormstedt & A Poe, 1857): 18, 31–34. "A Native Hill" was first published in 1969 in *The Long-Legged House* by Wendell Berry. The selections here are taken from *The Art of the Commonplace: The Agrarian Essays of Wendell Berry*, edited and introduced by Norman Wirzba

(Washington, DC: Shoemaker and Hoard, 2002): 10–12, 20–21, 25, 30–31. The quote by Berry cited in the introduction appears on 7.

Tracy Kidder, "September" is from *Among Schoolchildren* (Boston: Houghton Mifflin, 1989): 3–11.

Part Four

The quotation by Edwin Way Teale is from *Autumn Across America* (New York: Dodd, Mead & Co., 1956): 77. The Meusan prayer from Ethiopia is taken from John Mbiti, *The Prayer of African Religion* (Maryknoll, NY: Orbis Books, 1976): #15, p. 33; it is also reprinted in George Appleton, ed., *The Oxford Book of Prayer* (New York: Oxford University Press, 1985): #1055, p. 348. David's poem is found in Psalm 65:9–13; it is here printed in the King James Version. The reference to the animals of Rabbit Hill is from Robert Lawson, *Rabbit Hill* (New York: Viking Press, 1944): 120–127.

This translation of the book of Ruth is by the editors.

The excerpt from "The Apple" may be found in John Burroughs, *Winter Sunshine* (Boston: Houghton, Mifflin and Co., 1903): 120–127.

"After Apple-Picking" was published in Robert Frost, *North of Boston* (New York: Henry Holt & Co., 1914): 73–75. "My November Guest" and "A Late Walk" were published in Robert Frost, *A Boy's Will* (New York: Henry Holt & Co., 1915): 14, 17.

"Around the Horn" represents chapter 13 of Wyman Richardson's *The House on Nauset Marsh.* It was originally published in Boston by the Atlantic Monthly Company in 1947; it is currently available in an edition published in Woodstock, Vermont, by the Countryman Press (1997), from which this selection is taken.

"Autumnal Tints," by Henry David Thoreau, was first published several months after his death in the *Atlantic Monthly* 10, no. 60 (October 1862): 385–402; the present text is taken from this edition, with the idiosyncratic capitalization and punctuation retained intact. The essay was collected the next year by his sister, Sophia Thoreau, and William Ellery Channing in a posthumous volume titled *Excursions* (Boston: Ticknor and Fields, 1863). It has been newly edited and is today most accessible in William Rossi, ed., *Wild Apples and Other Natural History Essays by Henry D. Thoreau* (Athens: The University of Georgia Press, 2002): 108–39.

These journal entries are from Donald Culross Peattie, *An Almanac for Moderns* (New York: G. P. Putnam's Sons, 1935): 205, 206, 217, 239, 246.

The Showings of Divine Love, comprising sixteen mystical visions, survive in a long and a short version in four manuscripts. The present text is taken from the longer version, modernized from the transcription provided by the Christian Classics Ethereal Library (Grand Rapids, MI).

The Vedic harvest prayers are reprinted from Raimundo Panikkar, *The Vedic Experience: Mantramañjari* (Berkeley: University of California Press, 1977): #21–21, pp. 273–74. The "Verse of the Throne," from Sura 2:256, was translated by George Sale in 1734; it may be found in George Sale, *The Koran, commonly called the Alkoran of Mohammed* (New York: A. L. Burt, n.d. [before 1900]): 81. The hymn "Come, Ye Thankful People, Come" was written by Henry Alford in 1844, with numerous adaptations since. It is sung to the tune St. George's Windsor. "Sing to the Lord of Harvest" is another German hymn, written in 1866 by John S. B. Monsell; it is based on Psalm 65: 9–13. It is sung to the tune *Wie Lieblich ist der Maien*. The African harvest prayers are reprinted from John S. Mbiti, *The Prayers of African Religion* (Maryknoll, NY: Orbis Books, 1976): #70–75, pp. 70–71.

Part Five

The selection from Samuel Lane's diary has been published by Charles Lane Hanson, ed., *A Journal for the Years 1739–1803* (Concord, NH: New Hampshire Historical Society, 1937): 21–22. The journal is owned by the New Hampshire Historical Society.

This translation of the book of Ruth is by the editors.

William Bradford's description of the first Thanksgiving in his *History of Plymouth Plantation* first appeared when that history was first edited by Charles Deane (Boston: Little, Brown and Co., 1856): 105; the cited passage is taken from this first edition. The standard source for this text is *History of Plymouth Plantation, 1620–1647,* edited by Samuel Eliot Morison (New York: Random House, 1952). The selection from *A Relation Or Journall of the English Plantation Settled at Plimoth in New England* was almost certainly written by William Bradford and Edward Winslow, and first printed in London in 1622. Today, it is accessibly published in a facsimile edition as *Journall of the English Plantation at Plimoth* (Ann Arbor, MI: University Microfilms, 1966): 60–61. The editors have regularized the spelling and punctuation of this selection.

Sarah Josepha Hale, from *Northwood: A Tale of New England* (Boston: Bowles and Dearborn, 1827): I: 108–112, 116–117; and "The Thanksgiving of the Heart," from *Traits of American Life* (Philadelphia: E. L. Carey & A. Hart, 1835): 209–210.

Hahm Dong-seon's "A Rough Sketch of Autumn," "Autumn Sanjo," and "Landscape" are all to be found in Yu Jung-yul and James Kimbrell, trans., *Three Poets of Modern Korea* (Louisville, KY: Sarabande Books, 2002): 31, 34, 39.

"October" is from David Kline, *Great Possessions: An Amish Farmer's Journal* (New York: North Point Press, 1990): 178–181. This selection was first published in the Amish magazine *Family Life*. The quote from Wendell Berry occurs on p. xiii.

"I Am the Clock-Winder" is from Garret Keizer, *A Dresser of Sycamore Trees* (Boston: David R. Godine, 2001): 79–98. The book was first published by Viking Penguin in 1991.

"An Autumn Effect" by Robert Louis Stevenson was first published in 1875 in *The Portfolio* 6 (April and May) under the title "In the Beechwoods." It is collected in volume 30 of the Tusitala Edition of Stevenson's complete works (London: Heinemann, 1924); it is here printed from *Essays of Travel* by Robert Louis Stevenson (London: Chatto & Windus, 1905): 106–30.

"Sunday, 5th October," is taken from P. D. James, *Time to Be in Earnest: A Fragment of Autobiography* (New York: Alfred A. Knopf, 2000): 84–90.

Printed in the USA
CPSIA information can be obtained
at www.ICGtesting.com
JSHW022210140824
68134JS00018B/962

9 781683 365570